Arts & Crafts Across the U.S.A.

by Douglas M. Rife & Gina Capaldi

illustrated by Gina Capaldi

Teaching & Learning Company

1204 Buchanan St., P.O. Box 10

Carthage, IL 62321-0010

This book belongs to

_____

Cover design by Sara King

Teaching & Learning Company
1204 Buchanan St., P.O. Box 10
Carthage, IL 62321-0010

Acknowledgements

We would like to acknowledge the following people who granted permission to use the State Seals and Coat of Arms used in this book and explained the state and district laws governing their use:

Alabama: Secretary of State Nancy Worley
Alaska: Scott Clark, Notary Administrator; Annette Kreitzer, Chief of Staff for Lieutenant Governor Loren Leman
Arizona: Secretary of State Jan Brewer
Arkansas: Dr. David Ware, Capitol Historian
California: Secretary of State; Constituent Affairs
Colorado: Deputy Secretary of State William A. Hobbs
Connecticut: Deputy Secretary of State Maria M. Greenslade, Esq.; Barbara Sladek, Records and Legislative Services Assistant Coordinator
Delaware: Secretary of State Harriet Smith Windsor, Ed.D; Connie Stultz, Deputy Principal Assistant
District of Columbia: Secretary of the District of Columbia Sherryl Hobbs Newman; Arnold R. Finlayson, Director, Office of Documents and Administrative Issuances
Georgia: Governor Sonny Perdue; Billy C. Johnson, Jr., Special Assistant to Executive Council
Florida: D.H. Penton, Assistant General Counsel; Danielle M. Harrison, Executive Assistant to the General Counsel for the Department of State
Hawaii: Lieutenant Governor James R. Aiona, Jr.; Robert N.E. Piper, Esq.; Deputy Chief of Staff and General Counsel
Idaho: Patricia Herman, Webmaster, Secretary of State's Office
Illinois: Secretary of State Jesse White
Indiana: Secretary of State Todd Rokita; Sandy Gerster, Constituent Services
Iowa: Secretary of State Chet Culver; Michelle Bauer, Secretary of State's Office; Kristin Hardt, Legal Assistant, Governor's Office; Gary Dickey, Jr., General Counsel, Office of Governor Thomas J. Vilsak
Kansas: Secretary of State Ron Thornburgh; Nicole Romine, Law Clerk
Kentucky: Lillian Troop, Director of Administration, Secretary of State's Office
Louisiana: Steve Hawkland, Attorney Supervisor for the Secretary of State
Maryland: Secretary of State Karl Aumann; Aja C. Foster, Public Information Officer; Amy S. Lackington, Executive Assistant, Office of the Secretary of State
Massachusetts: Joseph Walsh, Staff Attorney, Office of the Secretary of State
Michigan: Patti Hayden, Office of Communications
Minnesota: Secretary of State Mary Kiffmeyer; Amber Galer, Assistant
Mississippi: Mandy Scott, Director of Publications, Secretary of State's Office
Missouri: Gary Schmidt, Legal Counsel for the Secretary of State's Office
Montana: Secretary of State Bob Brown; Shannon H. Stevens, Legislative Specialist, Secretary of State's Office
Nebraska: Secretary of State John A. Gale; Greg Lemon and Shelly Harrold from the Secretary of State's Office
Nevada: Brenda J. Erodes, Legislative Counsel; Kevin Honkomp, State Printer; Sallie Lincoln, Executive Assistant; Jackie Brantley, Office of the Governor
New Hampshire: Karen Ladd, Assistant Secretary of State
New Jersey: Kathleen M. Kisko, Assistant Secretary of State
New Mexico: Secretary of State Rebecca Vigil-Giron
New York: Glen T. Bruening, General Counsel, Office of the Secretary of State
North Carolina: George Jeter, Director of Communications, Secretary of State
North Dakota: Secretary of State Al Jaeger
Ohio: Carol Taylor, APR, Director of Public Affairs, Office of J. Kenneth Blackwell, Secretary of State; James G. Tassie, Deputy Chief Legal Counsel
Oklahoma: Secretary of State Susan Sarage; Kathy Jekel, Assistant to the Secretary of State
Oregon: James A. Austin, State Seal Use Coordinator, Secretary of State's Office
Pennsylvania: Christal Pike-Nase, Assistant Counsel, Governor's Office of General Counsel, Department of State
South Dakota: Secretary of State Chris Nelson
Tennessee: Secretary of State Riley Darnell; Judy Bond-McKissack, Chief Legal Counsel
Texas: Guy J. Joyner, Chief Legal Support Unit, Statutory Documents, Office of the Secretary of State
Vermont: Secretary of State D. Markowitz; Gregory Sanford, State Archivist
Virginia: Bernard Henderson, Deputy Secretary of the Commonwealth, Office of the Governor
Washington: Steve Excell, Assistant Secretary of State
West Virginia: Secretary of State Joe Manchin, III
Wisconsin: Secretary of State Doug La Follette
Wyoming: Karla Stackis, Administrative Assistant, Secretary of State's Office

Table of Contents

Alabama 5

Alaska 10

Arizona 14

Arkansas 19

California 23

Colorado 27

Connecticut 32

Delaware 37

District of Columbia 43

Florida 47

Georgia 51

Hawaii 54

Idaho 58

Illinois 62

Indiana 66

Iowa 70

Kansas 74

Kentucky 79

Louisiana 83

Maine 87

Maryland 91

Massachusetts 95

Michigan 100

Minnesota 104

Mississippi 110

Missouri 114

Montana 119

Nebraska 123

Nevada 127

New Hampshire 131

New Jersey 135

New Mexico 140

New York 143

North Carolina 148

North Dakota 152

Ohio 157

Oklahoma 161

Oregon 166

Pennsylvania 171

Rhode Island 175

South Carolina 180

South Dakota 184

Tennessee 188

Texas 194

Utah 198

Vermont 202

Virginia 208

Washington 212

West Virginia 216

Wisconsin 221

Wyoming 225

Reproducible Puzzle Pages 230

Answer Key 240

Dear Teacher or Parent,

The United States is one of the largest countries on Earth. It is a diverse and fascinating land. Each state within the United States is unique and holds treasures within it that are particular to it alone. The histories, cultures and people of each state are varied, too. To give students an insight to that diversity and richness, classroom teachers in every state in nearly every 4th, 5th or 6th grade are asked to teach about the U.S. This book aids in that teaching process.

This book is divided into 51 units, each focusing on one state and the District of Columbia. Within that unit, students are given "Fun Facts" about the state. These include the origins of the state's name, as well as a list of the items the state has designated to represent the state: motto, nickname, bird, tree or flower. In many cases, states have also named state amphibians, rocks, dinosaurs and insects. In most cases, students are given the common name, as well as, the scientific name.

In the second part of the "Fun Facts" section other important facts are listed in an almanac style so students have information about the state at their fingertips: date the state achieved statehood, order of admission to the Union, population, area, highest and lowest points, capital and largest city. Last in this section is a brief mention of the state's major crops and industries.

In a section called "Did You Know?" things of interest within the state are highlighted ranging from the history of Jell-O™ to the invention of the parking meter. These are always fun and fascinating! Each state's flag and seal or coat of arms is described and pictured along with a list of famous scientists, entertainers, Presidents and politicians born in the state, including names, birth and death dates, what they are best known for and birthplaces.

Each unit has a craft to be done by individual students or the entire class. Each craft is tailored to teach students something unique about the state's history, people, geography or culture.

As students work their way through the pages and activities of this book, they will discover fun and fascinating facts about the United States and its people and places. Let the journey begin!

Sincerely,

Douglas M. Rife and Gina Capaldi

Fun Facts

Amphibian: Red Hills Salamander (Phaeognathus hubrichti Highton)

Bird: Yellowhammer (Picus auratus)

Game Bird: Wild Turkey (Meleagris gallopavo)

Freshwater Fish: Largemouth or Black Bass (Micropterus salmoides)

Saltwater Fish: Fighting Tarpon (Tarpon atlanticus)

Flower: Camellia (Camellia japonica)

Wildflower: Oak-Leaf Hydrangea (Hydrangea quercifolia)

Fossil: Zeuglodon (Basilosaurus cetoides)

Gem: Star Blue Quartz (Silicon dioxide)

Insect: Monarch Butterfly (Danaus plexippus)

Mascot: Eastern Tiger Swallowtail (Papilio glaucus)

Mineral: Hematite (Red Iron Ore)

Motto: "Audemas jura nostra defendere" (We Dare Defend Our Rights)

Nickname: No official nickname, though, Alabama is often referred to as "The Heart of Dixie." This has also appeared on state license plates since the 1950s.

Nut: Pecan

Reptile: Alabama Red-Bellied Turtle (Pseudemys alabamensis)

Rock: Marble

Shell: Scaphella Junonia Johnstonae

Song: "Alabama" by Julia S. Tutwiler

Tree: Southern Longleaf Pine (Pinus palustris Miller)

Statehood: December 14, 1819; 22nd state admitted to the Union

Population: (2001 estimate) 4,464,356

Area: 52,423 square miles of land and water; 30th largest state

Highest Point: Cheaha Mountain; 2407 feet above sea level

Lowest Point: Gulf of Mexico

Capital: Montgomery

Largest City: Birmingham

Major Crops: Poultry, eggs, hogs, cattle, nursery stock, milk, fruits, peanuts, cotton, corn

Major Industry: Paper, lumber and wood products, chemicals, rubber, plastics, automobile production, iron and steel production, coal production

Alabama

Alabama is one of the many states that has a name of Native American origin. The word Alabama is a Creek word that means "tribal town."

Did You Know?

George Washington Carver, one of the greatest agricultural researchers and educators in America's history, became director of research at the Tuskegee Institute in Alabama. Carver was invited by Booker T. Washington to lead the research effort at the Institute. Carver quickly became an advocate for lessening the South's dependence on crops such as cotton and tobacco that leeched nutrients from the soil. Carver recommended that Southern farmers grow other crops that were native to the South such as sweet potatoes and peanuts. Through his research and experiments, more than 100 products from sweet potatoes and over 300 products from peanuts were developed. Carver worked exhaustively to teach better farming practices and became recognized worldwide for his progressive agricultural techniques that replenished the soil and stopped the destruction of native forests.

Flag: The present design of the flag of Alabama, a crimson cross of St. Andrew on a field of white, was adopted by the Alabama Legislature on February 16, 1895. The act requires that the bars on the flag be not less than six inches wide and that they must extend diagonally across the flag from side to side.

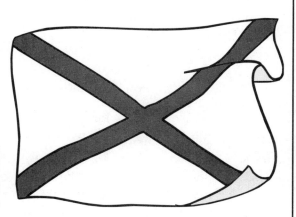

Seal: The circular state seal shows a map of the state of Alabama and its major rivers, along with the states that border Alabama—Mississippi, Tennessee, Georgia and Florida. The words *Alabama* and *Great Seal* appear in the outer circle of the state seal.

Celebrating History with Official Quilts

On December 1, 1965, a slight African American woman named Rosa Parks, boarded a bus in Montgomery, Alabama. The "established" rule in the old American south demanded that African Americans must surrender their seats to any white passengers and move to the back of the bus. When it came time for Mrs. Parks to surrender her seat, she would not! She did not argue with the bus driver but she did not move either. The police were called in and she was arrested.

At the same time, Dr. Martin Luther King, Jr., who was the pastor at Dexter Avenue Baptist Church in Montgomery, Alabama, called a meeting with other African American leaders. Together they began a movement of peace but protested against Mrs. Parks' arrest. Within five days, African American residents boycotted all the buses of Montgomery. The boycott continued for an entire year and caused great financial hardship for the city and state. Supporting the boycott was a hardship for the African Americans, too, but they would not give up. In the meantime, the Federal Supreme Court declared that Alabama state segregation laws were illegal. Not only was the boycott successful but the Civil Rights Movement had begun!

To honor Alabama's history and community, on March 11, 1997, the Pine Burr Quilt was designated the state's official quilt. The design was created by the Freedom Quilting Bee, which was organized during the Civil Rights Movement in 1966. This African American women's organization has received national attention for their quilt designs, which date back 140 years. The originators of the Freedom Quilting Bee maintain their African American culture and history by re-creating the life, customs and artifacts of their ancestors. The Pine Burr Quilt represents vision, community and tradition. Its pattern involves hundreds of colored swatches meticulously sewn together. It is a celebration of ancestors who lived, loved and suffered through the time of slavery and up to the Civil Rights Movement.

Make a bold statement during African American month by creating a wall hanging based on the official quilt of Alabama, the Pine Burr Quilt.

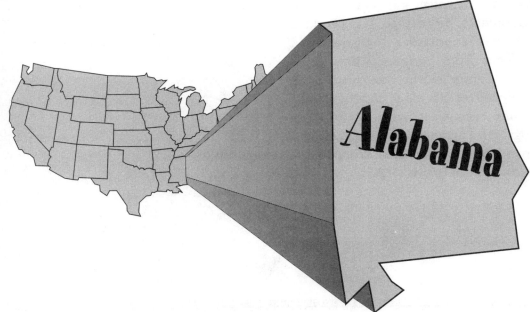

Notable Natives

Henry Louis (Hank) Aaron (1934-), baseball player, Mobile

Ralph Abernathy (1926-1990), civil rights activist, Linden

Courtney Cox Arquette (1964-), actress, Birmingham

Tullulah Bankhead (1903-1968), actress, Huntsville

Alva Ertskkin Belmont (1853-1933), feminist, reformer, Mobile

Hugo LaFayette Black (1886-1971), U.S. Supreme Court Justice, Harlan

Nat "King" Cole (Nathaniel Adams Coles) (1919-1965), singer, Montgomery

Zelda Fitzgerald (1900-1947), writer, Montgomery

William Crawford Gorgas (1854-1920), military doctor, Mobile

Mia Hamm (1972-), soccer player, Selma

W.C. Handy (1873-1958), musician, composer, Florence

Emmylou Harris (1947-), country singer, Birmingham

Kate Jackson (1948-), actress, Birmingham

Dean Jones (1931-), actor, Morgan City

Helen Keller (1880-1968), author, educator, Tuscumbia

Coretta Scott King (1927-), civil rights leader, Marion

Harper Lee (1926-), Pulitzer Prize-winning writer, Monroeville

Carl Lewis (1961-), Olympic gold-medal athlete, Birmingham

Joe Louis (1914-1981), world champion boxer, Lexington

Willie Mays (1931-), baseball player, Fairfield

Jim Nabors (1930-), actor, singer, Sylacauga

Jesse Owens (1913-1980), Olympic gold-medal runner, Danville

Rosa Parks (1913-), civil rights activist, Tuskegee

Lionel Richie (1949-), singer, Tuskegee

Hank Williams (1923-1953), country singer, Mount Olive

History Quilts

Materials

* card stock
* 30" x 56" white cotton fabric
* fabric squares that color coordinate
* 26" x 26" medium cotton batting
* 8—6" curtain rings
* curtain pole 34" long
* pencil
* scissors
* fabric glue
* straight pins
* needles and thread
* basting to match

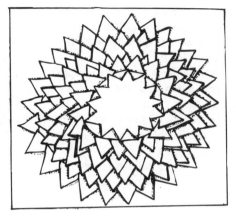

Figure 1

Instructions

1. Trace around the triangle template on page 9 on card stock to make a sturdy pattern. Enlarge if necessary. The smaller the triangle the more material is required to complete the interior design of the quilt. (Figure 1)
2. Trace the triangle on various pieces of color fabric and cut them out. Make at least 30 fabric triangles.
3. Lay out the triangle shape in a design on a large piece of white fabric. Glue the design on the white cotton. (Figure 2)
4. Lift the quilt up and slip cotton batting underneath the shape. Pin it down making sure that the batting is centered. (Figure 3)

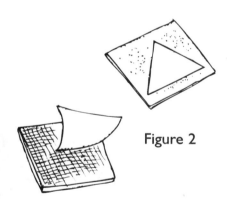

Figure 2

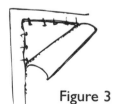

Figure 3

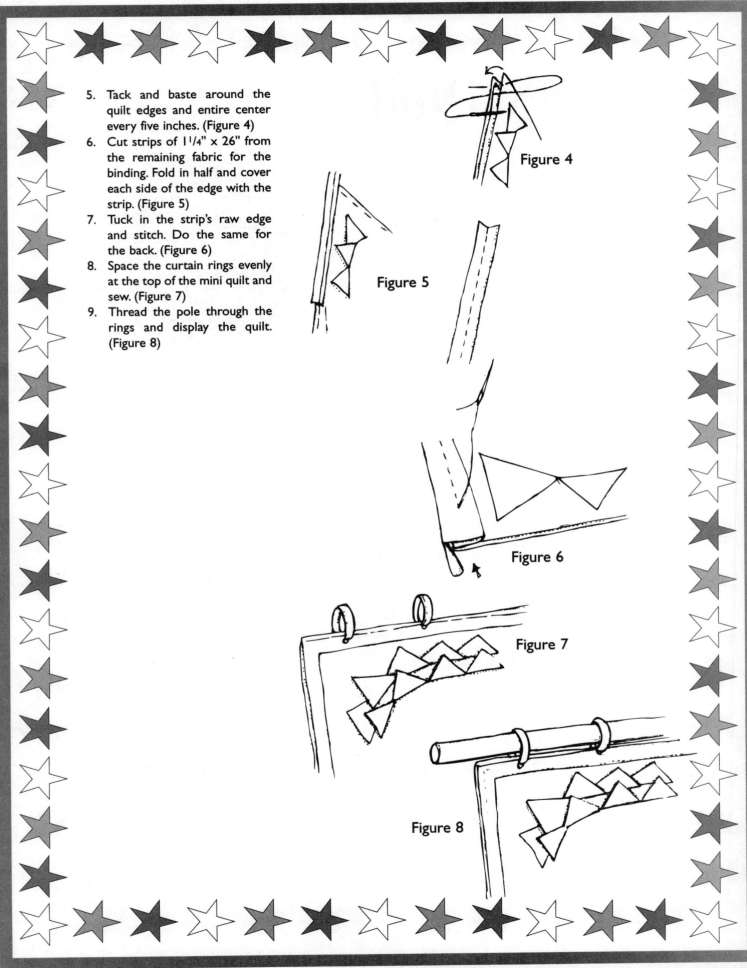

5. Tack and baste around the quilt edges and entire center every five inches. (Figure 4)

6. Cut strips of 1¹/₄" x 26" from the remaining fabric for the binding. Fold in half and cover each side of the edge with the strip. (Figure 5)

7. Tuck in the strip's raw edge and stitch. Do the same for the back. (Figure 6)

8. Space the curtain rings evenly at the top of the mini quilt and sew. (Figure 7)

9. Thread the pole through the rings and display the quilt. (Figure 8)

Figure 4

Figure 5

Figure 6

Figure 7

Figure 8

Triangle for Pine Burr Quilt

Enlarge or reduce as desired.

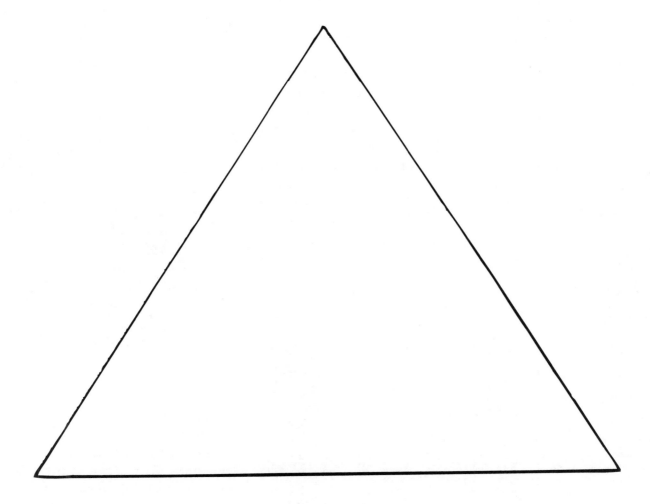

Fun Facts

Bird: Willow Ptarmigan (Lagopus albus)

Fish: Giant King Salmon, also called Chinook Salmon (Oncorhynchus tshawytscha)

Flower: Forget-Me-Not (Myosotis alpestris)

Fossil: Wooly Mammoth (Mammuthus primigenius)

Gem: Jade (Nephrite)

Insect: Four Spot Skimmer Dragonfly (Libellula quadrimaculata)

Land Mammal: Moose (Alces alces)

Marine Mammal: Bowhead Whale (Balaena mysticetus)

Mineral: Gold (Aurum)

Motto: "North to the Future"

Nickname: Last Frontier

Song: "Alaska's Flag" by Marie Drake

Tree: Sitka Spruce (Picea sitchensis)

Statehood: January 3, 1959; 49th state admitted to the Union

Population: (2000 estimate) 626,932

Area: 656,425 square miles of land and water; 1st largest state

Highest Point: Mt. McKinley; 20,320 feet

Lowest Point: At sea level where land meets Pacific Ocean, Bering Sea or Arctic Ocean

Capital: Juneau

Largest City: Anchorage

Major Crops: Seafood, fisheries, dairy, livestock

Major Industry: Petroleum, natural gas, gold and mining, food processing, lumber and wood products, furs, tourism

Alaska

Name: The state name Alaska is derived from the Aleut word Alakshak meaning "great lands" or "peninsula" obviously referring to the incredible natural beauty of the state and the fact that it is surrounded by water on three sides.

Did You Know?

On October 18, 1867, the United States government purchased Alaska from Russia for $7.2 million. While that was a great deal of money at the time, it did not represent very much money per acre—only two cents per acre! Nonetheless, the purchase was considered quite controversial by some. The Secretary of State, William Seward, who brokered the land deal, was mocked in the press. Many American critics of Seward, who thought the purchase was too expensive, called Alaska "Seward's Folly." But the purchase of Alaska greatly increased the amount of land owned by the United States. And Alaska is the largest state in the Union, 425 times bigger than the state of Rhode Island, America's smallest state.

North Star, are emblazoned on a field of dark blue. *Ursa Major* means "big bear a symbol of great strength." The blue represents the sky, water and the state flower—the forgot-me-not—of Alaska. The North Star represents Alaska as the northernmost state in the Union.

Seal: The state seal encircles a scene of mountains with rays spreading above them to represent the Northern Lights. A smelter symbolizes the mining industry in the state. The scene also shows a train and ships which denote Alaska's early trade by train and sea. The trees represent the forests of Alaska. The farmer, horse and three shocks of wheat demonstrate the importance of agriculture for the economy of the state. The fish and seals shown portray the importance of wildlife to the economy of the state.

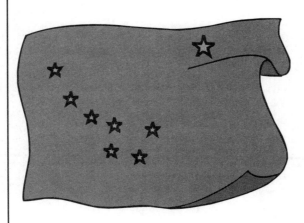

Flag: The Alaska state flag was designed by a seventh grade Aleut student. Eight stars, seven in the shape of the big dipper (Ursa Major) and one representing the

Aurora Borealis

The Aurora Borealis can be seen all over the world and particularly in Alaska. For centuries, human beings have tried to explain away the mystery of these northern lights through folklore and legends. But it is through science that the Aurora Borealis is understood.

Northern lights are a natural phenomena in the sky that continually move like giant colored curtains of red, violets, yellow, blues and green. In simple terms, it is a huge space storm that is created by wind blasting past the Earth to the sun. This storm is called a "solar wind." Generally, we cannot feel this unusual space weather because the Earth is protected by a magnetic field. However, the space storm can be seen as an Aurora Borealis in starburst shapes, twists, waves and even swirls.

The source of the Auroras is the sun which gives off high-energy charged particles, or ions. These ions blast through space up to 400 miles per second. When the solar wind hits the Earth's magnetic field its particles begin to bounce and vibrate. But some of the particles become trapped in the Earth's magnetic field called the ionosphere. When the ionic particles strike the ionosphere, they create a glow that corresponds to different gasses in the ionosphere. Nitrogen in the ionosphere gives off a blue or violet light whereas oxygen gives a green or red light.

In the following project you will re-create the colors, illusion and drama of the Aurora Borealis without the aid of the magnetic field.

Notable Natives

Carlos Boozer (1981-), basketball player, Juneau

William Egan (1914-1984), governor, Valdez

Rosey Fletcher (1975-), snowboard champion, Anchorage

Scott Gomez (1979), football player, Anchorage

Travis Hall (1972-), football player, Kenai

Eben Hopson (1922-1980), founder of the Inuit Circumpolar Conference, Barrow

Lisa Murkowski (1957-), U.S. senator, Ketchikan

Northern Lights

Materials

* 8½" x11" black or dark blue paper
* oil-based paints: purple, red, yellow, green, light blue
* turpentine
* stick, knitting needle or other instrument for stirring
* comb
* shallow mixing tray or shallow basin
* water
* small jar for each color
* heavy book (place in plastic bag to protect)
* newspaper and blotting paper

Figure I

Instructions

1. Place several pieces of newspaper around your work space. Copy the Aurora Borealis shapes on page 13 and decide which type of look you want to create for your Northern Lights project.
2. Fill a shallow mixing tray or basin with water.
3. Squeeze a few pea-size shapes of one oil paint color into the jar. Mix with turpentine until it becomes the consistency of heavy cream. (Figure 1)
4. Drop the color into the water in various places. Spread them throughout. (Figure 2)
5. Take a comb or knitting needle and blend the color streams together in swirls, curtains, etc., that resemble the designs on page 13. Use a comb to make the Aurora's curtain shapes. Add contrasting paint colors. (Figure 3)
6. When you have created your Aurora Borealis, lower the sheet of paper onto the surface of the water. Hold the paper at both ends and curve the center of the paper into the water. Move the entire paper over the surface of the mixture. Do not immerse. (Figure 4)
7. Carefully lift the paper and place it, faceup, on the newspaper. In some cases you can continue to manipulate the colors while the paper begins to dry. Allow the paper to lie still for half an hour.
8. Remove the colored Aurora Borealis paper from the newspaper and place it on a fresh sheet of newspaper. Place blotting paper on top of the inked side and place the book on top to keep the paper from wrinkling. (Figure 5)
9. Place additional books on top to weigh it down.

Figure 2

Figure 3

Figure 4

Figure 5

Name _____

Aurora Borealis Shapes

curtains

waves

twists

swirls

Fun Facts

Amphibian: Arizona Tree Frog (Hyla eximia)

Bird: Cactus Wren (Campylorpynchus brunncicapillum)

Fish: Apache Trout (Salmo apache)

Flower: Saguaro Cactus Blossom (Carnegiea gigantea)

Fossil: Petrified Wood

Gem: Turquoise

Mammal: Ringtail Cat (Bassariscus astutus)

Motto: "Ditat Deus" (God enriches)

Nickname: Grand Canyon State

Reptile: Arizona Ridge-Nosed Rattlesnake (Crotalus willardi)

Songs: "Arizona March Song" by Margaret Rowe Clifford and "Arizona" by Rex Allen, Jr.

Tree: Yellow Palo Verde (Genera cericidium)

Statehood: February 14, 1912; 48th state admitted to the Union

Population: (2000 estimate) 5,130,632

Area: 114,006 square miles of land and water; 6th largest state

Highest Point: Humphrey's Peak; 12,633 feet above sea level

Lowest Point: Colorado River; 70 feet above sea level

Capital: Phoenix

Largest City: Phoenix

Major Crops: Cattle, calves, cotton, dairy products, lettuce, hay

Major Industry: Copper and other mining, electrical communications equipment, aeronautical equipment, food processing, tourism

Arizona

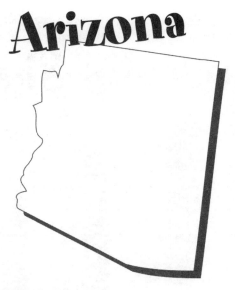

Name: Like many states, Arizona can trace the origin of its name to a Native American word. In fact, in this case, the state name can trace its origin back to two Native American words. Arizuma was an Aztec word meaning "silver bearing." Arizonac was a Pima word meaning "little spring place." No one is quite sure which of the two words is the exact origin of the state name.

Did You Know?

Arizona is one of the most important mining states in the United States. In fact, Arizona leads the nation in the production of copper. Copper is the metal used in the production of pipes and the production of pennies! Mining copper is so important to the state of Arizona, its history and economic development that copper is represented at the middle of the state flag by a large copper five-point star. In addition, the dome on the state capitol building is made of copper. In fact, there is enough copper on the Arizona state capitol building's dome to make 4,800,000 pennies. That would fill a lot of piggy banks!

inal 13 colonies and the rays of the setting sun. The red and yellow colors were chosen because they were the colors carried by the Spanish conquistador Coronado on his search for the Seven Cities of Cibola in 1540. The large copper star in the center of the flag represents the copper mined in the state. The bottom half of the flag is blue, representing liberty, the same blue found in the United States flag.

Seal: The state seal of Arizona has a shield in the center with the motto "Ditat Deus" on top of the shield. Below the motto inside the shield is a mountain range with the rising sun behind it. At the right side of the mountains is a reservoir showing irrigated fields and orchards. On the right are grazing cattle and a mill with a miner holding a pick and shovel. The miner symbolizes the importance of mining on the state's economy and early settlement.

Flag: The flag is divided into two halves. The top half has seven red and six light yellow rays emanating from a large copper five-point star in the direct center of the flag. The 13 rays are symbolic of the orig-

14

Painted Desert

In northeast Arizona stretches a land of brilliant and striking bands of color called the Painted Desert. This strange multicolored landscape covers 93,533 acres of wilderness. The Painted Desert is not only breathtaking, it offers an abundance of cultural, geological and historical features. The natural phenomena of the Painted Desert was developed in a unique variety of ways. The red shades are a result of iron oxide intermingling with streaks of white from gypsum deposits, and even volcanic ash. These minerals mixed with bentonite clay and created irregular layers of sediment. Other hues and tones were created by varieties of metal oxides that were deposited over the land when this region was submerged under water millions of years ago. Creating intricate patterns and deep ravines of sediment, resulting in the Painted Desert.

Notable Natives

Michael Carbajal (1967-), champion boxer, Phoenix

Lynda Carter (1951-), actress, Phoenix

Cesar Estrada Chavez (1927-1993), labor leader, Yuma

Cochise (?-1874), Apache chief, Arizona Territory

Barbara Eden (1934-) actress who starred in *I Dream of Jeannie*, Tucson

Louie Espinoza (1962-), champion boxer, Chandler

Geronimo (1829-1909), Apache chief, Arizona Territory

Barry Goldwater (1909-1998), U.S. senator, 1964 Republican candidate for President, Phoenix

Carl Trumbull Hayden (1877-1972), U.S. senator, Hayden's Ferry now Tempe

Frank Luke, Jr. (1897-1918), WWI fighter ace, Phoenix

Charles Mingus (1922-1979), jazz musician, composer, Nogales

Stevie Nicks (1948-) singer, Phoenix

Linda Ronstadt (1946-), singer, Tucson

Kerri Strug (1977-), Olympic gold-medal gymnast, Tucson

Stewart Udall (1920-), Secretary of the Interior, Saint Johns

Arizona

Painted Desert

This project requires heat.

Materials

* ¹/₂ cup of sand or salt for each color and variations you create
* food coloring: red, yellow, green, blue
* container and lid for each color
* fine mesh sieve
* large bowl
* large glass jar with lid
* 1" x 3" cube of paraffin wax
* heating plate
* gloves
* newspaper
* mixing dishes for each color
* ¹/₃ cup water or alcohol

Optional:
  alcohol

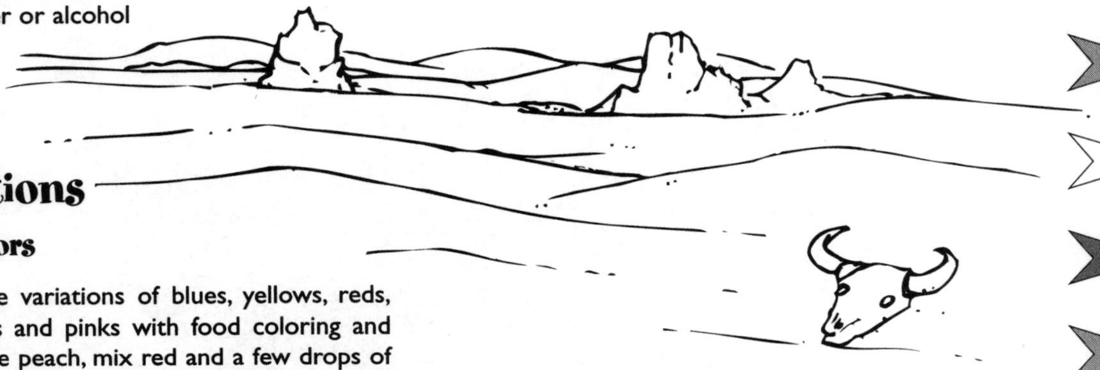

Instructions

Mixing Colors

You will make variations of blues, yellows, reds, oranges, grays and pinks with food coloring and water. To make peach, mix red and a few drops of yellow together. Burnt red is a blend of red with a few drops of green. Gray is a combination of all colors mixed together, muted with drops of water. Blue requires just a few drops to keep the color warm and subtle. White is the neutral and natural color of sand.

1. Mix the food coloring and water for each color in separate jars.
2. Pour the sand slowly into the jar and stir.
3. Allow the sand to sit in the colored water for at least 30 minutes.
4. Place the sieve over a sink and pour the colored sand and water into it. Shake out any remaining color.
5. Pour the sand out onto some newspaper and allow it to dry. If the sand is too light, repeat the color process.

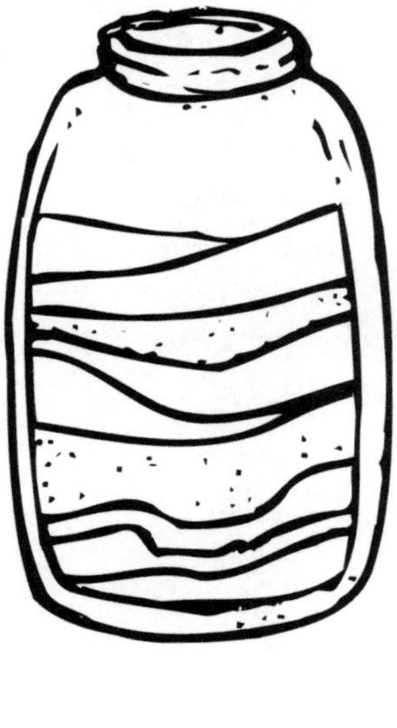

Optional Variation Using Salt

Salt takes less time to color and the color is more vibrant.

a. Pour salt into a container and stir in drops of food coloring.
b. Stir the salt until the color is evenly distributed.
c. Let the salt dry in jar. Repeat this process for each color.

Making the Sedimentary Layers

6. Copy the example of the Painted Desert layers from page 18.
7. Pour the first layer of color into the large jar. Move the glass jar to distribute the color, particularly against the glass. (Figure 1)
8. Continue layering the dried colors. Make the striations dynamic by occasionally pressing a pencil into the segments and against the side of the glass. (Figure 2)
9. When you have completed the layers, level them off with flattened material. (Figure 3)
10. Heat small chunks of wax in separate containers. Allow it to settle into a thick liquid. Pour it directly onto the leveled top of the colored layers. Let it dry. (Figure 4)

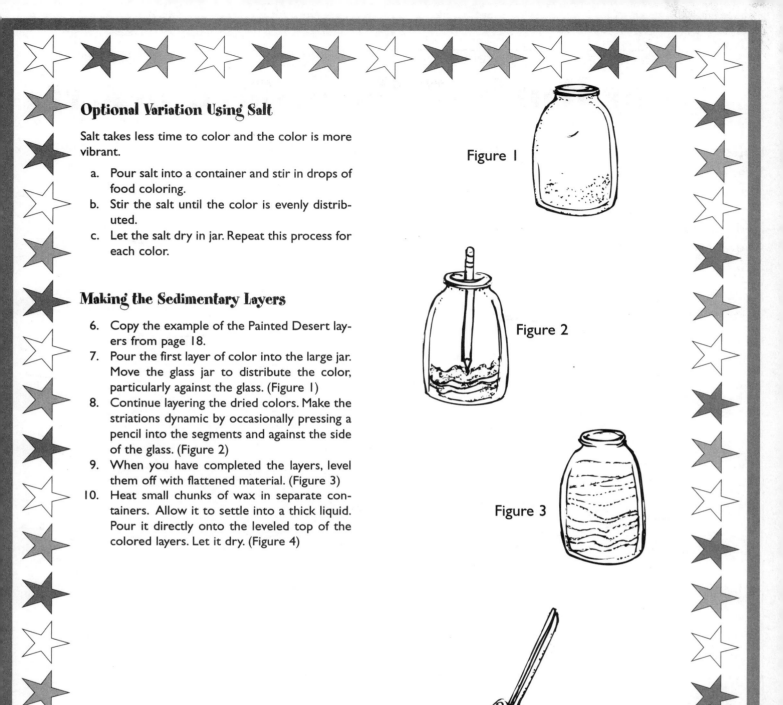

Figure 1

Figure 2

Figure 3

Figure 4

Color Bands of the Painted Desert

Color each area as indicated by the key.

Key
a. blue
b. red
c. yellow
d. white
e. peach
f. gray

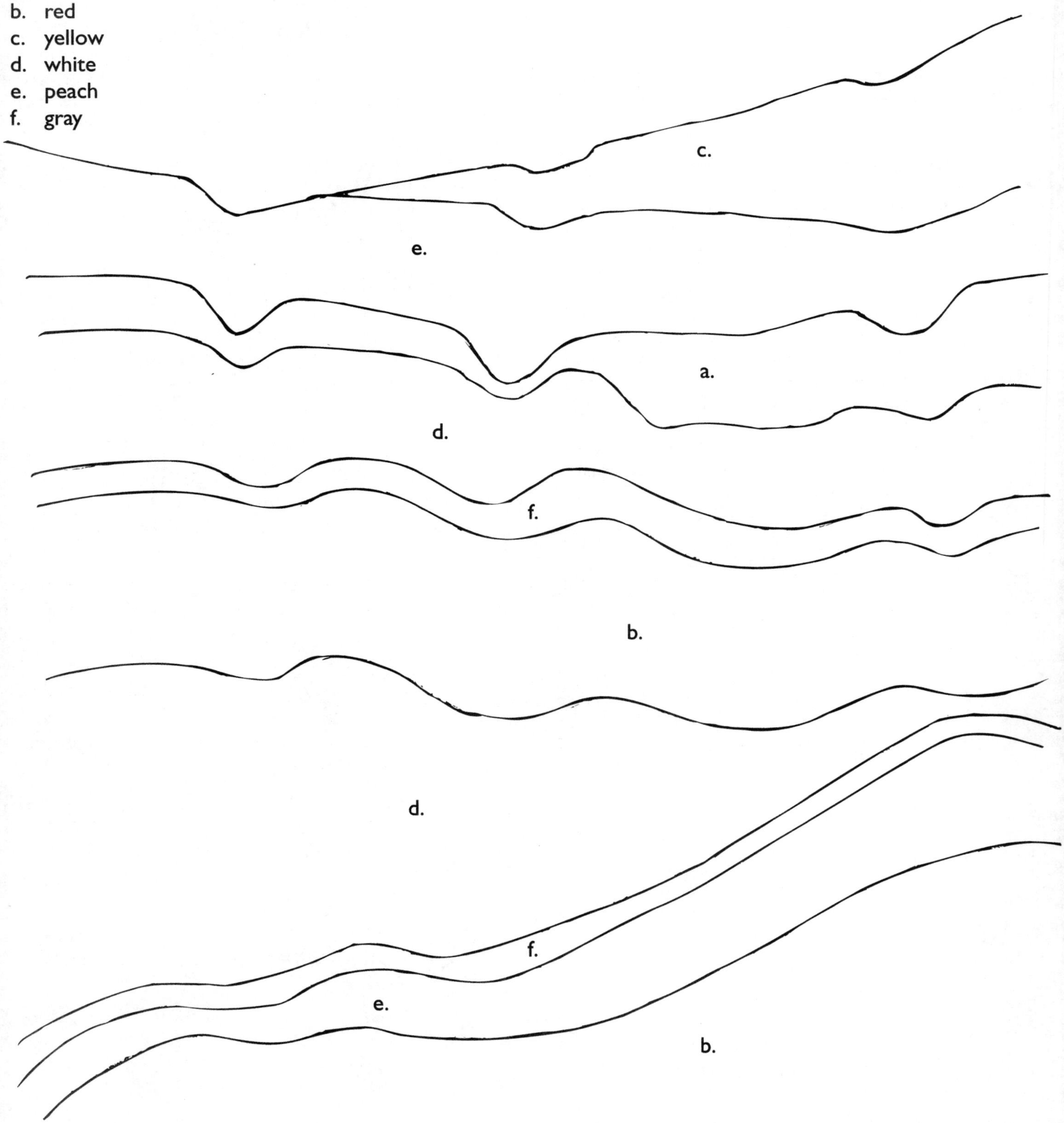

c.

e.

a.

d.

f.

b.

d.

f.

e.

b.

Fun Facts

Bird: Mockingbird (Mimus polyglottos)

Flower: Apple Blossom (Pyrus coronaria)

Fruit and Blossom: South Arkansas Vine Ripe Pink Tomato

Gem: Diamond

Insect: Honeybee (Apis mellifera)

Instrument: Fiddle

Mineral: Bauxite

Motto: "Regnat Populus" (The People Rule)

Nickname: Natural State

Rock: Quartz Crystal

Songs: "Arkansas" by Wayland Holyfield

"Oh, Arkansas" by Terry Rose and Gary Klaff

Trees: Loblolly Pine (Pinus taeda), Shortleaf Pine (Pinus echinata)

Statehood: June 15, 1836; 25th state admitted to the Union

Population: (2000 estimate) 2,673,400

Area: 53,182 square miles of land and water; 29th largest state

Highest Point: Magazine Mountain; 2753 feet above sea level

Lowest Point: Ouachita River; 55 feet above sea level

Capital: Little Rock

Largest City: Little Rock

Major Crops: Poultry, eggs, soybeans, sorghum, cattle, cotton, rice

Major Industry: Food processing, electrical equipment, bromine, vanadium, diamond mining, tourism

Arkansas

Did You Know?

A small variety store, that sold all sorts of items to customers was opened in Bentonville, Arkansas, by Sam Walton. It was the beginning of what we now know as the largest retailing store chain in the world—Wal-Mart! Over one million people work for Wal-Mart in all parts of the world, making it the world's largest private employer. Wal-Mart sells everything from toys to fishing hooks, and it all started in Bentonville, Arkansas.

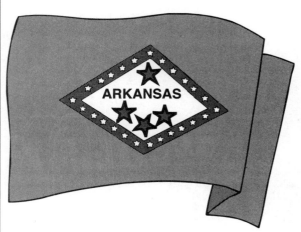

Flag: The state flag has a bright red background, with a blue and white diamond shape in the center, a reminder that Arkansas is the only state in the Union where diamonds have been found. The diamond shape is surrounded by 25 stars because Arkansas was the 25th state to join the Union. In the center of the white diamond is the word *Arkansas* with one five-point star above it, symbolic of

Name: The word Arkansas is derived from the Sioux word acansa. Acansa meant "downstream place" used to describe a river that the Quapaw tribal people lived near. When French explorers heard the word they pronounced it "ark-an-saw."

Arkansas' membership in the Confederacy during the Civil War and three five-point stars below it, representing Spain, France and the United States. Arkansas was once part of Spain, then France, then the United States.

Seal: The circular seal of the state is dominated by an eagle with its wings spread. On the eagle is a shield divided into three parts. The upper third displays a steamship, the middle third, a plow, and the lower third, a sheaf of wheat. The eagle has in its talons an olive branch on one side and arrows on the other. In the eagle's beak is a ribbon that bears the state's motto, "Regnat Populus." To the left of the eagle is an angel with the word *mercy* on a scroll. To the right of the eagle is a sword with the word *justice* on it. Above the eagle in a circle of 13 five-point stars is the figure of Liberty. The seal has an outer ring (which is not pictured) containing the words *Great Seal of the State of Arkansas.*

State Flag of 1913

In 1913, the Daughters of the American Revolution (D.A.R.) voted to present the Arkansas state flag to a battleship dedicated to their state. But no such flag existed!

They set out to change this problem by holding a statewide contest to choose a design for their state's first official flag. Sixty-five separate designs were entered into the contest. Some designs had crayon drawings while others were sewn on silk. The designs varied from apple blossoms to scattered stars. But the one design that stood out from the others was made by a member of the D.A.R., Willie Hocker, of Wabbaseka, Arkansas.

Though some final adjustments were made to Miss Hocker's initial design, the representations and symbols were specific to her beloved state. The general color scheme was red, white and blue which symbolized that Arkansas belonged to the United States of America. The flag was designed with a rectangular field of red and a large blue diamond reaching out to all sides. Three blue stars under the name, *Arkansas*, represented the state's early claims by France, then Spain and finally, the United States. The three stars also stood for 1803, the year the Louisiana Territory was purchased by the United States. And the three stars are a reminder that Arkansas was the third state created from the Louisiana Purchase, after Missouri and Louisiana.

Notable Natives

Cyrus Adler (1863-1940), religious educator, leader, Van Buren

Helen Gurley Brown, (1922-) editor of *Cosmopolitan* magazine, Green Forest

Paul William "Bear" Bryant (1913-1983), football coach, Kingsland

Glen Campbell (1936-), country singer, Delight

Johnny Cash (1932-2003), country singer, Kingsland

Eldridge Cleaver (1935-1998), civil rights activist, Wabbaseka

William (Bill) Jefferson Clinton (1946-), 42nd President (1992-2000), Hope

James Hal Cone (1938-), theologian, author, Fordyce

Jay Hanna "Dizzy" Dean (1911-1974), baseball player, Lucas

Jocelyn Elders (1933-), U.S. Surgeon General, Skaal

John Gould Fletcher (1886-1950), poet, Little Rock

John Grisham (1955-), writer, Jonesboro

Alan Ladd (1913-1964), actor, Hot Springs

Douglas MacArthur (1880-1964), five-star general, Little Rock

Arkansas Crate

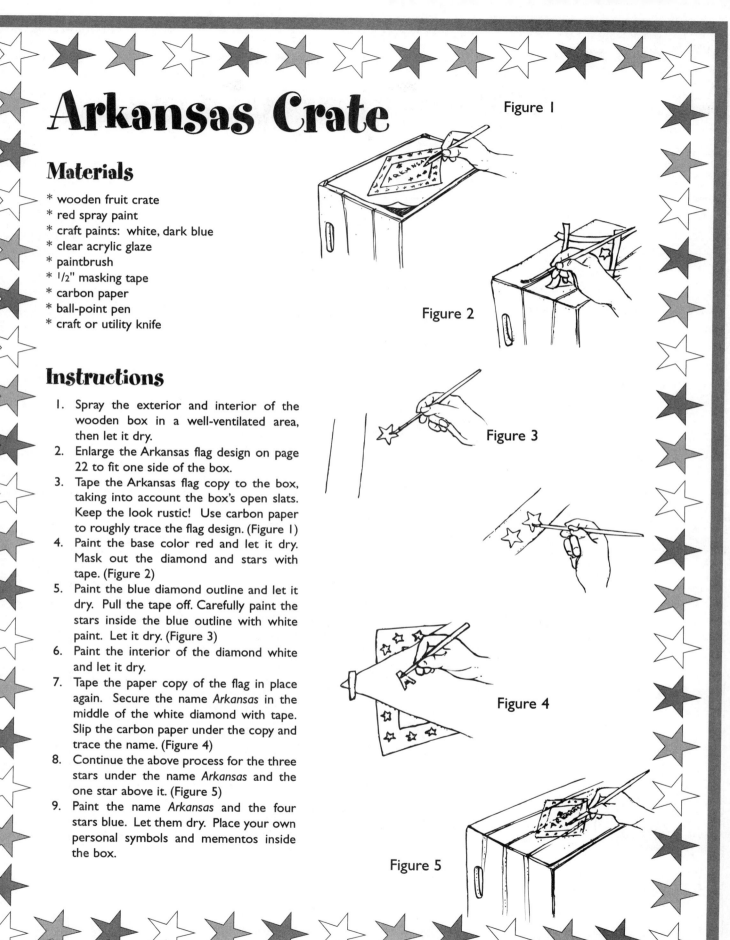

Figure 1

Figure 2

Figure 3

Figure 4

Figure 5

Materials

* wooden fruit crate
* red spray paint
* craft paints: white, dark blue
* clear acrylic glaze
* paintbrush
* 1/2" masking tape
* carbon paper
* ball-point pen
* craft or utility knife

Instructions

1. Spray the exterior and interior of the wooden box in a well-ventilated area, then let it dry.
2. Enlarge the Arkansas flag design on page 22 to fit one side of the box.
3. Tape the Arkansas flag copy to the box, taking into account the box's open slats. Keep the look rustic! Use carbon paper to roughly trace the flag design. (Figure 1)
4. Paint the base color red and let it dry. Mask out the diamond and stars with tape. (Figure 2)
5. Paint the blue diamond outline and let it dry. Pull the tape off. Carefully paint the stars inside the blue outline with white paint. Let it dry. (Figure 3)
6. Paint the interior of the diamond white and let it dry.
7. Tape the paper copy of the flag in place again. Secure the name *Arkansas* in the middle of the white diamond with tape. Slip the carbon paper under the copy and trace the name. (Figure 4)
8. Continue the above process for the three stars under the name *Arkansas* and the one star above it. (Figure 5)
9. Paint the name *Arkansas* and the four stars blue. Let them dry. Place your own personal symbols and mementos inside the box.

Arkansas State Flag

Fun Facts

Animal: Grizzly Bear
(Ursus californicus)

Bird: California Quail
(Lophortyx californica)

Fish: Golden Trout
(Salmo agua-bonita)

Marine Fish: Golden Orange Fish
(Hypsypops rubicundus)

Flower: California Poppy
(Eschholtzia californica)

Fossil: Saber-Tooth Cat
(Smilodon californicus)

Gem: Benitoite or Blue Diamond
(Barium Titanium Silicate)

Insect: California Dogface
Butterfly or Dog Head
(Zerene eurydice)

Marine Mammal: California
Whale (Eschrichtius robustus)

Motto: "Eureka"

Mineral: Gold (Aurum)

Nickname: Golden State

Reptile: Desert Tortoise
(Gopherus agassizii)

Rock: Serpentine

Song: "I Love You, California" by
F.B. Silverwood

Tree: California Redwood
(Sequoia sempervirens)
(Sequoia gigantea)

Statehood: September 9, 1850;
31st state admitted to the Union

Population: (2000 estimate)
33,871,646

Area: 163,707 square miles of
land and water; 3rd largest state

Highest Point: Mt. Whitney;
14,494 feet above sea level

Lowest Point: Death Valley; 282
feet below sea level

Capital: Sacramento

Largest City: Los Angeles

Major Crops: Truck vegetables,
fruits and nuts, dairy products,
cattle, grapes, wine

Major Industry: Aerospace,
defense manufacturing and
design, film production, biotech-
nology, food processing,
petroleum, natural gas, cement,
computers and computer
software, tourism

California

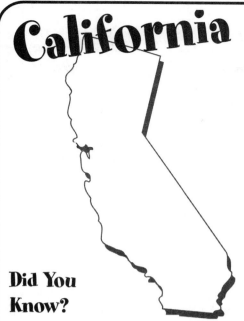

Name: Many people considered California a paradise because of its beautiful coastline, majestic mountains and year-round temperate weather. In fact, California was named after a mythical island paradise, Califia, first described by Spanish author Montalvo in 1510, in his book, _Las Serges Esplandian_.

Did You Know?

A & W Root Beer™ got its name from the initials of the two partners who made the thirst-quenching drink—Roy Allen and Frank Wright. Roy Allen first sold his root beer in Lodi, California, at a parade for soldiers returning from World War I. The drink was an instant hit. In 1922, Allen partnered with Wright to open a series of "drive-ins" that provided food and drinks from the restaurant directly to customers waiting in their cars. They called it curbside service. The drive-in restaurant was born.

Flag: Most of the California state flag is white, with the exception of a red bar across the bottom. In the center of the flag is a large bear walking on green grass over the words _California Republic_. A single, red five-point star appears in the upper left corner.

Seal: The seal is dominated by the figure of Minerva, Roman goddess of wisdom, seated to the right. At her feet are a grizzly bear, the official state animal, and a cluster of grapes. The bear represents the abundant and untamed wildlife of the state. The grapes symbolize the richness of the fruit and agriculture. Behind Minerva are mountains and the Sacramento River. Three sailing ships are on the river and a miner is busily working near the banks. _Eureka_, the state motto, which means "I have found it," is at the top center of the seal. The word refers to the discovery of gold that brought thousands of miners to California in search of fortune. Thirty-one five-point stars form a half crescent near the top of the seal to show that it was the 31st state in the Union. The words _The Great Seal of the State of California_ appear in the outer ring of the seal.

Bandboxes

Bandboxes were rural America's way of acquiring extra storage space in the 19th century. The bandboxes stored starched collars and ladies' bonnets, lacebands, gloves and other small accessories. As bandboxes increased in size, they were able to hold larger items and were soon built sturdy enough for stagecoach travel. Bandboxes were made of 100% cotton fiber, painted with distemper, usually lined with newspaper and covered with block print. Sometimes bandboxes had advertisements from local scenes or political themes on them. Others had images of 19th century changes (steamboats, canals and railroads) that were beginning to make an impact on the upper and middle classes of America.

The following bandbox project includes California landscape images that move through a black frame. The frame represents the movie industry, an important part of California culture.

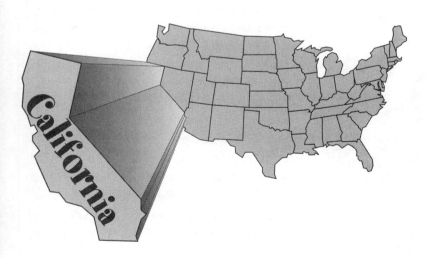

Notable Natives

Robert Grant Aiken (1864-1951), astronomer, Jackson

Gracie Allen (1895-1964), comedic actress, San Francisco

David Belasco (1853-1931), playwright, San Francisco

Victor Hugo Benioff (1899-1968), geophysicist, Los Angeles

Busby Berkeley (William Berkeley Enos) (1895-1976), choreographer, Los Angeles

Matt Biondi (1965-), Olympic gold-medal swimmer, Morego

Shirley Temple Black (1928-), childhood actress, ambassador, Santa Monica

Barry Bonds (1964-), baseball player, Riverside

Nicolas Cage (Nicolas Coppola) (1964-), Oscar-winning actor, Long Beach

Owen Chamberlain (1920-), Nobel Prize-winning physicist, San Francisco

Cher (1946-), actress, singer, El Centro

Julia Child (1912-2004), chef who pioneered television cooking shows, Pasadena

Coolio (1963-), musician, Los Angeles

Jami Lee Curtis (1958-), actress, Los Angeles

Lindsay Davenport (1976-), tennis player, Palos Verdes

Laura Dern (1967-), actress, Santa Monica

Cameron Diaz (1972-), actress, San Diego

Leonardo DiCaprio (1974-), actor, Hollywood

Joe DiMaggio (1914-1999), New York Yankees baseball player, Martinez

James Doolittle (1896-1993), heroic Air Force officer during World War II, Alameda

Isadora Duncan (1878-1927), dancer, San Francisco

Clint Eastwood (1930-), actor, Oscar-winning film director, San Francisco

Mia Farrow (Maria de Lourdes Villiers) (1945-), actress, Los Angeles

Peggy Fleming (1948-), Olympic gold-medal figure skater, San Jose

Jodi Foster (1962-), Oscar-winning actress, Los Angeles

Robert Frost (1874-1963), poet, San Francisco

Jerry Garcia (1942-1995), musician, San Francisco

William Randolph Hearst (1863-1951), newspaper publisher, San Francisco

Mariel Hemingway (1961-), actress, Mill Valley

Anthony Kennedy (1936-), U.S. Supreme Court Justice, Sacramento

Jack London (John Griffith Chaney) (1876-1916), writer, San Francisco

George Lucas (1944-), filmmaker, Modesto

Toby Maguire (1975-), actor, Santa Monica

Mark McGwire (1963-), baseball player, Pomona

Richard Milhous Nixon (1913-1994), 37th President (1969-1974), Yorba Linda

Ashley & Mary-Kate Olsen (1986-), actresses, Sherman Oaks

George Smith Patton, Jr. (1885-1945), major general in World War II, San Gabriel

Robert Redford (1937-), actor, Santa Monica

Sally Ride (1951-), astronaut, first U.S. woman in space, Los Angeles

William Saroyan (1908-1981), writer, playwright, Fresno

John Steinbeck (1902-1968), Nobel Prize-winning author, Salinas

Adlai Stevenson (1900-1965), governor, statesman, two-time Democratic presidential candidate, Los Angeles

Earl Warren (1891-1974), Chief Justice of the U.S. Supreme Court, Los Angeles

Eldrick "Tiger" Woods (1975-), golfer, Cypress

Bandboxes

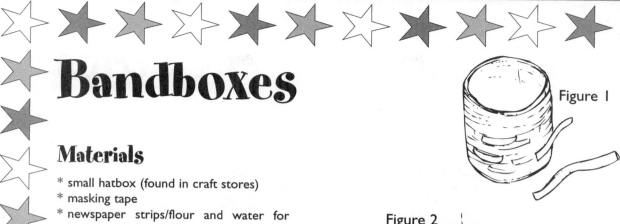

Figure 1

Materials

* small hatbox (found in craft stores)
* masking tape
* newspaper strips/flour and water for papier-mâché mix
* white glue
* newspaper
* white latex paint
* acrylic paint of your choice
* X-acto™ knife
* paint
* scissors
* saw

Figure 2

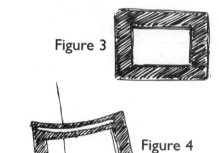

Figure 3

Instructions

1. Apply newspaper strips with water and flour to the interior and exterior of the hatbox and cover. Let it dry. (Figure 1)

2. Prime everything with white latex paint. Then paint the entire box with your favorite colors.

3. Make a copy of the movie frame and scene strips on page 26. Glue the squares together to make a strip that wraps around the bandbox and set aside. (Figure 2)

4. Cut out the movie frame. (Figure 3)

5. Apply a line of glue to the bottom and top edges (only) of the movie frame to the box—no more than 1/4" below both edges. (Figure 4)

6. Slip the movie strip through the black movie frame. (Figure 5)

7. Wrap the movie strip around the bandbox and glue the strip edges together. Move the California images through the black movie frame. (Figure 6)

Figure 4

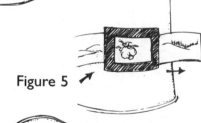

Figure 5

Figure 6

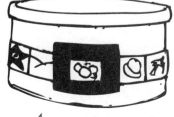

Movie Frame and Scene Strips

 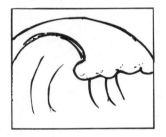 

 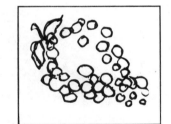 

Fun Facts

Animal: Rocky Mountain Bighorn Sheep (Ovis canadensis)

Bird: Lark Bunting (Calamospiza melanocoryus Stejneger)

Fish: Greenback Cutthroat Trout (Oncorhynchus clarki)

Flower: White and Lavender Columbine (Aquilegia caerules)

Fossil: Stegosaurus (Stegosaurus armatus)

Gem: Aquamarine (Berylium Aluminum Silicate)

Grass: Blue Grama Grass (Bouteloua gracilis)

Insect: Colorado Hairstreak Butterfly (Hypaurotis cysalus)

Mineral: Rhodochrosite (Manganese carbonate)

Motto: "Nil Sine Numine" (Nothing Without Providence)

Nickname: Centennial State

Song: "Where the Columbines Grow" by A.J. Fynn

Tree: Colorado Blue Spruce (Picea pungens)

Statehood: August 1, 1876; 38th state admitted to the Union

Population: (2000 estimate) 4,301,261

Area: 104,100 square miles of land and water; 8th largest state

Highest Point: Mt. Elbert; 14,433 feet above sea level

Lowest Point: Arikaree River; 3315 above sea level

Capital: Denver

Largest City: Denver

Major Crops: Cattle, dairy products, corn, hay, wheat

Major Industry: Food processing, electrical instruments, chemical products, gold and other mining, printing and publishing, tourism

Name: *Some of the earliest explorers in the area now known as Colorado were Spanish. The word they used to describe the river running through the area was* <u>Colorado</u>, *a Spanish word that means "colored red." The state got its name from the Colorado River. It is one of several states named for the river that runs through it.*

Did You Know?

The world's first rodeo was held in Deer Trail, Colorado, on July 4th, 1869. Crowds enjoy seeing the skills exhibited by horsemen and women. Denver claims to host the world's largest rodeo every year.

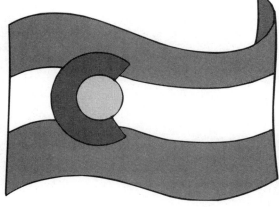

Flag: The state flag consists of three equal stripes of blue, white and blue. To the left of center is a large, bright red letter "C" with a golden disk inside it. The red, white and blue of the flag is consistent with the U.S. national flag.

Seal: The state seal carries the words, *State of Colorado, 1876,* the year Colorado was admitted to the Union, and "Nil Sine Numine," the state motto. In the center of the circular seal is a shield. On top of the shield is the eye of God in a triangle with rays emanating from it. Underneath are Roman fasces and a battle-ax. Inside the shield are three snow-covered mountains with a pick and a sledgehammer underneath.

The Professor & Pike's Peak

The mountains of Colorado inspire all who see them. This was especially true in 1880 when poet and professor of English literature, Katharine Lee Bates, witnessed the majesty of America from Pike's Peak* in the Colorado mountains. Professor Bates was so taken by the beauty, she wrote what became a beloved national hymn, "America the Beautiful." It was originally published as a poem in the *Congressionalist* journal on July 4, 1895. Professor Bates later revised some sections of the poem and published it in the *Boston Evening Transcript* in November 1904. Some critics mocked the word *beautiful* in the poem because they believed it lacked ingenuity. Professor Bates refused to change the word because she believed it best described what she had seen from Pike's Peak. The poem was later set to music by Silas G. Pratt.

* Pike's Peak was named after the explorer, Lieutenant Zebulon Montgomery Pike, who explored the western portion of the Louisiana Purchase in 1806.

Katharine Lee Bates

Born on August 12, 1859, Katharine Lee Bates attended Wellesly College in 1880. She later taught at Wellesly as a professor of literature. Professor Bates wrote 32 books. It is believed that she created the character, Mrs. Claus, first introduced in the book, *Goody Santa Claus on a Sleigh Ride*, published in 1889.

Topographical Mapmaking

Imagine looking off in the distance from the summit of Pike's Peak at land that seems to stretch on forever. Standard maps rarely give us an idea of true topography. We'll use topographical maps to begin this project. By filling in the details, we'll gain a better understanding of what inspired Katharine Lee Bates to write "America the Beautiful."

Notable Natives

Tim Allen (1953-), actor, Denver

Lon Chaney (1883-1930), actor, Colorado Springs

Kristin Davis (1965-), actress, Boulder

Laura Gilpin (1891-1979), photographer, Austin Bluffs

William Harrison (Jack) Dempsey (1895-1983), world heavyweight boxer, Manassa

Erick Hawkins (1909-1994), dancer, choreographer, Trinidad

Douglas Fairbanks (1883-1939), actor, Denver

Byron Raymond White (1917-2002), U.S. Supreme Court Justice, Fort Collins

Jan-Michael Vincent (1944- actor, Denver

Colorado

Topographical Maps

This project requires heat.

Materials

* Gesso™ or white latex paint
* corrugated cardboard
* carbon paper
* pencil
* tape
* white glue
* X-acto™ knife
* acrylic or tempera paints: brown, purple, green, white
* 2 cups Styrofoam™ peanuts

Materials for Papier-Mâché Mixture

* newspaper
* ¹/₂ teaspoon white glue
* 5 teaspoons wallpaper paste
* 1 teaspoon plaster of Paris
* ¹/₂ teaspoon linseed oil
* saucepan
* water
* blender
* reusable plastic container

Instructions

Reading topographical maps is a handy skill. Begin by examining the map on page 31. Topographical maps vary from simple to complex, but the most basic show the contour of an area at each elevation of the Earth's surface. The hachure marks show the depressions of the Earth's surface.

From the contour map, a topographic map is created. Making a two-dimensional object into a three-dimensional form is an abstract idea.

1. Make a copy of the contour map of Pike's Peak on page 31.
2. Tape the copy onto a large piece of cardboard with a sheet of carbon paper between them. Firmly pressing down with your pencil, trace over the lines. Then cut out the pieces with an X-acto™ knife. (Figure 1)

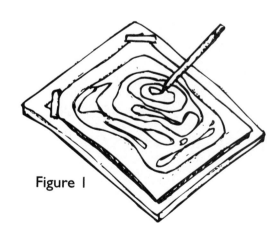

Figure 1

3. Cut a Styrofoam™ peanut in quarters. Glue a few of the pieces in strategic places on one of the larger cardboard shapes. (Figure 2)
4. Make additional contour layers of various sizes, adding Styrofoam™ pieces to build the layers up. (Figure 3)
5. Let the glue dry as you begin making a papier-mâché mixture.
6. Tear newspaper into small pieces. Place the newspaper in a small saucepan and cover with water. Simmer for a half an hour or more. Cool. (Figure 4)
7. Pour or spoon the mixture into a blender and liquefy it into a mash. (Figure 5)
8. Add white glue, plaster of Paris, linseed oil and wallpaper paste to the mixture.
9. Scoop the mixture up into your hands and begin to cover the contour layers to form Pike's Peak. When complete, let it dry, then paint it. (Figure 6)

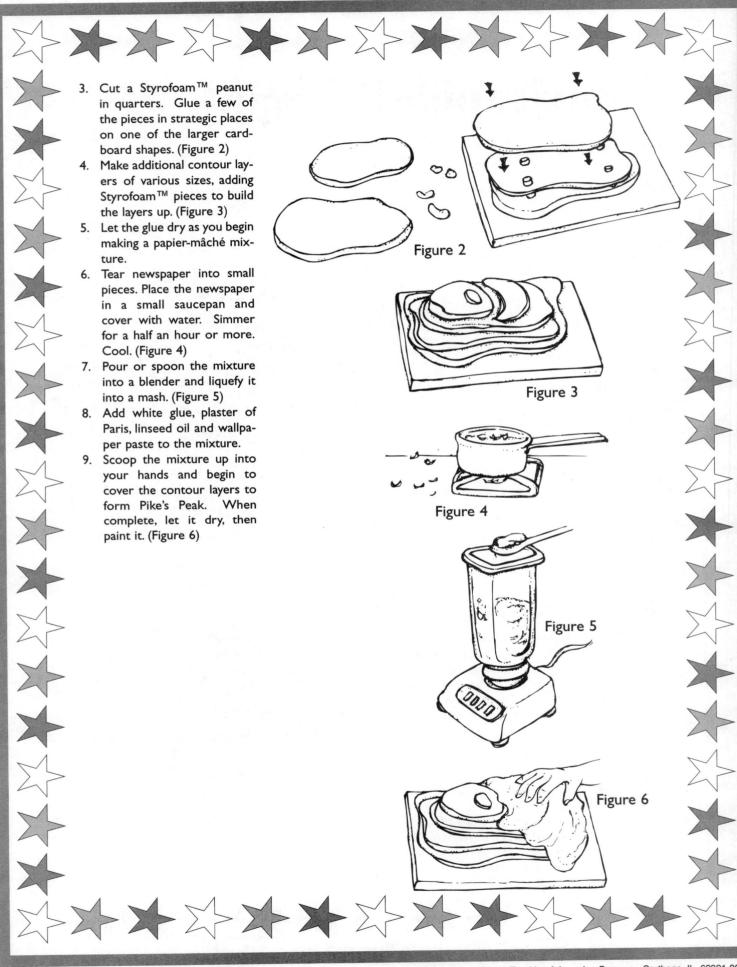

Figure 2

Figure 3

Figure 4

Figure 5

Figure 6

Name _____

Pike's Peak Contour Map

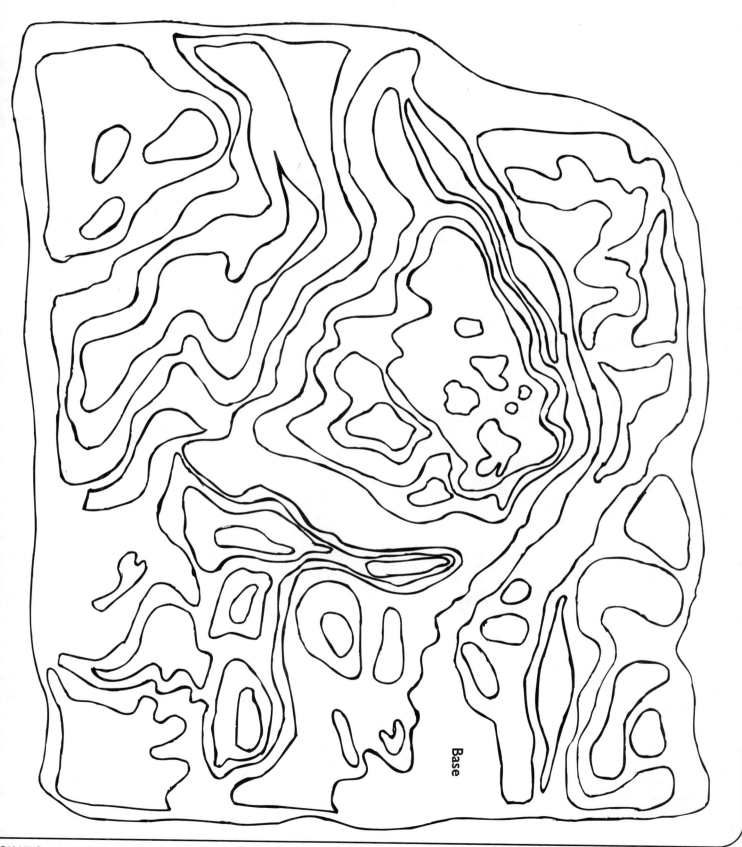

Base

Fun Facts

Animal: Sperm Whale
(Physeter macrosephalus)

Bird: American Robin
(Turdus migratorius)

Flower: Mountain Laurel
(Kalmia latifolia)

Fossil: Dinosaur footprint of
Eubrontes giganteus

Insect: European Mantis
(Mantis religiosa)

Mineral: Garnet
(Almadine garnet)

Motto: "Qui Transtulit
Sustinet" (He who
transplants sustains)

Nicknames: Constitution
State, Nutmeg State

Shellfish: Eastern Oyster
(Crassostera virginica)

Song: "Yankee Doodle" by
Francis Hopkinson

Trees: Charter Oak, White
Oak (Quercus alba)

Statehood: January 9, 1788;
5th state admitted to the
Union

Population: (2000 estimate)
3,405,565

Area: 5544 square miles of
land and water; 48th largest
state

Highest Point: Mt. Frissell;
2380 feet above sea level

Lowest Point: Long Island
Sound

Capital: Hartford

Largest City: Bridgeport

Major Crops: Oysters,
poultry, eggs, dairy products,
pears, peaches, mushrooms,
cattle

Major Industry: Tourism,
insurance, silverware,
hardware, chemical prod-
ucts, scientific instruments,
defense weapons and
jet engines

Connecticut

Did You Know?

Children love the sweet taste of lollipops, those yummy candies on sticks. Since they were so popular, someone made a machine to mass produce them.

The speedy lollipop machine was invented by George Smith in New Haven, Connecticut, in 1908. The lollipop was named after a popular horse that could run fast!

Flag: The state flag of Connecticut has a white shield in the center of an azure blue background. Inside the shield are three grape vines, each bearing three bunches of purple grapes. Under the shield are the words *Qui Transtulit Sustinet* on a white rib-bon. The vines represent the English who transplanted themselves from England to Connecticut.

Name: *Like many states, Connecticut owes its name to Native Americans. The word* <u>Connecticut</u> *can be traced back to Mohican and Algonquin words meaning "long river place" or "beside the long tidal river." Both Native American tribes lived in the area.*

Seal: The seal is an oval showing three posts. Each has a grapevine with three bunches of grapes growing on the vine. Under the vines is the state motto, "Qui Transtulit Sustinet," which means "He who transplants sustains," in a ribbon. Around the outer rim of the oval are the words *Sigillum Reipublicae Connecticutensis.*

Charter Oak

A tree in Connecticut's history was so sig-nificant, it is called the Charter Oak. This single oak is the symbol of strength, free-dom and resistance against tyranny. Though the tree fell in a great storm on August 21, 1856, many of its seedlings sur-vive today.

The story of the charter oak began on April 26, 1662. When the Connecticut General Court received a charter from King Charles II. Charters secured the rights enjoyed by British colonies in the new world, such as the right to vote and self-govern. However, when Charles II died, his successor, King James, grew con-temptuous of the colonial charters. He wanted to bring all the colonies together under a new consolidated patent which would give him complete control. Each colony was forced to give back its charter to the crown, but Connecticut's citizens refused!

King James, furious, appointed the aggressive governor of New York, Sir Edmund Andros, to put pressure on Connecticut officials. They were threatened with treason if they did not hand over the document. Still, they refused. Sir Andros insisted on meeting with the Connecticut officials at Moses Butler's Tavern in Hartford.

Connecticut citizens knew that refusing to give up their charter was a treasonous act, but they believed Sir Andros' attempt to claim the charter was illegal. On the designated day, they gathered arms and lined up on the road to Hartford as Sir Andros and his 70 armed soldiers moved through the town. Inside the tavern, Governor Treat, Captain Joseph Wadsworth, Assemeblyman Stanley, Andrew Leete and others pleaded to keep their charter to no avail. Eventually, the governor acquiesced and directed Wadsworth to get the charter hidden at the home of Ruth Wylly. While Wadsworth went to find the charter, those in the tavern continued to plead and argue over the charter's validity. Sir Andros sat and glared. Finally, the charter was brought in and laid on the table. Connecticut citizen, Andrew Leete, though deathly ill, pleaded again. He swung his hands dramatically through the air, then suddenly grabbed his chest, fell forward onto the table and knocked over the candelabra, the only light in the room. The room went dark. When the candles were finally relit, the charter had disappeared.

Legend says the theft of the charter was prearranged by the governor, Stanley, Leete and Wadsworth. In the darkness, Stanley grasped the charter and passed it through an open window to Wadsworth who was standing outside. With the precious document under his arm, Wadsworth ran back to Wylly's house. Ruth Wylly suggested they hide the charter in the hollow of an old oak tree that grew on her property.

Sir Edmund Andros was never able to find the charter.

Connecticut

Notable Natives

Dean Acheson (1893-1971), statesman, Pulitzer Prize-winning author, Middletown

George A. Akerof (1940-), Nobel Prize-winning economist, New Haven

Bronson Alcott (1799-1888), teacher, Transcendentalist, near Wolcott

Ethan Allan (1738-1789), American Revolutionary War hero, Litchfield

Benedict Arnold (1741-1801), American Revolutionary War general, traitor, Norwich

Joel Barlow (1754-1812), poet, statesman, Redding

Henry Barnard (1811-1900), first U.S. Commissioner of Education, Hartford

P.T. Barnum (1810-1891), circus owner, showman, Bethel

Moses Yale Beach (1800-1868), journalist, Wallingford

William Beaumont (1785-1853), surgeon, author, Lebanon

Henry Ward Beecher (1813-1887), clergyman, abolitionist, Litchfield

Michael Bolton (1967-), singer, New Haven

Ernest Borgnine (1917-), actor, Hamden

Charles Loring Brace (1826-1890), Children's Aid Society founder, Litchfield

David Brainerd (1718-1747), missionary, Haddam

John Brown (1800-1859), abolitionist, Torrington

Gary Burghoff (1943-), actor, Bristol

George Walker Bush (1946-), 43rd President (2001-), New Haven

Al Capp (Alfred Gerald Caplin) (1909-1976) L'il Abner cartoonist, New Haven

Russell Henry Chittenden (1856-1943), physiological chemist, New Haven

Frederick Edwin Church (1826-1900), landscape painter, Hartford

Glenn Close (1947-), actress, Greenwich

Samuel Colt (1814-1862), inventor, Hartford

Brian Dennehy (1938-), actor, Bridgeport

Jonathan Edwards (1703-1858), theologian, preacher, East Windsor

Linda Evans (1942-), actress, Hartford

Charles Goodyear (1800-1860), inventor of vulcanized rubber, New Haven

Nathan Hale (1755-1776), American Revolutionary War hero, Coventry

Katharine Hepburn, (1907-2003), Oscar-winning actress, Hartford

Norman Lear (1922-), writer, television producer, New Haven

Annie Leibovitz (1949-), photographer, Westbury

John Pierpont Morgan (1837-1913), banker, financier, Hartford

Kevin Nealon (1953-), comedian, actor, Bridgeport

Frederick Law Olmsted (1922-2003), landscape architect, Hartford

Kenneth Olsen (1926-), computer engineer, mini computer pioneer, Bridgeport

Adam Clayton Powell, Jr. (1908-1972), U.S. congressman, New Haven

Meg Ryan (1961-), actress, Fairfield

Benjamin Spock (1903-1998), pediatrician, author, New Haven

Harriet Beecher Stowe (1811-1896), writer, Litchfield

Noah Webster (1758-1843), lexicographer, West Hartford

Charter Oak

Figure 1

Materials

* paper towel tube
* 30 florist medium stub wires
* brown florist tape
* fine brass wire
* green crepe paper
* white glue
* brown acrylic paint
* aluminum foil
* wire cutters or old scissors
* paper towel tube
* scissors
* paintbrush
* tea bag
* 1/4" wide red ribbon
* sealing wax or red crayon
* 7 sheets newspaper
* 4 teaspoons white glue
* 4 teaspoons plaster of Paris
* 5 teaspoons wallpaper paste
* 1 teaspoon linseed oil

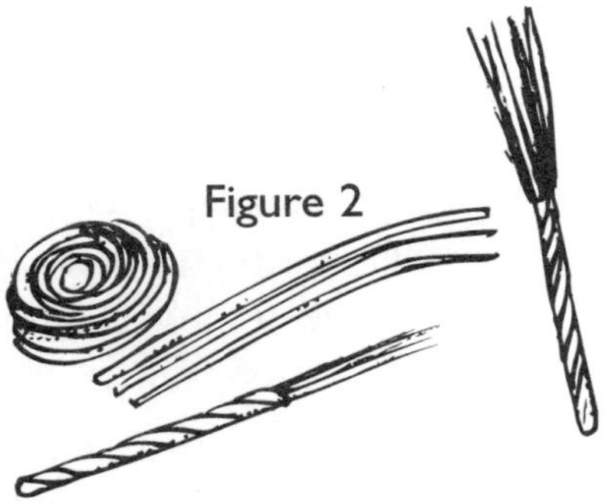

Figure 2

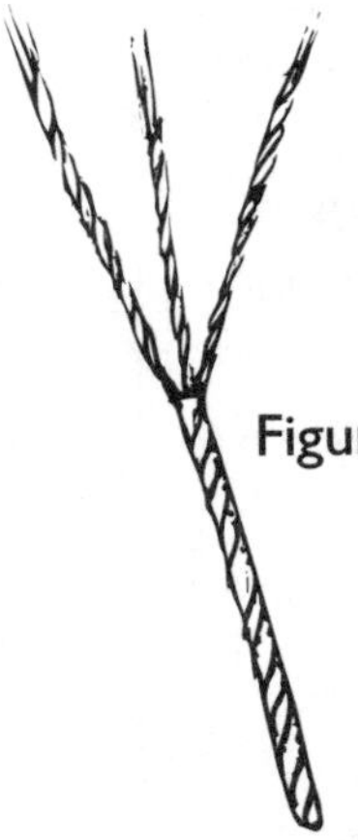

Figure 3

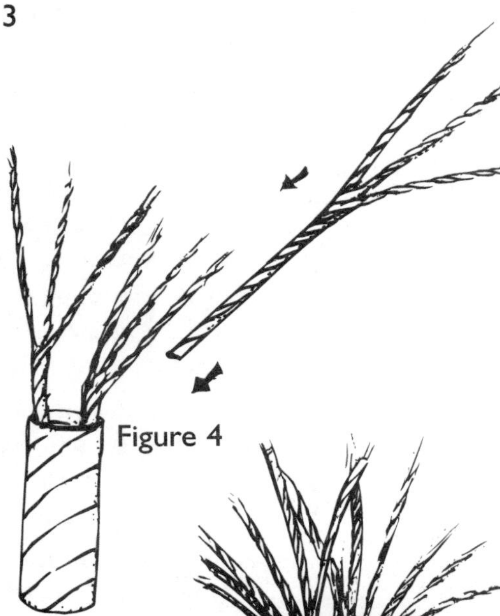

Figure 4

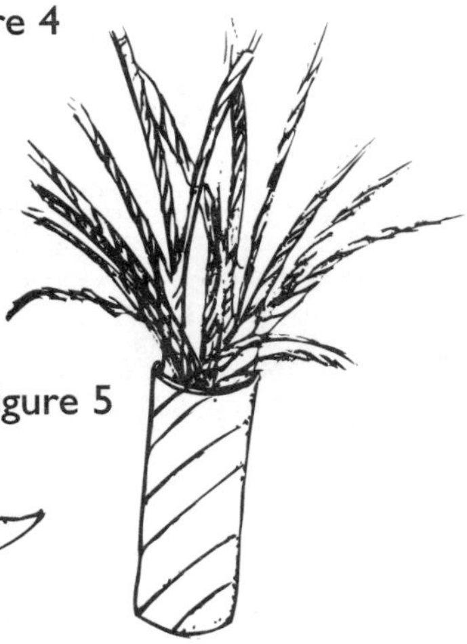

Figure 5

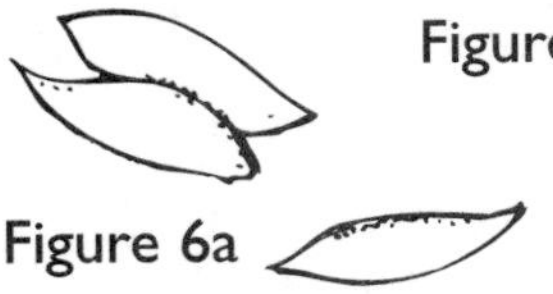

Figure 6a

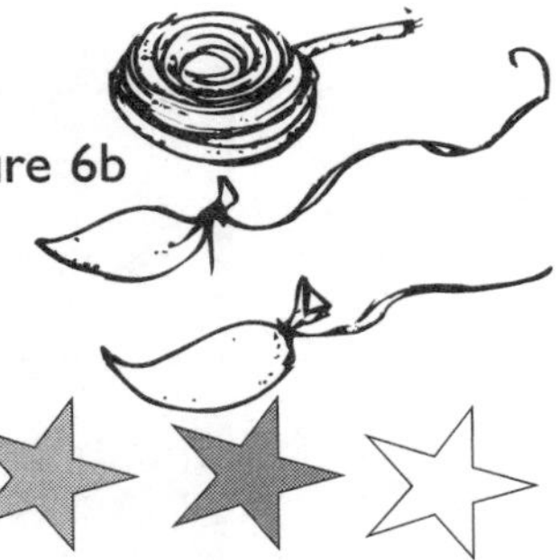

Figure 6b

Instructions

1. Cut the paper towel tube to 6" high. Tape upright to aluminum foil. (Figure 1)
2. Trim 30 pieces of stub wire to 10". Bind six wires together with brown florist tape, 6" from the bottom. (Figure 2)
3. Divide the wires into three pairs and bind them into branches. (Figure 3)
4. Set every other bundle against the paper towel tube and tape them to its side. Space out evenly. Do the same with the remaining bundles but place them on the inside of the tube. (Figure 4)
5. Spread out the branches for each bundle. (Figure 5)
6. Cut out several small leaves from green crepe paper and wrap the edges with the fine brass wire. Leave a few inches of wire dangling from the leaf. (Figures 6a and 6b)

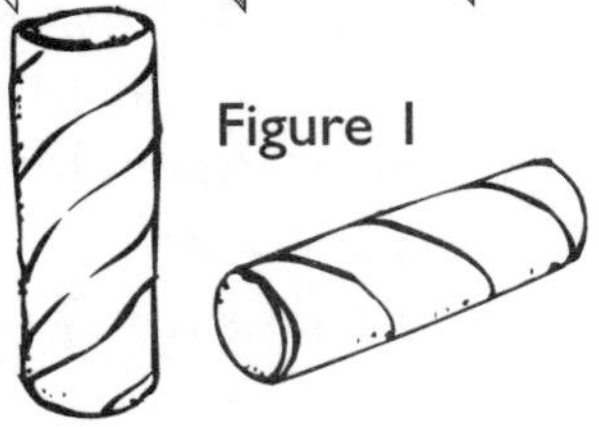

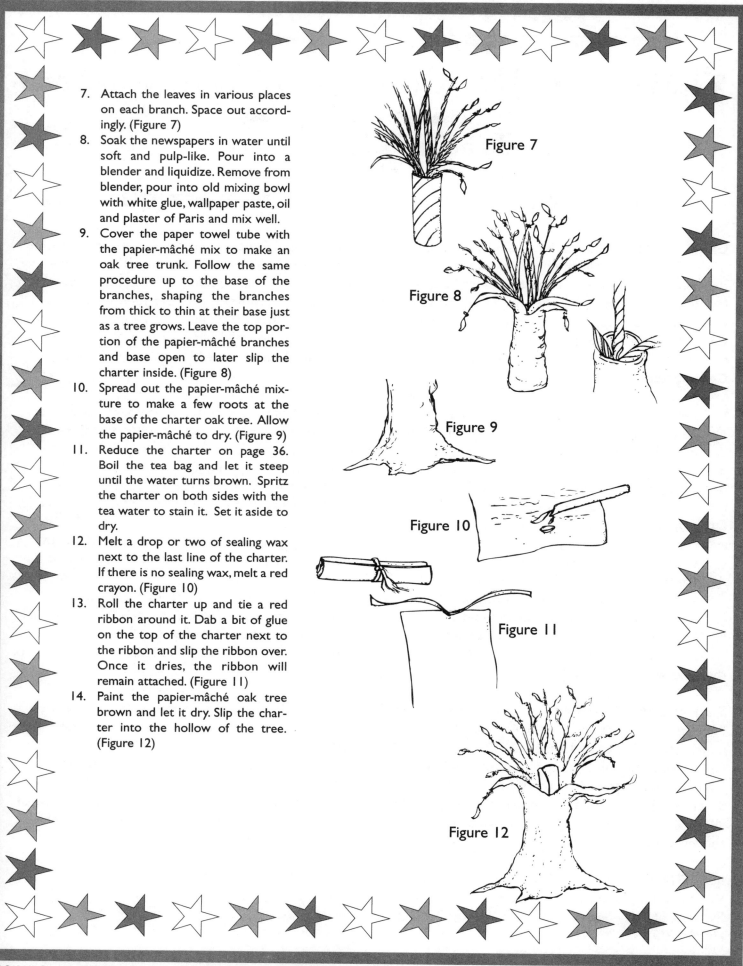

7. Attach the leaves in various places on each branch. Space out accordingly. (Figure 7)

8. Soak the newspapers in water until soft and pulp-like. Pour into a blender and liquidize. Remove from blender, pour into old mixing bowl with white glue, wallpaper paste, oil and plaster of Paris and mix well.

9. Cover the paper towel tube with the papier-mâché mix to make an oak tree trunk. Follow the same procedure up to the base of the branches, shaping the branches from thick to thin at their base just as a tree grows. Leave the top portion of the papier-mâché branches and base open to later slip the charter inside. (Figure 8)

10. Spread out the papier-mâché mixture to make a few roots at the base of the charter oak tree. Allow the papier-mâché to dry. (Figure 9)

11. Reduce the charter on page 36. Boil the tea bag and let it steep until the water turns brown. Spritz the charter on both sides with the tea water to stain it. Set it aside to dry.

12. Melt a drop or two of sealing wax next to the last line of the charter. If there is no sealing wax, melt a red crayon. (Figure 10)

13. Roll the charter up and tie a red ribbon around it. Dab a bit of glue on the top of the charter next to the ribbon and slip the ribbon over. Once it dries, the ribbon will remain attached. (Figure 11)

14. Paint the papier-mâché oak tree brown and let it dry. Slip the charter into the hollow of the tree. (Figure 12)

Figure 7

Figure 8

Figure 9

Figure 10

Figure 11

Figure 12

Name _____

Charter of the Colony of Connecticut

Edited version with original spelling
*The original Charter of the Colony of Connecticut, 1662, is on permanent exhibition at
the Museum of Connecticut History, 231 Capitol Ave., Hartford.

*CHARTER OF THE COLONY OF CONNECTICUT, 1662

CHARLES THE SECOND, BY THE GRACE OF GOD, King of England, Scotland, France and Ireland, defender of the Faith, &c.; To all to whome theis presents shall come Greetinge: WHEREAS, wee have byn informed by the humble Peticon of our Trusty and welbeloved John Winthrop, John Mason, Samuell Willis, Henry Clerke, Mathew Allen, John Tappen, Nathan Gold, Richard Treate, Richard Lord, Henry Woolicott, John Talcott, Daniell Clerke, John Ogden, Thomas Wells, Obedias Brewen, John Clerke, Anthony Haukins, John Deming and Mathew Camfeild, being Persons Principally interested in our Colony or Plantacon of Connecticut in New England, that the same Colony or the greatest parte thereof was purchased and obteyned for greate and valuable Consideracons.

WEE HAVE thought fitt, and att the humble Peticon of the Persons aforesaid, and are graciously pleased to Create and Make them a Body Pollitique and Corporate, with the powers and Priviliges herein after men-coned; And Accordingly Our will and pleasure is, and of our especiall grace, certeine knowledge and meere mocon wee have Ordeyned, Constituted and Declared. The said John Winthrop, whoe is herein before nominated and appointed the present Governour of the said Company, shall take the said Oath before one or more of the Masters of our Court of Chancery for the tyme being, vnto which Master of Chancery WEE DOE, by theis presents, give full power and authority to administer the said Oath to the said John Winthrop accordingly. And the said John Mason, whoe is herein before nominated and appointed the present Deputy Governour of the said Company, shall take the said Oath before the said John Winthrop, or any twoe of the Assistants of the said Company, vnto whome WEE DOE by these presents, give full power and authority to Administer the said Oath to the said John Mason accordingly. And the said Samuell Willis, Henry Clerke, Mathew Allen, John Tappen, Nathan Gold, Richard Treate, Richard Lord, Henry Woolcott, John Talcott, Daniell Clerke, John Ogden and Thomas Welles, whoe are herein before Nominated and appointed the present Assistants of the said Company, shall take the Oath before the said John Winthrop and John Mason, or one of them, to whome WEE DOE

TO HAVE AND TO HOLD the same vnto the said Governor and Company, their Successors and Assignes, for ever vpon Trust and for the vse and benefitt of themselves and their Associates, freemen of the said Colony, their heires and Assignes, TO BEE HOLDEN of vs, our heires and Successors, as of our Mannor of East Greenewich, in Free and Common Soccage, and not in Capite nor by Knights Service, YULMLDING AND PAYINGE therefore to vs, our heires and Successors, onely the Fifth parte of all the Oare of Gold and Silver which from tyme to tyme and at all tymes hereafter shall bee there gotten, had or obteyned, in liew of all Services, Dutyes and Demaunds whatsoever, to bee to vs, our heires or Successors, therefore or thereout rendered, made or paid.

IN WITNES whereof, we have caused these our Letters to be made Patent; WITNES our Selfe, att Westminister, the three and Twentieth day of Aprill, in the Fowerteenth yeare of our Reigne.
By writt of Privy Seale
HOWARD

Fun Facts

Bird: Blue Hen (Gallus gallus)

Butterfly: Tiger Swallowtail (Pterourus glaucus)

Fish: Weakfish (Cynoscion genus)

Flower: Peach Blossom (Prunus persica)

Fossil: Belemnite (Belemnitella americana)

Herb: Sweet Goldenrod (Solidago odora)

Insect: Ladybug (Coccinella novemnotata)

Marine Animal: Horseshoe Crab (Limulus polyphemus)

Mineral: Sillimanite (Aluminum Silicate)

Motto: "Liberty and Independence"

Nicknames: First State, Diamond State, Small Wonder

Song: "Our Delaware" by George B. Hynson

Tree: American Holly (Ilex opaca Aiton)

Statehood: December 7, 1787; 1st state admitted to the Union

Population: (2000 estimate) 783,600

Area: 2489 square miles of land and water; 49th largest state

Highest Point: Ebright Azimuth; 447 feet above sea level

Lowest Point: Atlantic coastline

Capital: Dover

Largest City: Wilmington

Major Crops: Poultry, broiler chickens, soybeans, milk, corn, hay, potatoes, crabs, clams

Major Industry: Chemical products, medical supplies, textiles, food processing, paper products, vulcanized fiber, rubber and plastic products

Delaware

Name: Delaware is one of several states named after a person. It got its name from Lord De La Warr, an early governor of Virginia. The name Delaware was first used to describe a river in the state. It was later given to a Native American tribe, then later applied to the state.

Did You Know?

The Du Pont family established the chemical industry in Delaware. Their business has been responsible for many innovations and inventions throughout the company's history. Du Pont Laboratories in Delaware were the first to produce nylon. The plant at Seaford, which first produced it, earned the town the nickname, "The Nylon Capital of the World." Can you think of products made of nylon?

DELAWARE PUBLIC ARCHIVES
Delaware restricts the use of the Seal. Written permission to use the Seal must be requested of the Secretary of State.

DECEMBER 7, 1787

Flag: The flag is blue and buff, the colors of George Washington's uniform. In the center of the flag is Delaware's coat of arms. Centered beneath it is the date, *December 7, 1787,* the date on which Delaware adopted the U.S. Constitution. Delaware was the first state in the Union to do so.

Seal: In the center of the circular seal are a farmer holding a hoe and a militiaman with a musket. Between them is a cartouche. Above the cartouche is a ship representing Delaware's shipbuilding past. In the top portion of the cartouche is a sheaf of wheat denoting the importance of agriculture to the state. Below that is water, representing the Delaware River. Below that is a lone ox, representing the importance of animal husbandry. In a ribbon underneath the shield is the state motto: "Liberty and Independence." Three dates, *1704, 1776, 1787,* are at the bottom of the seal.

Salt Glaze Pottery Tribute to Thomas Garrett

The state of Delaware has been home to many wonderful people and inventions. Courageous people fought for independence during the Revolutionary War in the 1700s and for the abolishment of slavery in the 1800s. One abolitionist was Thomas Garrett.

At the same time, Delaware's soil has been important to the farming and survival. Early colonists dug up the rich, abundant clay and made unique ceramics. One of the more significant ceramists was William Hare (1814-1885). He is known for his salt glaze stoneware, and is the only known regional ceramist to have signed his work, the mark of a true artisan.

Pay tribute to the state of Delaware, Thomas Garrett and the brave abolitionists who helped thousands of runaway slaves to freedom with a period-like ceramic.

Notable Natives

Valerie Bertinelli (1960-), actress, Wilmington

Annie Jump Cannon (1863-1941), astronomer, Dover

Pierre Samuel du Pont (1870-1954), industrialist, Wilmington

Oliver Evans (1755-1819), inventor of the high-pressure steam engine, Newport

Louis Plack Hammett (1894-1987), physical chemist, Wilmington

Howard Pyle (1853-1911) artist, Wilmington

George Read (1733-1798) signer of the Declaration of Independence, New Castle

Judge Reinholt (1957-), actor, Wilmington

Caesar Rodney (1728-1784), signer of the Declaration of Independence, Dover

Elizabeth Shue (1963-), actress, Wilmington

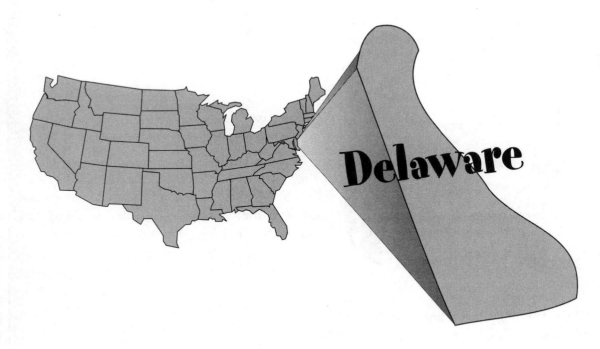

Hare Pottery

Figure 1

Materials

* self-hardening clay
* water
* clay carving tools
* rolling pin
* acrylic paints: yellow, white, blue, black
* acrylic varnish
* carbon paper
* masking tape
* newspaper or towels
* toothpicks
* thick paintbrush
* thin paintbrush

For decorative purposes only—not to be used as a cake pan

Figure 2

Instructions

1. Copy the images of Thomas Garrett and the flower and tendril designs on pages 42.
2. Soften the clay to make it pliable. Roll the clay into an evenly flat form no less than 1/4" thick, 6" x 8" long. (Figure 1)
3. Make wedge cut pieces for the sides of your Hare pottery. For the two long top and bottom sides, make two 8" x 1 1/2" x 1/4" slabs. For the final two right and left sides, make 1/4"-thick slabs that are 6" long and 1 1/2" wide. (Figure 2)
4. Lay the bottom edge of each of the four pieces down and measure 1 1/4" of the bottom edge. Slice it off at an angle. (Figure 3)
5. Incise the wedged bottom by scoring with a clay tool. (Figure 4)
6. Do the same at the edge of the large main slab. (Figure 5)
7. Dab some water on the edges and press them together. (Figure 6)

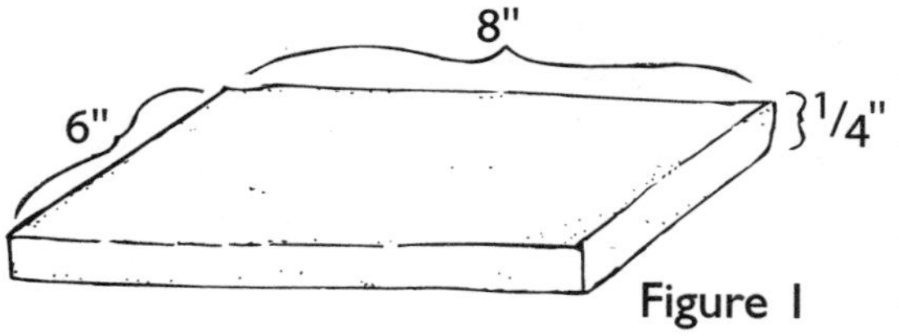

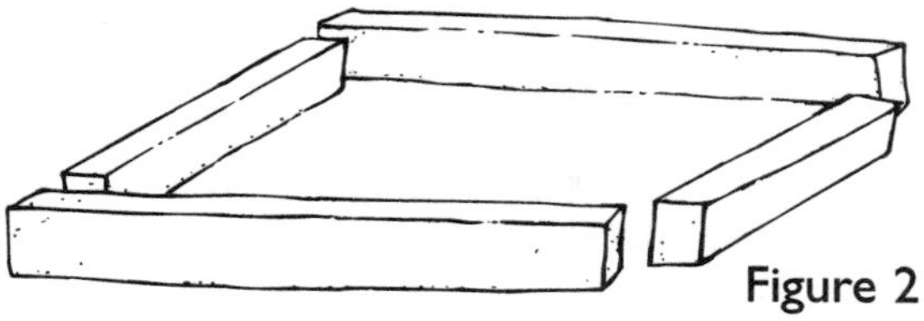

Figure 3

Figure 4

Figure 5

Figure 6

8. Place toothpicks in the sides of the clay to hold in place. (Figure 7)

9. Attach the smaller sides with the same technique. Adjust the size of these slabs to fit. Let them dry. (Figure 8)

10. Paint the entire cake pan a creamy yellow color by mixing yellow and white paint. Let it dry.

11. Tape the leaf and tendril designs on the side of the cake pan. Slip carbon paper under it and trace the lines. Pull everything off and paint by following the lines. (Figure 9)

12. Tape the Thomas Garrett picture in the center of the cake pan. Slip the carbon paper underneath it and trace the lines to make a light impression of the work. (Figure 10)

13. Outline the image of Thomas Garrett by following the drawn lines with your paint and brush. Let it dry and varnish the entire cake pan.

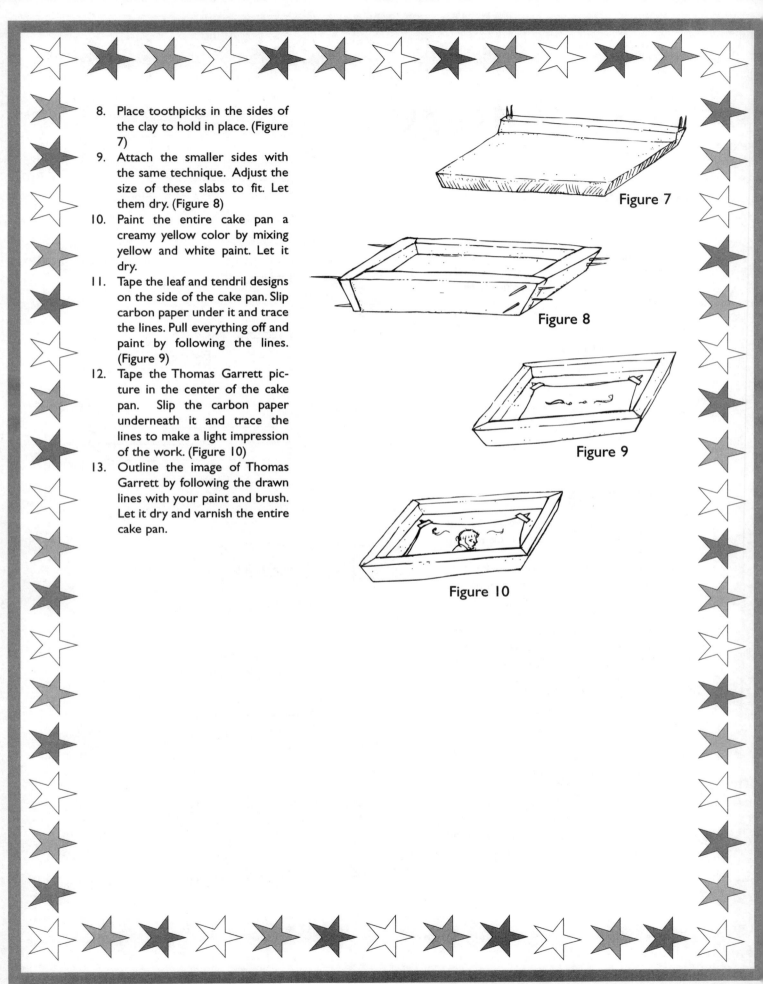

Figure 7

Figure 8

Figure 9

Figure 10

Thomas Garrett

Thomas Garrett was a Quaker who moved from his native state, Pennsylvania, to Delaware in 1822. Delaware was a border state and Garrett was determined to help runaway slaves to freedom through the Underground Railroad. From his home at 227 Shipley Street, Garrett broke the law, aiding slaves with food, refuge, clothing and secret exile into Canada or other regions of the country that were considered free. He was befriended by the great abolitionists of his day, Frederick Douglass and Harriet Tubman. In 1848,

Garrett was brought to trial for aiding runaway slaves. At the end of the three-day trial he was found guilty along with fellow abolitionist, John Hunn. Garrett was fined $5400, and Hunn was fined $2500. When the judge imposed the fine he stated, "I hope you will never be caught at this business again." Garrett, true to his beliefs, spoke these famous words: "I haven't a dollar in the world, but if thee knows a fugitive who needs a breakfast, send him to me."

Flower & Tendril Designs

Thomas Garrett Design

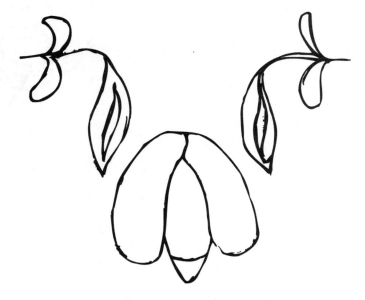

Leaf and tendril design made around 1850-1875

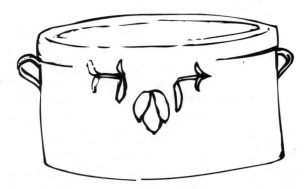

William Hare Ceramic Cake Pan Design

Salt glazed container
attributed to William Hare

Fun Facts

Bird: Wood Thrush (Hylocichla mustelina)

Flower: American Beauty Rose (Rosa "American Beauty")

Motto: Justica Omnibus (Justice for All)

Nickname: D.C.

Song: "The Star-Spangled Banner" by Francis Scott Key

Tree: Scarlet Oak (Fagaceae Quercus coccinea)

Founded: 1790

Population: (2000 estimate) 572,059

Area: 68.25 square miles

Highest Point: Tenleytown; 410 feet above sea level

Lowest Point: Potomac River

Major Industry: Government and tourism

District of Columbia

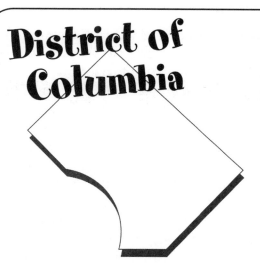

Name: Washington, D.C., is a city as well as a federal district. The district was established by Congress at a location personally chosen by George Washington in 1791. Washington is the city within the District of Columbia. The District was named after the explorer Christopher Columbus. The city was named in honor of the first United States President, George Washington.

Did You Know?

Lobby groups or special interest groups in Washington, D.C., are well known for the work they do on Capitol Hill, trying to convince members of Congress to adopt points of view on certain topics to help shape legislation. The term *lobbyist* originated in Washington, D.C., during President Ulysses Grant's time. He referred to the special interest groups who gathered in the opulent lobby of the Willard Hotel as lobbyists. He didn't mean it as a compliment.

Seal: The circular seal of the District bears the words *District of Columbia* and shows a woman, representing justice, hanging a wreath at the base of a statue of George Washington. In the background is the Capitol building. Beneath the statue is the American eagle.

Flag: The District's flag, a red and white banner, has three five-point red stars spread evenly across the top white band. Below are four stripes: red, then white, then red, then white. The design is based on George Washington's family coat of arms.

Tribute to Pershing's Own

After World War I, one of the first proposals for a war memorial was from the Society of the First Division, American Expeditionary Forces (AEF). They proposed a memorial in the nation's capital as a tribute to commemorate the lives of 5516 First Division fallen soldiers.

The soldiers had served under the leadership of General John J. Pershing. The Division was formed shortly after the United States declared war on Germany in April 1917. The soldiers of the First Division were the first to arrive in France in 1917, and the last to leave Europe in 1919. General Pershing was proud of his First Division because their high morale never broke in spite of hardships, difficult circumstances of battle and the sacrifices they made. This unique Division was affectionately called "Pershing's Own."

In October 1919, the First Division Memorial Association was organized. They raised funds and oversaw the entire memorial project. The final cost of this monument was $115,000, paid for by private donations from families and friends across the nation. The memorial still stands in front of the Old Executive Office Building, conveying the "spirit of triumph, sacrifice and service." The bronze statue of Victory stands on the world, holding a flag in her right hand. The left hand extends in a gesture of benediction for the fallen whose names are on the base of the monument.

Notable Natives

Pat Buchanan (1938-), journalist

Stephen Carter (1954-), law professor

Al Gore, Jr. (1948-), U.S. senator, Vice President, 2000 presidential candidate

J.C. (Joshua Scott Chasez) (1976-), member of the band NSYNC

Goldie Hawn (1945-), Oscar-winning actress

Kristen Johnston (1967-) actress best known for her role on *3rd Rock from the Sun*

Jayne Kennedy (1951-), sportscaster, actress

Michael Learned (1939-) actress best known for her role on *The Waltons*

James McDaniel (1958-) actor

Christopher Meloni (1961-), actor

Chita Rivera (Delores Conchita Figueroa del Rivero) (1933-), Tony-winning actress, dancer

Henry Rollins (1961-), punk musician

Rip Taylor (1934-), actor

Peter Tork (1942-), singer in the group The Monkees

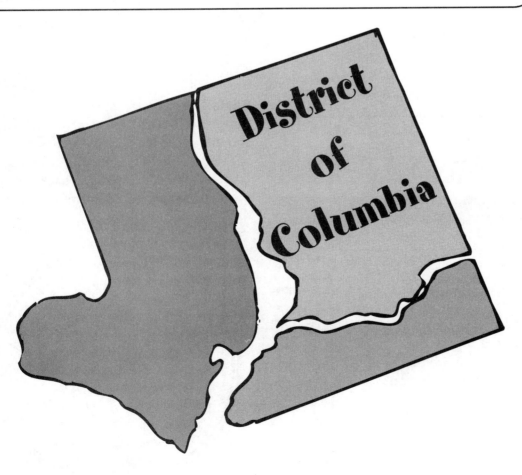

First Division Memorial

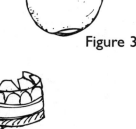

Figure 2

Materials

* paper towel tube
* 4 cups plaster of Paris
* scissors
* toothpicks
* felt-tip pen
* white paper tape
* white spray paint
* water
* 8¹/₂" x 11" poster board
* glue
* 1¹/₂" Styrofoam™ ball
* sandpaper

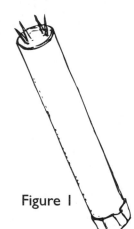

Figure 1

Figure 3

Figure 4

Instructions

1. Seal one end of the paper towel tube with tape. Mix the plaster into a syrupy texture and pour it into the unsealed end of the paper towel tube. Stick four toothpicks in the middle of the plaster and set upright. Allow it to dry. (Figure 1)

2. Copy the Victory image on page 46 and mount it on poster board. Cut it out and set it aside. (Figure 2)

3. Mix ¹/₂ cup of plaster with water and spread it over the Styrofoam™ ball, except at the bottom and top. Set aside to dry. (Figure 3)

4. Copy the Ionic trim on page 46. Mount it on poster board and set it aside. Do the same for the base. (Figure 4)

5. Cut a ¹/₂" slit ¹/₄" deep into the top of the plastered Styrofoam™ ball. Attach the Victory figure to the ball. Glue it for support. (Figure 5)

6. Remove the cardboard tube from the column and clean off by scraping as necessary. Sand the bottom of the plaster base to make it flat. Stand it upright.

7. Dab glue on the toothpick tips, then slip the plaster Victory ball on them. Press down to secure in place.

8. Lightly spray all but Victory in white and allow it to dry.

9. Slip the Ionic trim around the top of the tube and glue in place. Glue the base trim at the bottom of the tube. (Figure 6)

Figure 5

Figure 6

First Division Memorial

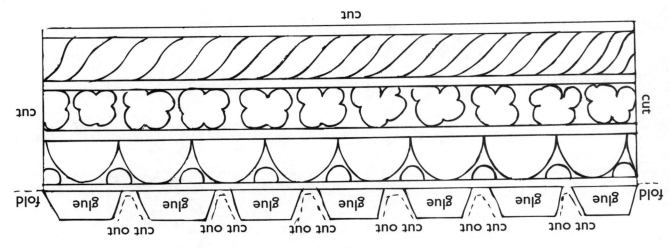

Ionic Trim

Base

Fun Facts

Animal: Florida Panther (Felis concolor coryi)

Bird: Mockingbird (Mimus polyglottos)

Butterfly: Zebra Longwing (Heliconius charitonius)

Freshwater Fish: Largemouth or Black Bass (Micropterus salmoides)

Saltwater Fish: Sail Fish (Istiophorus platypterus)

Flower: Orange Blossom (Citrus sinensis)

Wildflower: Coreopsis (Coreopsis grandiflora)

Gem: Moonstone (Potassium Aluminum Silicate)

Marine Mammal: Manatee (Tricheus manatus laterostris)

Saltwater Mammal: Porpoise (Tursiops truncates)

Motto: "In God We Trust"

Nickname: Sunshine State

Reptile: Alligator (Alligator mississippiensis)

Shell: Horse Conch (Pleuroploca gigantea)

Song: "The Swanee River" by Stephen C. Foster

Stone: Agatized Coral

Tree: Sabal Palm (Sabal palmetto)

Statehood: March 3, 1845; 27th state admitted to the Union

Population: (2000 estimate) 15,982,378

Area: 65,758 square miles of land and water; 22nd largest state

Highest Point: Britton Hill; 345 feet above sea level

Lowest Point: Atlantic and Gulf coasts

Capital: Tallahassee

Largest City: Jacksonville

Major Crops: Citrus fruit, strawberries, vegetables, peanuts, melons, cattle, sugarcane, dairy products

Major Industry: Tourism, electrical equipment, food processing, machinery, printing and publishing

Florida

Name: *On Easter Sunday 1513, the Spanish explorer, Ponce de Leon, was traipsing through tropical and lush countryside looking for the fountain of youth. He named the land "Pascua Florida." Pascua Florida is Spanish for "flowery Easter." Today it's called simply Florida.*

Did You Know?

When athletes participate in sports such as football, baseball, soccer and basketball, they run and jump and exert themselves which causes them to sweat. Sweating causes the athletes to lose water from their bodies. Since the body needs lots of water to function properly, the water needs to be replenished. When University of Florida sports doctors noticed that their football players were tired during the game, they realized that they needed a drink to replenish the water lost from sweating. Dr. Robert Cade and Dr. Dana Shires invented a sports drink they called Gatorade™ to keep the "Gators" (the nickname for the University of Florida football players) hydrated.

Flag: The background of the Florida flag is white, with a red X across the flag. In the center of the X is the state seal.

Seal: The scene on the seal shows the sun's rays over a high land in the distance, a sabal palmetto tree, a sailing steamboat on the water and a Seminole woman scattering flowers in the foreground, encircled by the words *Great Seal of the State of Florida: In God We Trust.*

Florida's Sugar Plantations

The ruins of the Bulow Plantation are reminiscent of an era gone by. Plantation life, slaves and Native American raids colored the plantation's past. Now overrun by growth, the remnants of this sugar plantation can still be seen near Flagler Beach, Florida. The plantation's original owner was Major Charles Bulow. In 1821, he bought 4675 acres of Floridian wilderness that bordered a tidal creek. Over 300 slaves cleared 2000 acres of the dense vegetation by hand. Then the land was tilled and planted with sugarcane, indigo, cotton and rice. Under Bulow's direction a sugar house was soon erected and raw sugar was extracted from the cane. Barrels of the raw sugar were loaded at the tidal creek docks and shipped north to other states. Wealth came quickly to Major Bulow. However, in January 1836, a band of Seminole Indians resisted their removal from the area and the second Seminole war erupted. In retaliation, the Native Americans pillaged and burned the plantation. The Bulow Plantation never recovered from the destruction. All that remains of this stately frontier plantation are the walls of the sugar mill's chimney.

Notable Natives

Pat Boone (1934-), singer, Jacksonville

Steve Carlton (1944-), baseball player, Miami

Jacqueline Cochran (1910-1980), aviatrix, Pensacola

Faye Dunaway (1941-), actress, Bascom

Chris Evert (1954-), tennis player, Fort Lauderdale

Deborah Harry (1945-), singer, actress, Miami

Catherine Keener (1959-), actress, Miami

Butterfly McQueen (1911-1995), actress, Tampa

Jim Morrison (1943-1971), singer, Melbourne

Sidney Poitier (1927-), Oscar-winning actor, Miami

Janet Reno (1938-), first woman U.S. Attorney General, Miami

Ben Vereen (1946-), actor, Miami

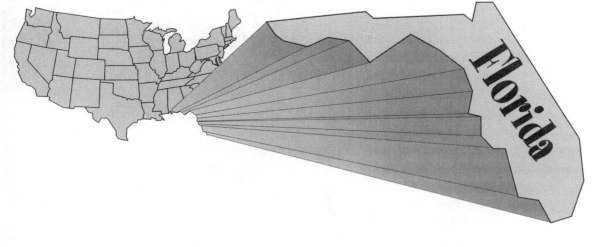

Rock Candy Crystals

This project requires heat.

Materials

* ½ cup water
* 1½ cups granulated sugar
* saucepan
* wooden spoon
* 1½" deep tray
* 12" piece of cotton string
* pencil
* paper clip
* pot holders

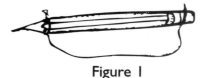

Figure 1

Instructions

1. Tie the ends of the string to the ends of a pencil. (Figure 1)
2. Moisten the string with a drop of water and add a little sugar. (Figure 2)
3. Lay the pencil across the tray with the string dangling in the middle. (Figure 3)
4. Boil ½ cup of water in the saucepan.
5. Add 1½ cups of sugar to the boiling water and stir until the sugar dissolves.
6. Carefully remove pan from heat and pour the sugar water into the tray.
7. Crystals will begin to form along the string within a few days. Continue to let them grow for up to 10 days.

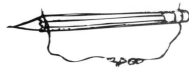

Figure 2

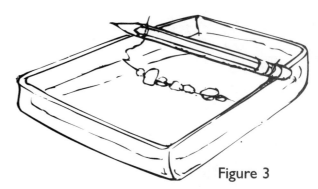

Figure 3

Name _____

Ruins of the Bulow Plantation

Color this page according to the color key.

Color Key
a. gray
b. green
c. red

Fun Facts

Bird: Brown Thrasher (Toxostoma rufum)

Butterfly: Tiger Swallowtail (Papilio glaucus)

Fish: Largemouth or Black Bass (Micropterus salmoides)

Flower: Cherokee Rose (Rosa laevigata)

Fossil: Shark Tooth

Fruit: Peach (Prunus persica)

Game Bird: Bobwhite Quail (Colinus virginianus)

Gem: Quartz (Silicon dioxide)

Insect: Honeybee (Apis mellifera)

Marine Mammal: Right Whale (Eubabalena glacialis)

Mineral: Staurolite (Iron Aluminum Silicate Hydroxide)

Motto: "Wisdom, Justice, and Moderation"

Nickname: Peach State

Reptile: Gopher Tortoise (Gopherus polyphemus)

Seashell: Knobbed Whelk (Busycon carica gmelin)

Song: "Georgia on My Mind" by Stuart Gorrell

Tree: Live Oak (Quercus virginiana)

Vegetable: Vidalia Sweet Onion

Statehood: January 2, 1788; 4th state admitted to the Union

Population: (2000 estimate) 8,186,453

Area: 59,441 square miles of land and water; 24th largest state

Highest Point: Brasstown Bald; 4784 feet above sea level

Lowest Point: Atlantic sea coast

Capital: Atlanta

Largest City: Atlanta

Major Crops: Poultry, eggs, cotton, tobacco, soybeans, peanuts

Major Industry: Textiles, resins, turpentine, apparel, food processing, paper products, chemical products, marble, bauxite, tourism

Georgia

Name: Like several U.S. states, Georgia was named in honor of an English monarch, King George II of England. James Edward Oglethorpe, a member of Parliament, suggested that a colony be formed in America for debtors who were suffering in English prisons. Parliament granted money for the formation of the colony and King George II of England granted the land for Georgia to be established.

Did You Know?

Coca-Cola™, one of the most popular drinks in the world, was invented in 1886 in Atlanta, Georgia, by Dr. John S. Pemberton. His bookkeeper, Frank Robinson, suggested the name to him. The soda concoction was first sold at Jacob's Pharmacy in Atlanta by Willis Venable.

Flag: The Georgia state flag has the state seal emblazoned on a blue canton, surrounded by 13 stars symbolizing that Georgia was one of the original colonies. The flag has three broad horizontal stripes, two red and one white. The United States' motto, "In God We Trust" is written below the seal.

Seal: The Georgia state seal shows three pillars supporting an arch. On the arch is the word *Constitution*. The pillars have ribbons on which are the words: *Wisdom, Justice* and *Moderation*. The three pillars represent the three branches of government—legislative, judicial and executive—which support the Constitution. A colonial man bearing a drawn sword stands under the arch to defend the Constitution and the principles of wisdom, justice and moderation. The date on the seal, *1776,* is the year the United States declared its independence from England.

Native American Game of Dish

In 1995, the peach was designated as Georgia's official state fruit. Peaches have had a long history with Native Americans, especially the Iroquois-speaking Cherokee who lived in Georgia.

Dish is a game that is part of the legend and culture of the Cherokee. It is believed that the game originated with the Cherokee god and his twin brother. It had been used for centuries as a part of special medicine ceremonies as a game of fate, to gain insight into the mind of the god. By today's standards we understand that it was an example of mathematical probabilities.

The following project is one that challenges the use of math in everyday life by incorporating simple game structure and rules.

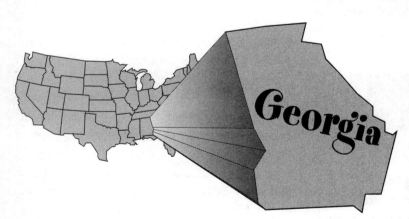

Notable Natives

Robert Sengstacke Abbott (1868-1940), newspaper publisher, civil rights advocate, St. Simons Island

Conrad Potter Aiken (1889-1973), Pulitzer Prize-winning poet, Savannah

Kim Basinger (1953-), actress, Athens

Alfred Blalock (1899-1964), surgeon, Culloden

Daniel Joseph Boorstin (1914-), author, Librarian of Congress, Atlanta

Jim Brown (1936-), football player, actor, St. Simons Island

Erskine Caldwell (1903-1987), writer, White Oak

James (Jimmy) Earl Carter (1924-), 39th President (1977-1981), Plains

Ray Charles (1930-2004), singer, Albany

Ty Cobb (1886-1961), baseball player, Narrows

James Lafayette Dickey (1923-1997), poet, novelist, Atlanta

Father Divine (George Baker) (1877-1965), charismatic preacher, Savannah

Thomas A. Dorsey (1899-1993), considered "The Father of Gospel Music," Villa Rica

Teresa Edwards (1964-), three-time Olympic gold-medal basketball player, Cairo

Laurence Fishburne (1961-), actor, Augusta

John Charles Fremont (1813-1890), explorer, politician, Savannah

Jeff Foxworthy (1958-), actor, comedian, Atlanta

Josh Gibson (1911-1947), baseball player, Buena Vista

Amy Grant (1960-), Christian singer, Augusta

Oliver Hardy (1892-1957), comic actor, Harlem

Joel Chandler Harris (1848-1908), journalist, author, Eatonton

Larry Holmes (1949 -), boxer, Cuthbert

Holly Hunter (1958-), actress, Conyers

Harry James (1916-1983), trumpeter, big band leader, Albany

Martin Luther King, Jr. (1929-1968), civil rights leader, Atlanta

Gladys Knight (1941-), singer, Atlanta

Brenda Lee (1944-), singer, Lithonia

Spike Lee (1957-), film maker, Atlanta

Carson McCullers (1917-1967), writer, Columbus

Margaret Mitchell (1900-1949), Pulitzer Prize-winning author, Atlanta

Otis Redding (1941-1967), singer, Dawson

Burt Reynolds (1937-), actor, Waycross

Little Richard (1932-), singer, Macon

Julia Roberts (1967-), actress, Smyrna

Jackie Robinson (1919-1972), baseball player, Cairo

Dean Rusk (1909-1994), U.S. Secretary of State, Cherokee County

Nipsey Russell (1924-), comedian, Atlanta

Wyomia Tyus (1945-), Olympic gold-medal runner, Griffin

Alice Walker (1944-), Pulitzer Prize-winning writer, Eatonton

Joanne Woodward (1930-), actress, Thomasville

Dish

Generally, the Cherokee sanded peach stones, then blacked one side with smoke or fire and kept the opposite side its natural color.

Two or more people can play this game of chance. Each must have 100 counters to toss into the pot.

Materials

* 100 counters (butter beans, corn kernels, small pebbles or toothpicks) for each player
* 6 peach stones
* black permanent marker
* sandpaper
* medium-sized bowl or basket

Instructions

1. Sand the peach stones as smooth as possible. Blacken one side of the peach stones with black marker.
2. Review some of the mathematical possibilities of the game on this page.
3. Each person takes a turn shaking the peach stones in a bowl or basket, tossing them in the air and letting them fall naturally. Peach stone combinations represent 1 to 5 points as shown below.
4. Keep an account of how many points you accumulate. The first player to get 100 points wins.

Rules of Dish

6 burnt or 6 neutral peach stones = 6B or 6N = 5 points
5 burnt or 5 neutral peach stones = 5B or 5N = 1 point
Anything else earns zero points and a lost turn.

Mathematical Probability Equation

Probability of an event is explained mathematically as P(E) or, it equals the number of likely ways (E) the event can happen. P(E) is divided by the total number of equally likely things that can happen, or n/N.

Description	Formula
Probability, in one toss, of getting no blacks =	$P(E) = 1/64$
Probability, in one toss, of getting one black =	$P(E) = 6/64$
Probability, in one toss, of getting two blacks =	$P(E) = 15/64$
Probability, in one toss, of getting three blacks =	$P(E) = 20/64$
Probability, in one toss, of getting four blacks =	$P(E) = 15/64$
Probability, in one toss, of getting five blacks =	$P(E) = 6/64$
Probability, in one toss, of getting six blacks =	$P(E) = 1/64$

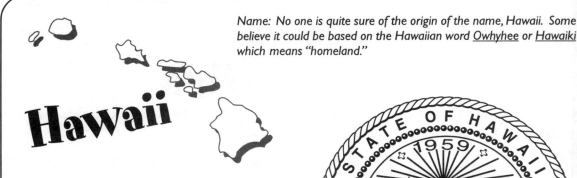

Hawaii

Fun Facts

Bird: Nene or Hawaiian Goose (Branta sandwicensis)

Fish: Humuhumunukunuku Apua'a (Rhinecanthus rectangulus)

Flower: Hibiscus or Pua Aloalo (Hibiscus brackenridgei)

Gem: Black Coral (Antipathes subpinnata)

Marine Mammal: Humpback Whale (Megaptera novaengliae)

Motto: "Ua mau ke ea o ka aina i ka pono" (The life of the land is perpetuated in righteousness)

Nickname: Aloha State

Song: "Hawaii Ponoi" by Hawaii's own King David Kalakaua

Tree: Kukui (Aleurites moluccana)

Statehood: August 21, 1959; 50th state admitted to the Union

Population: (2000 estimate) 1,211,537

Area: 10,932 square miles of land and water; 43rd largest state

Highest Point: Mauna Kea; 13,796 feet above sea level

Lowest Point: Pacific coast

Capital: Honolulu

Largest City: Honolulu

Major Crops: Sugarcane, coffee, bananas, pineapples, flowers macadamia nuts, livestock

Major Industry: Tourism, food processing, clothing

Name: No one is quite sure of the origin of the name, Hawaii. Some believe it could be based on the Hawaiian word Owhyhee or Hawaiki which means "homeland."

Did You Know?

Hawaii grows more of the pineapples sold throughout the United States than any other state, nearly 97%. One-third of the world's supply are grown in Hawaii, but the pineapple is not native to Hawaii. It was first discovered in South America, but Spanish and Portuguese traders transplanted it to Europe. In fact, when Christopher Columbus first saw a pineapple, he thought it looked like a big pinecone and called it *pina,* the Spanish word for *pine.* That's how it got its name. The pineapple wasn't introduced to the Hawaiian islands until the 1700s.

Flag: The Hawaiian state flag, designed for King Kamehameha, has a Union Jack in the upper left section or canton, and eight horizontal stripes of equal width white, red and blue. The Union Jack, or British flag represents the long relationship the British had with Hawaii. The white, red and blue stripes represent the eight main Hawaiian Islands.

Seal: Hawaii was ruled by a royal family whose history is represented on the seal. On the circular seal is the standing figure of King Kamehameha the Great with one arm outstretched and the other holding a staff. He was the first to unify the islands under one rule. On the other side stands the Goddess of Liberty. Between the two figures is a modified royal shield with a star in the center and paddles on either side. Above the shield is a rising sun with the date, 1959, the year Hawaii became a state. Below the shield is a rising Phoenix. In the outer circle are the words *State of Hawaii* and the state motto, "Ua Mau Ke Ea O Ka Aina I Ka Pono," which translates into English as, "The life of the land is perpetuated in righteousness."

Celebrate Hawaii's Lei Day in May

The history of the lei is centuries old. During the Paleolithic time, leis were made of ivory, bones, shells and teeth. In early Hawaii, leis were symbolic of the esteem of the gods and loved ones. They were also given to express a form of friendship and of gratitude. Hawaiians fashioned their leis so beautifully, they remain a dynamic and joyful aspect of their culture. Natural materials of the islands, flowers, seeds, pods and vines, were selected for their beauty, color, healing powers, symbolism, freshness and durability. Many were sewn together with coconut husks or banana fibers. About 90 percent of Hawaii's animals and plants exist nowhere else on the planet, but many have become extinct. Today, making leis with contemporary materials rather than traditional ones has become the norm.

Some traditional lei makers have become amateur botanists, dedicating themselves to replanting and restoring native plants, especially rare ones.

Contemporary leis, called "fresh leis," are a mixture of flowers, leaves, mosses, blossoming grasses and vines. Some permanent leis are made of silk, satin, paper and ribbons. Yarn, candy and money are also used for various occasions.

Lei Day in Hawaii, when leis are made, worn and given away, is traditionally the first day of May. Public schools have lei-making contests that are so popular, school districts coordinate their contests to avoid conflict.

In 1923, the Territorial Legislature of Hawaii designated specific emblems and colors to each island. All emblems, except the lokelani rose which represents Maui, are natural fauna specific to each island. This includes the pupu shell which represents Ni`ihau.

Notable Natives

Samuel Chapman Armstrong (1839-1893), educator, Wailuku, Maui

Hiram Bingham (1875-1956), archaeologist, author, politician, Honolulu

Tia Carrere (1967-), singer, Honolulu

Sanford Ballard Dole (1844-1926), first territorial governor of Hawaii, Honolulu

Don Ho (1930-), singer, Kakaako, Oahu

Daniel Inouye (1924-), U.S. senator, Honolulu

Kamehameha the Great (1758?-1819), first Hawaiian king, North Kohala, Hawaii

Kaahumanu (1777-1824), Hawaiian Queen, wife of Kamehameha the Great, Maui

Nicole Kidman (1967-), actress, Honolulu

Queen Liliuokalani (1838-1917), last Hawaiian Queen, Honolulu

Ellison Onizuka (1946-1986), astronaut, Kealakekua, Kona, Hawaii

These are the emblems and colors for each Hawaiian island
as designated by the Territorial Legislature in 1923.

Island	Color	Flower
Hawaii	red	lehua
Kaho`olawe	silver gray	hinahina
Kaua`i	violet	mokihana
Lana`i	orange	kaunoloa
Maui	pink	damask rose or lokelani
Moloka`i	silver green	kukui
Ni`ihau	white	pupu shells
O`ahu	yellow	ilima

Stringing Leis

There are six basic methods of the haku lei (lei maker).
1. kipu`u: knotting with short vines or leaves with a long stem
2. hili: plaiting or braiding with only one material
3. haku: braiding with a mixture of flower, leaf or fern
4. wili: winding with no knots till the end
5. humu papa: the traditional head lei sewn to a foundation
6. kui: strung rather than knotted, plaited or braided

Hawaii

Basic Lei

Materials

* crepe paper or tissue paper of various colors
* plastic straws or pasta noodles
* string 24" to 36" long
* scissors
* hole punch

Optional
* fresh flowers (pansies, baby's breath, ferns)

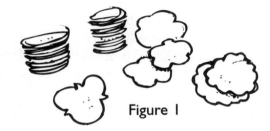

Figure 1

Instructions

1. Cut a piece of string to the appropriate length of a necklace.
2. Copy the flower designs on page 57. Cut out the flower shapes and lay them on tissue or crepe paper. Cut enough flowers to fill a necklace from end to end. (Figure 1)
3. Punch a hole in the center of each flower. (Figure 2)
4. Cut the straws into 1/4" to 1/2" pieces. (Figure 3)
5. Tie a knot in one end of the string and thread a piece of straw on it. Add the paper flower on the string. Continue with straw pieces and flowers until you have completed the lei. (Figure 4) Tie both ends of the string together.

* If you use fresh flowers, push a needle through the middle of each flower to pull it onto the string.

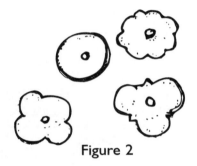

Figure 2

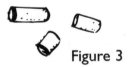

Figure 3

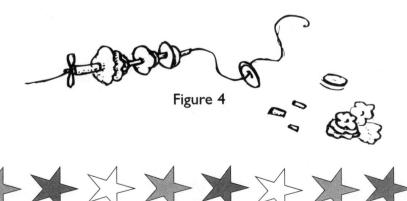

Figure 4

Flower Designs

Fun Facts

Bird: Mountain Bluebird
(Sialia arcticia)

Fish: Cutthroat Trout
(Salmo clarki)

Flower: Syringa
(Phiadelphus lewisii)

Fossil: Hagerman Horse
Fossil (Equus simplicidens)

Fruit: Huckleberry
(Vaccinium membranaceum)

Gem: Idaho Star Garnet

Horse: Appaloosa
(Equus caballus)

Insect: Monarch Butterfly
(Danaus plexippus)

Motto: "Esto Perpetua"
(Let it be perpetual.)

Nickname: Gem State

Song: "Here We Have Idaho"
by McKinley Helm and
Albert J. Tompkins

Tree: Western White Pine
(Pinus monticola pinaceae)

Vegetable: Potato (Solanum
tuberosum Linnaeus)

Statehood: July 3, 1890; 43rd
state admitted to the Union

Population: (2000 estimate)
1,293,953

Area: 83,574 square miles of
land and water; 14th largest
state

Highest Point: Borah Peak;
12,662 feet above sea level

Lowest Point: Snake River;
710 feet above sea level

Capital: Boise

Largest City: Boise

Major Crops: Cattle, apples,
potatoes, dairy products,
wheat, sugar beets, barley,
hops

Major Industry: Food
processing, lumber and
wood products, chemical
products, paper products,
mercury, silver, zinc, cobalt,
lead, phosphate, tourism

Idaho

Name: Some people believe the name <u>Idaho</u> came from a Native American phrase meaning "gem of the mountains," but apparently the word was invented or created.

Did You Know?

When most people think of Idaho, the first thing that comes to mind is the potato. Though many different kinds of agricultural goods are raised in Idaho, the potato is the most important to the state. It ranks first in potato production in the United States. Nearly a third of all potatoes raised in the U.S. are grown in Idaho. Over 15% of all the income generated in the state is from the production and processing of potatoes!

Flag: The state flag is a deep blue background with the state seal in the middle. Below the seal are the words *State of Idaho* surrounded by gold embroidery.

Seal: The state seal of Idaho is quite ornate. In the center of the circular seal is a shield depicting the beautiful and dramatic landscape of the state. The large fir tree symbolizes the forests of the state. The farmer represents agriculture. The river is a great stream of majestic beauty. A woman holding a spear in one hand topped with the liberty cap, and the scales of justice in the other represents freedom and justice. The man on the other side represents strength, mining and industry. Giving the man and woman equal representation on the seal, symbolizes their equality in the state. Above the shield is an elk's head representing the protection of wild animals. Below it is a sheaf of wheat, symbolizing agricultural riches. Two cornucopias symbolize horticulture. Above the elk's head a ribbon displays the state's motto, "Esto Perpetua," which means, "Let it be perpetual." In the outer circle surrounding the seal are the words *Great Seal of the State of Idaho.*

58

Soda Springs

Soda Springs, Idaho, has the only manmade geyser in the world and was featured in *Ripley's Believe It or Not*. The geyser was created accidentally in 1937 when a drill struck a subterranean chamber filled with water and carbon dioxide. The geyser was capped and put on a timer. It now "erupts" every hour on the hour! When emigrants traveling on the Oregon Trail 150 years ago refreshed themselves on the special waters, some suggested that one spring tasted like beer. Others believed it tasted like soda water. Some people sweetened the spring's water with sugar to make a tasty drink.

Notable Natives

Gutzon Borglum (1867-1941), sculptor of Mt. Rushmore, Bear Lake

Frank Forrester Church (1924-1984), U.S. senator, Boise

Harmon Killebrew (1936-), baseball player, Payette

Ezra Pound (1885-1972), poet, Hailey

Picabo Street (1971-), Olympic gold-medal skier, Triumph

Lana Turner (1920-1995), actress, Wallace

Soda Geyser

This project requires heat.

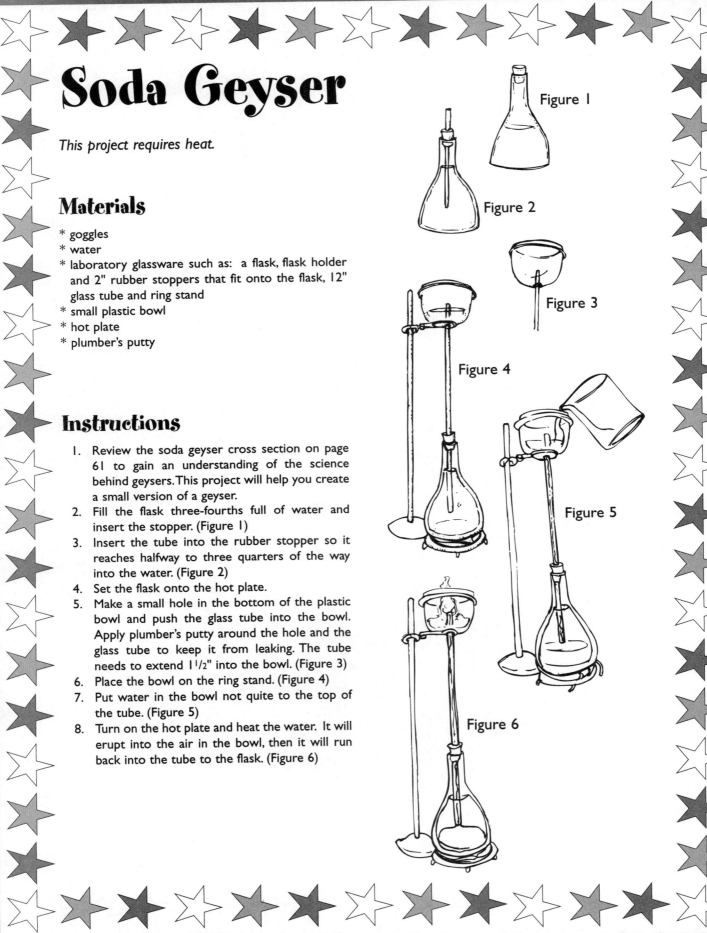

Figure 1

Figure 2

Figure 3

Figure 4

Figure 5

Figure 6

Materials

* goggles
* water
* laboratory glassware such as: a flask, flask holder and 2" rubber stoppers that fit onto the flask, 12" glass tube and ring stand
* small plastic bowl
* hot plate
* plumber's putty

Instructions

1. Review the soda geyser cross section on page 61 to gain an understanding of the science behind geysers. This project will help you create a small version of a geyser.
2. Fill the flask three-fourths full of water and insert the stopper. (Figure 1)
3. Insert the tube into the rubber stopper so it reaches halfway to three quarters of the way into the water. (Figure 2)
4. Set the flask onto the hot plate.
5. Make a small hole in the bottom of the plastic bowl and push the glass tube into the bowl. Apply plumber's putty around the hole and the glass tube to keep it from leaking. The tube needs to extend 1 1/2" into the bowl. (Figure 3)
6. Place the bowl on the ring stand. (Figure 4)
7. Put water in the bowl not quite to the top of the tube. (Figure 5)
8. Turn on the hot plate and heat the water. It will erupt into the air in the bowl, then it will run back into the tube to the flask. (Figure 6)

Soda Geyser Cross Section

Color this page according to the color key.

Color Key
a. brown
b. red
c. black

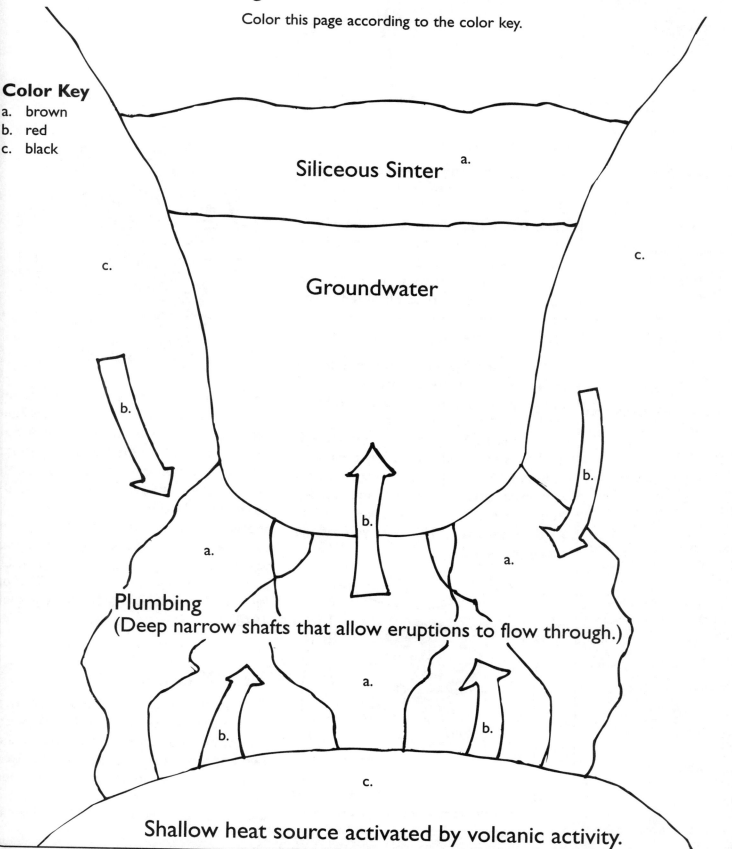

Siliceous Sinter   a.

c.   c.

Groundwater

b.

b.   b.

a.   a.

Plumbing
(Deep narrow shafts that allow eruptions to flow through.)

a.

b.   b.

c.

Shallow heat source activated by volcanic activity.

Fun Facts

Animal: White-Tailed Deer (Odocoileus virginianus)

Bird: Cardinal (Cardinalis cardinalis)

Fish: Bluegill (Lepomis macrochirus)

Flower: Purple Violet (Viola sororia)

Fossil: Tully Monster (Tullimonstrum gregarium)

Insect: Monarch Butterfly (Danaus plexippus)

Mineral: Flourite (Calcuim fluoride)

Motto: "State Sovereignty, National Union"

Nickname: Prairie State

Prairie Grass: Big Bluestem (Andropogon gerardii)

Song: "Illinois" by Charles H. Chamberlin

Tree: White Oak (Quercus alba)

Statehood: December 3, 1818; 21st state admitted to the Union

Population: (2000 estimate) 12,419,293

Area: 57,918 square miles of land and water; 25th largest state

Highest Point: Charles Mound; 1235 feet above sea level

Lowest Point: Mississippi River; 279 feet above sea level

Capital: Springfield

Largest City: Chicago

Major Crops: Corn, hay, soybeans, sorghum, hogs, cattle, dairy

Major Industry: Food processing, computer equipment, chemical products, oil production, printing and publishing, coal mining, meat packing

Illinois

Name: <u>Illinois</u> was named after the French word <u>Illini</u> Algonquin for "warriors."

Did You Know?

Cracker Jacks™, the famous caramel popcorn treat, was invented in Illinois by German immigrant Frederick William Ruekheim in the 1870s. Ruekheim experimented with many different recipes until, after years of trial and error, he found just the right blend of flavors. Not until the early 1890s was the recipe finalized, which makes the recipe for the delicious popcorn treat more than 100 years old!

At first Cracker Jacks™ were sold on the street in a cart to people walking by. Eventually it was produced and sold to stores in large containers. In 1899, Cracker Jacks™ was packaged in individual boxes so people could buy a package at a time. Prizes appeared in the boxes a few years later. Sailor Jack and his dog Bingo were added on the boxes in 1918. As the slogan says, "The more you eat, the more you want!"

Flag: The state seal is emblazoned on the center of a white flag with the name *Illinois* underneath.

Seal: On the state seal of Illinois an American eagle holds a shield with a blue field with 13 five-point stars on it, beneath that seven red stripes and six white stripes. The ribbon in the eagle's mouth bears the state's motto: "State Sovereignty, National Union." Two dates appear directly below the eagle, 1868, the year the seal was adopted, and 1818, the year Illinois became a state. On the outer circle are the words *Seal of the State of Illinois* and the date of statehood, *Aug. 26th 1818.*

Mrs. O'Leary's Cow

The Great Chicago Fire was started by a cow the evening of October 9, 1871, or so the legend goes. Early testimonies of the two-and-a-half-day fire determined that Mrs. O'Leary was in her barn milking her cow when it suddenly knocked over a kerosene lamp. The fire started a blaze in the hay and straw. Before the fire died out on October 10, it had cut a swath through Chicago that left 100,000 people homeless and 300 people dead.

Historians agree that the fire started in the O'Leary barn, but careful analysis suggests an accident not by a cow but by a neighbor who housed his cow in the same barn. It is believed that the match that lit the neighbor's pipe might have started the tremendous fire. Other historians speculate that the fire was ignited by a spark from a nearby chimney. No one will ever know the true story.

O'Leary's house remained standing after the fire. In 1955 it was finally demolished. Ironically, the Chicago Fire Academy was built on the same property. On the first floor of the academy at the supposed location where the Great Chicago Fire started, a cross was painted.

The following craft plays on the suggestion that Mrs. O'Leary's cow knocked over the kerosene lamp in the barn and set off one of the most infamous fires in history. The rolling cow toy reflects the time, character and toys of that time period.

Notable Natives

Jane Addams (1860-1935), social worker, Nobel Prize winner, Cedarville

Mary Astor (Lucille Langhanke) (1906-1987), actress, Quincy

Jack Benny (Benjamin Kubelsky) (1894-1974), comedian, Waukegan

Black Hawk (1767-1838), Sauk Indian Chief, Saukenuk

Harry Blackmun (1908-1999), U.S. Supreme Court Justice, Nashville

Herbert Lawrence Block (pen name, Herblock) (1909-2001), three-time Pulitzer Prize-winning political cartoonist, Chicago

Ray Bradbury (1920-), science fiction writer, Waukegan

William Jennings Bryan (1860-1925), three-time Democratic candidate for President, Salem

Edgar Rice Burroughs (1875-1950), writer, creator of Tarzan, Chicago

Dick Butkus (1942-), football player, Chicago

Hillary Rodham Clinton (1947-), First Lady, U.S. senator, Chicago

Jimmy Connors (1952-), world champion tennis player, East St. Louis

Cindy Crawford (1966-), super model, De Kalb

Richard J. Daley (1902-1976), mayor of Chicago, Chicago

Miles Davis (1926-1991), jazz trumpeter, musician, Alton

Walt Disney (1901-1966), animator, creator of Mickey Mouse and Disneyland, Chicago

Edward Adelbert Doisy (1893-1986), Nobel Prize-winning physiologist, Hume

Harrison Ford (1942-), actor, Chicago

Paul John Flory (1910-1985), Nobel Prize-winning chemist, Sterling

Betty Friedan (1921-), writer, feminist, Peoria

Benny Goodman (1909-1986), big band leader, clarinetist, Chicago

Frederick William Goudy (1865-1947), printer, type designer, Bloomington

Dorothy Hamill (1956-), ice skater, Chicago

Ernest Hemingway (1899-1961), Nobel Prize-winning writer, Oak Park

Ricky Henley Henderson (1958-), baseball player, Chicago

Charlton Heston (Charles Carter) (1923-), Oscar-winning actor, Evanston

"Wild Bill" Hickok (1837-1876), famous personality from the old West, Troy Grove

Robert William Holley (1922-1993), Nobel Prize-winning physiologist, Urbana

Rock Hudson (Roy Scherer, Jr.) (1925-1985), actor, Winnetka

Burl Ives (1909-1995), ballad singer, Oscar-winning actor, Hunt

Quincy Jones (1933-), composer, music producer, Robinson

David Mamet (1947-), playwright, Chicago

Bill Murray (1950-), actor, Wilmette

Richard Pryor (1940-), comedian, actor, Peoria

Ronald Wilson Reagan (1911-2004), 40th President (1981-1989), Tampico

Carl Sandburg (1878-1967), Pulitzer Prize-winning poet, writer, Galesburg

Raquel Welch (Raquel Tejada) (1940-), actress, Chicago

Robin Williams (1951-), comedian, actor, Chicago

Mrs. O'Leary's Cow

Materials

* 1 piece of thick tagboard or plywood, 7" square and at least $^1/_{16}$" thick
* 2 pieces of wood, 14" x $^1/_2$" x $^1/_2$"
* dowel, $1^7/_8$" x $^1/_4$"
* mason line or other strong string
* drill
* acrylic paints: black, white
* paintbrush
* paper clips or thin wire
* wire cutters

Instructions

1. Drill two $^1/_{16}$" holes $^1/_4$" from the top of the two 14" pieces of wood. (Figure 1)
2. Drill additional holes at least 5" from the bottom of both 14" pieces of wood. Glue and insert the dowel into the holes. Let it dry. (Figure 2)
3. Transfer the pattern on page 65 to the plywood or tagboard. Paint as specified, using the color key. Drill holes where specified with $^1/_{16}$" bit. (Figure 3)
4. Cut the paper clips or wire into "L" shapes and use them to attach both front and back legs to the body of the cow. Bend them over to secure. (Figure 4)
5. Thread the mason line or string through the holes at the top of one 14" piece of wood.
6. Twist the two pieces of string halfway. (Figure 5)
7. Slip the cow's front leg through the twisted piece of string. (Figure 6)
8. Make a full twist in the string and slip the other front leg through it. (Figure 7)
9. Make another half twist in the string, then thread the string through the two holes of the other 14" pieces of wood. Pull the string snuggly and tie to secure. (Figure 8)
10. Make Mrs. O'Leary's cow kick by squeezing the lower portion of the two 14" pieces of wood. The quicker you squeeze, the faster the cow kicks up its feet! (Figure 9)

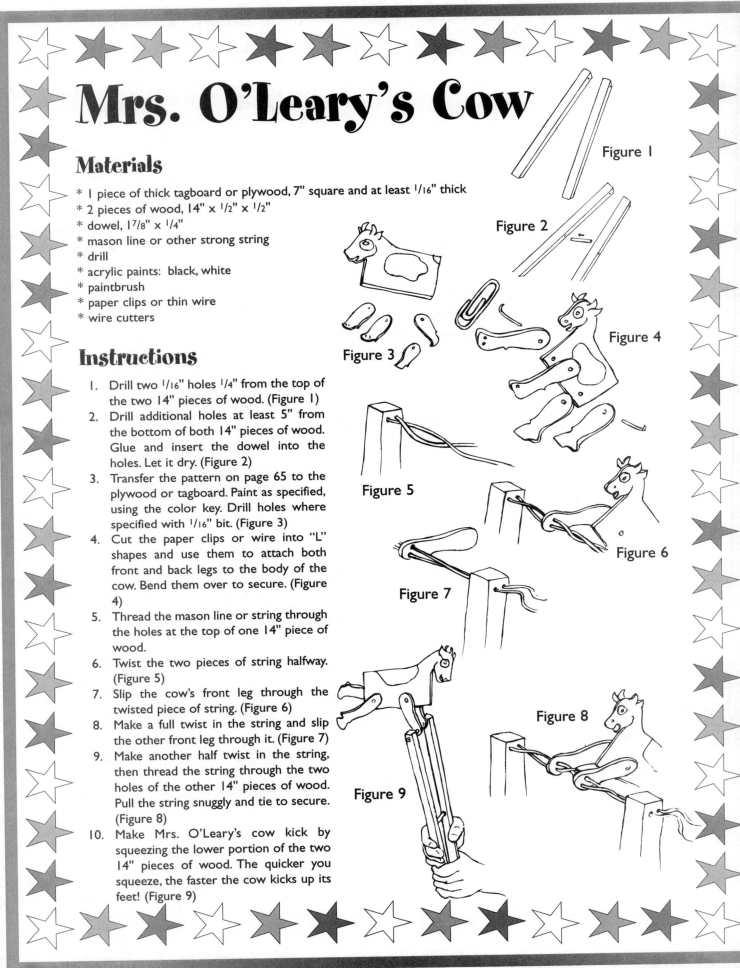

Figure 1

Figure 2

Figure 3

Figure 4

Figure 5

Figure 6

Figure 7

Figure 8

Figure 9

Name _____

Mrs. O'Leary's Cow

Color Key
a. black
b. white

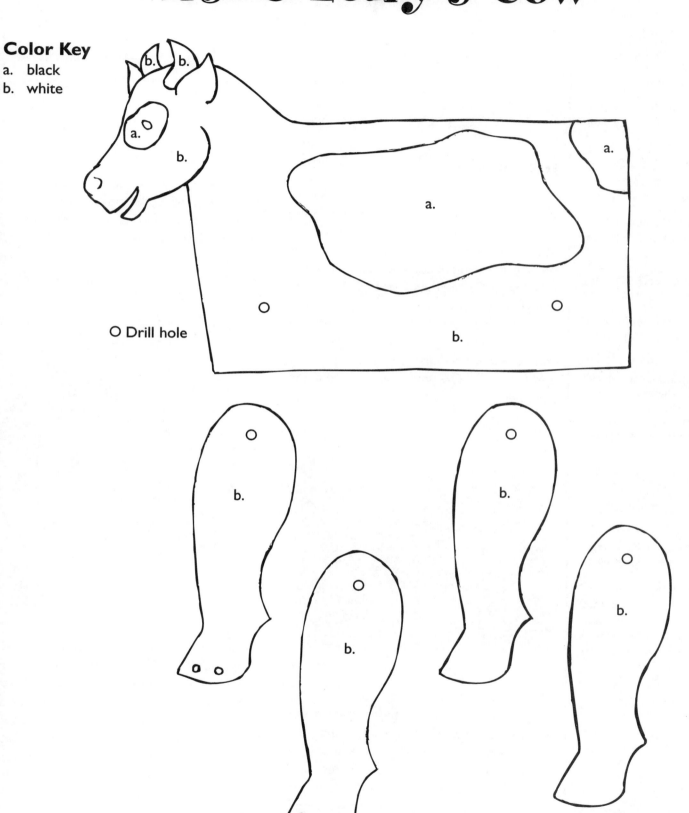

O Drill hole

Fun Facts

Bird: Cardinal (Cardinalis cardinalis)

Flower: Peony (Paeonie)

Motto: "The Crossroads of America"

Nickname: Hoosier State

Stone: Limestone

Song: "On the Banks of the Wabash, Far Away" by Paul Dresser

Tree: Tulip Tree or Tulip Poplar (Liriodendron tulipifera)

Statehood: December 11, 1816; 19th state admitted to the Union

Population: (2000 estimate) 6,080,485

Area: 36,420 square miles of land and water; 38th largest state

Highest Point: Hoosier Hill; 1257 feet above sea level

Lowest Point: Southwest boundary; 320 feet above sea level

Capital: Indianapolis

Largest City: Indianapolis

Major Crops: Corn, oats, rye, onions, soybeans, hogs, cattle, dairy products, eggs

Major Industry: Steel, iron, chemical products, car part production, mobile homes, farm machinery, pharmaceuticals, limestone, petroleum, coal products

Name: _Indiana_ comes from a Latin word which means the "land of Indians."

Did You Know?

A grocer named Gilbert Van Camp discovered his customers really liked his family recipe for pork and beans cooked in a special tomato sauce. It was so popular, he began selling it commercially. This led to a bigger demand as word spread about the delicious pork and beans. Eventually the Van Camp family had to open a canning company to produce enough for all the people who wanted Van Camp's Pork and Beans™. Do you have any old family recipes?

star, bigger than the others, to represent the state, is directly above the flame of the torch, and inside the outer circle of stars. The word _Indiana_ is centered over it. Straight lines emanate from the torch, radiating to the star above the torch and three stars on each side of the torch on the outer circle of stars.

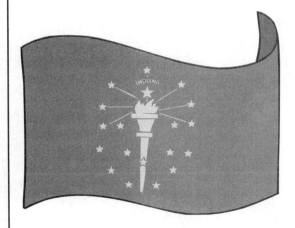

Flag: The Indiana flag is a rectangle with a blue field with 19 five-point stars and a flaming gold torch. Thirteen of the stars are arranged in a circle, representing the original 13 states. Five stars are arranged in a half circle inside the outer circle of stars, to represent the other states admitted to the Union before Indiana. The 19th

Seal: The state seal encircles a scene with three hills in the background and a setting sun shining rays toward the sky. To the right are two sycamore trees. A woodsman is cutting the larger of the two with an axe. A buffalo in the foreground faces left, his tail up, front feet on the ground, back feet in the air, as he jumps over a log. The foreground shows bluegrass.

The Town of Santa Claus

In 1852 the little town of Santa Fe was renamed Santa Claus because another town in Indiana had already been named Santa Fe! Legend says that the city elders toyed with other names but could not agree on one suggestion. It was Christmas Eve and they vacillated back and forth until they heard a child yell "It's Santa Claus," outside their building. From that moment on, they called their town *Santa Claus*. Today, the Santa Claus postmaster receives over one million letters to Santa each Christmas. Yes, Virginia, there really is a Santa Claus, and he is in Indiana!

Make a Christmas card with your own wish list and mail it to Santa Claus, Indiana, 47579.

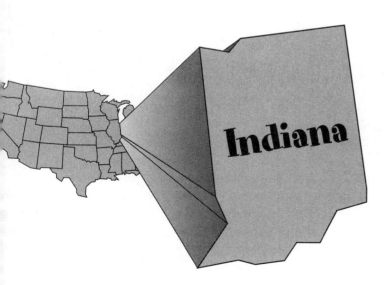

Notable Natives

George Ade (1866-1944), humorist, playwright, Kentland

Anne Baxter (1923-1985), actress, Michigan City

Charles Austin Beard (1874-1948), historian, Knightstown

Mary Ritter Beard (1876-1958), feminist, historian, Indianapolis

Lawrence Dale Bell (1894-1956), aircraft designer, businessman, Mentone

John Shaw Billings (1838-1913), physician, founder of the National Library of Medicine, Switzerland County

Larry Bird (1956-), basketball player, French Lick

Bill Blass (1922-2002), clothing designer, Fort Wayne

Ambrose Everett Burnside (1824-1881), Civil War general, U.S. senator, Liberty

Hoagy Carmichael (1899-1981), songwriter, Bloomington

William Merritt Chase (1849-1916), painter, Franklin

James Dean (1931-1955), actor, Marion

Eugene Debs (1855-1926), socialist activist, union leader, Terre Haute

Henry Dodge (1782-1867), soldier, politician, Vincennes

Theodore Herman Albert Dreiser (1871-1945), novelist, Terre Haute

James Buchanan Eads (1820-1887), salvager, inventor, Lawrenceburg

Edward Eggleston (1837-1902), preacher, writer, Vevay

Janet Flanner (1892-1978), novelist, journalist, Indianapolis

Vivica Fox (1964-), actress, Indianapolis

George Brown Goode (1851-1896), ichthyologist, New Albany

Michael Graves (1934-), postmodernist architect, Indianapolis

John Hay (1838-1905), private secretary to President Lincoln, politician, Salem

Florence Henderson (1934-), actress, Dale

James Hoffa (1913-1975), labor leader, Brazil

Greg Kinnear (1963-), actor, Logansport

David Letterman (1947-), comedian, talk show host, Indianapolis

Shelley Long (1949-), actress, Fort Wayne

Karl Malden (1912-), actor, Gary

John Mellencamp (1951-), singer, Seymour

Sarah Purcell (1948-), actress, Richmond

J. Danforth Quayle (1947-), politician, Vice President, Indianapolis

James Whitcomb Riley (1849-1916), poet, Greenfield

Axl Rose (1962-), musician, Lafayette

David Lee Roth (1955-), singer, Bloomington

Red Skelton (1913-1997), comedian, Vincennes

Twyla Tharp (1941-), dancer, Portland

Kurt Vonnegut, Jr. (1922-), writer, Indianapolis

Wilbur Wright (1867-1912), aviation pioneer, near Millville

Santa Claus Card

Materials

* masking tape
* adhesive foam pads (found in craft stores) or silicone adhesive
* 8½" x11" heavy card stock
* markers, paints or crayons
* pre-cut blank art card and slightly larger envelope (found in stationery stores)
* glitter
* white glue
* craft knife

Instructions

1. Copy (enlarge if necessary) on heavy card stock the card designs on page 69. Color them with crayons, paints or markers.
2. Cut them out, cover some parts with glue and sprinkle on glitter. (Figure 1)
3. Write your town's name on the banner design.
4. Sketch where you want your cut-outs to go on the blank art card. Color the background with the same medium as you colored the card designs. (Figure 2)
5. Glue adhesive foam pads to the back of the cut-out designs. (Figure 3)
   Optional: Dab a pea-size drop of silicone adhesive in various places on the back of the cut-out designs. (Figure 4)
6. Layer the designs on the painted card to create a Christmas scene. (Figure 5)
7. Write your Christmas greetings on the card to a special friend and mail it. You may need extra postage.

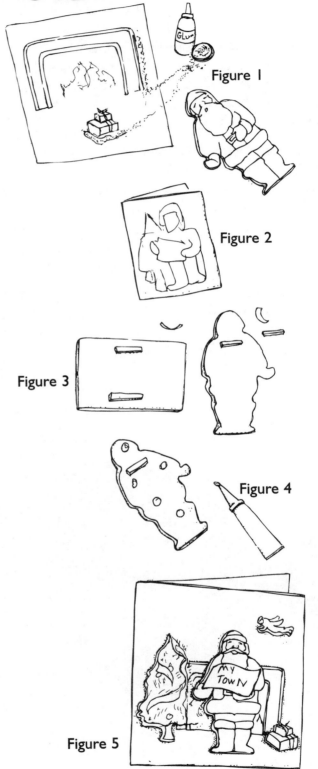

Figure 1

Figure 2

Figure 3

Figure 4

Figure 5

Card Designs

a. Santa Claus
b. tree
c. gifts
d. interior of a house
e. fireplace
f. miscellaneous articles
g. banner

f.

g.

c.

d.

e.

b.

a.

Fun Facts

Bird: Eastern Goldfinch (Carduelis tristis)

Flower: Wild Prairie Rose (Rosa pratincola or Rosa arkansana)

Motto: "Our liberties we prize and our rights we will maintain"

Nickname: Hawkeye State

Rock: Geode

Song: "The Song of Iowa" by S.H.M. Byers

Tree: Oak (Quercus species)

Statehood: December 28, 1846; 29th state admitted to the Union

Population: (2000 estimate) 2,926,324

Area: 56,276 square miles of land and water; 26th largest state

Highest Point: High Point; 1670 feet above sea level

Lowest Point: Junction of the Des Moines and Mississippi Rivers; 480 feet above sea level

Capital: Des Moines

Largest City: Des Moines

Major Crops: Corn, soybeans, popcorn, hogs, oats, cattle, dairy products

Major Industry: Food processing, RV production, hardwood lumber, gypsum, gravel, farm machinery, printing and publishing

Name: Iowa is a Native American word which means "beautiful land."

Did You Know?

Many actors and actresses start their careers in acting with new names, better sounding for the movies. Two actors who have done that were born in Iowa. John Wayne, the famous western actor, born in Earlham, Iowa, was named Marion Michael Morrison at birth. Donna Reed, best remembered for her television show, *The Donna Reed Show*, and her role in the Frank Capra movie, *It's a Wonderful Life*, was born with the name Donnabelle Mullenger in Denison, Iowa.

United States from France. An American eagle with wings outspread holds a blue ribbon in its beak with the state motto, "Our liberties we prize and our rights we will maintain." *Iowa* is written in red underneath.

Seal: The seal shows a citizen soldier holding an American flag in one raised hand and a rifle in the other. In the background to the left is a sheaf of wheat with farm tools (sickle, rake, plow). On the right is a lead furnace, and a pile of pig lead. In the far background is the Mississippi River. On the river is the steamer, *Iowa*. Above the scene is an American eagle, a banner in its beak with the state motto: "Our liberties we prize and our rights we will maintain."

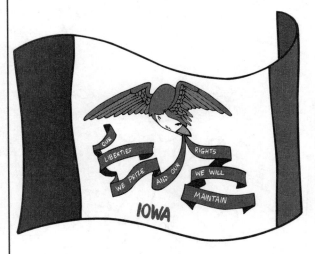

Flag: The state flag has three broad vertical stripes of blue, white and red like the French Tri-color, paying tribute to the fact that Iowa was once part of the Louisiana Territory which was purchased by the

American Gothic Mosaic

The painting, *American Gothic*, is one of America's most recognized images. It typifies rural Iowa's homesteads and farmers. Hundreds of takeoffs and parodies have been created featuring the house, the farmer and his daughter. Painted in 1930, it brought the artist, Grant Wood, instant fame and has become a cultural icon. The house pictured in the painting has been on the National Register of Historical Places since 1974 and was donated to the State Historical Society in 1992.

Every year the second Saturday in June is designated as Gothic Day in Eldon, Iowa.

Notable Natives

Bill Bailey (Dale D. Bales) (1886-1966), vaudevillian, Maxwell

Carl Lotus Becker (1873-1945), historian, Waterloo

Bix Beiderbecke (1903-1931), jazz musician, cornettist, Davenport

Norman Ernest Borlaug (1914-), Nobel Prize-winning plant geneticist, Cresco

Perry Byerley (1897-1978), geophysicist, Clarinda

Bill Bryson (1951-), writer, Des Moines

Wallace Hume Carothers (1896-1937), nylon inventor, Burlington

Johnny Carson (1925-2005), talk show host, Corning

"Buffalo Bill" Cody (1846-1917), creator of the Wild West Shows, near Le Claire

Edwin Harris Colbert (1905-), paleontologist, Clarinda

Lee De Forest (1873-1961), U.S. "Father of Radio," inventor, Council Bluffs

Leonard Eugene Dickson (1874-1954), mathematician, Independence

Mamie Geneva Doud Eisenhower (1896-1979), First Lady, Boone

Simon Estes (1938-), opera singer, Centerville

William Frawley (1887-1966), actor who played "Fred" on *I Love Lucy*, Burlington

George Gallup (1901-1984), opinion pollster, Jefferson

Susan Glaspell (1882-1948), short story writer, novelist, Davenport

Janet Guthrie (1938-), first woman racecar driver to compete in the Indy 500, Iowa City

Vincent T. Hamlin (1900-1993), cartoonist, creator of *Alley Oop*, Perry

Harry Frederick Harlow (1905-1981), psychologist, Fairfield

Alan J. Heeger (1936-), Nobel Prize-winning chemist, Sioux City

Bruce Charles Heezen (1924-1977), oceanographer, Vinton

Herbert Hoover (1874-1964), 31st President (1929-1933), West Branch

Harry Hopkins (1890-1946), administrator, FDR advisor, Sioux City

Ann Landers (Esther Pauline Friedman) (1918-2002), advice columnist, Sioux City

John Lewis (1880-1969), labor leader, Lucas County

Glenn Miller (1904-1944), big band leader, trombonist, Clarinda

Kate Mulgrew (1955-), actress, Dubuque

John Naughton (1915-1999), inventor of the reclining dentist chair, Parnell

Harriet Nelson (1909-1994), actress, Des Moines

Robert Noyce (1927-1990), inventor of the microchip, Burlington

Harry Olson (1901-1982), acoustic systems inventor, Mount Pleasant

Harry Reasoner (1923-1991), television journalist, *60 Minutes* reporter, Dakota City

Donna Reed (Donnabelle Mullenger) (1921-1986), actress, Denison

Lillian Russell (Helen Louise Leonard) (1861-1922), actress, singer, Clinton

Loren J. Shriver (1944-), astronaut, Jefferson

Wallace Stegner (1909-1993), author, near Lake Mills

Billy Sunday (1862-1935), evangelist, Ames

James A. Van Allen (1914-), space physicist, Mount Pleasant

Abigail Van Buren (Pauline Esther Friedman) (1918-), advice columnist, Sioux City

Henry A. Wallace (1888-1965), U.S. Vice President, Adair

John Wayne (Marion Michael Morrison) (1907-1979), actor, Earlham

Andy Williams (1927-), singer, Wall Lake

Meredith Willson (1902-1984), composer, Mason City

Grant Wood (1892-1942), artist most famous for *American Gothic*, Anamosa

American Gothic Mosaic

This project requires heat.

Materials

* 2¹/₂ cups cornstarch
* 3¹/₄ cups baking soda
* 2¹/₂ cups water
* cooking pot
* spoon
* knife
* flour
* rolling pin
* aluminum foil
* cookie sheet
* oven
* sandpaper
* acrylic paints: yellow, white, brown, green, red, blue, peach or beige, black
* medium-point, permanent black marker
* brushes
* white glue
* 10¹/₂" x 13¹/₂" heavy cardboard

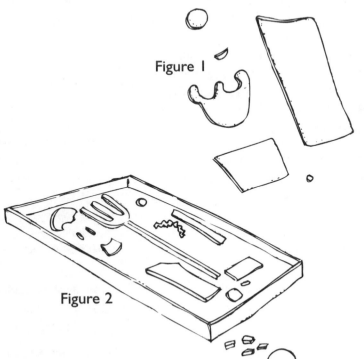

Figure 1

Figure 2

Instructions

1. Copy the American Gothic mosaic design on page 73. Cut out the shapes and set them aside. (Figure 1)
2. Mix the first three ingredients in a pot on low heat. Stir the mixture constantly so none sticks to the bottom.
3. Remove the pot when the mixture turns soupy and let it cool.
4. Gather the mixture together and knead the dough on a floured surface until soft.
5. Roll the dough out to approximately ¹/₄" thick.
6. Lay each piece of the paper American Gothic design on the dough and cut it out. Place the dough shapes gently on the cookie sheet. (Figure 2)
7. Make sure all the pieces of dough match the mosaic design. (Figure 3)
8. Bake in an oven at a low heat until the pieces are hardened. Make sure the heat is low so the dough does not curl. Remove from oven and let it cool.
9. Lay the pieces down according to the design on page 73. Sand any pieces that do not fit. (Figure 4)
10. Follow the color key on page 73, to paint each solid mosaic piece. Do not saturate. Let the pieces dry. (Figure 5)
11. Glue the shapes to the cardboard sheet.

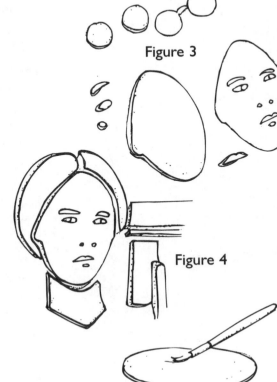

Figure 3

Figure 4

Figure 5

Name _____

American Gothic Mosaic Designs

Color Key

a. brown
b. peach or beige
c. yellow
d. white
e. blue
f. green
g. red
h. black

Fun Facts

Amphibian: Barred Tiger Salamander (Ambystonia tigrinum mavortium)

Animal: American Buffalo or Bison (Bison bison)

Bird: Western Meadowlark (Sturnella neglecta)

Flower: Native Sunflower (Helianthus annuus)

Insect: Honeybee (Apis mellifera)

Motto: "Ad Astra Per Aspera" (To the stars through difficulty)

Nickname: Sunflower State

Reptile: Ornate Box Turtle (Terrapene ornata)

Song: "Home on the Range" by Brewster Higley

March: "The Kansas March" by Duff E. Middleton

Tree: Cottonwood (Populus deltoids)

Statehood: January 29, 1861; 34th state admitted to the Union

Population: (2000 estimate) 2,688,418

Area: 82,282 square miles of land and water; 15th largest state

Highest Point: Mt. Sunflower; 4039 feet above sea level

Lowest Point: Verdigris River; 680 feet above sea level

Capital: Topeka

Largest City: Wichita

Major Crop: Cattle, wheat, sorghum, soybeans, oats, barley, hogs, corn, potatoes

Major Industry: Aircraft manufacturing, food processing, zinc, coal, lead, helium production

Kansas

Name: Like many states, Kansas gets its name from a Native American word. <u>Kansas</u> is a Sioux word that means "south wind people."

Did You Know?

One of America's favorite foods is pizza. Millions of Americans eat it for lunch or dinner, or even cold for breakfast! The largest pizza restaurant company in the world is Pizza Hut™. It started with one small restaurant in Wichita, Kansas, opened in 1958 by brothers Dan and Frank Carney. The first restaurant was tiny with room for only 25 customers, but much has changed since those first days. Today Pizza Hut™ has more than 12,000 restaurants in over 90 countries!

You might wonder how the Carney brothers came up with the name. The sign they purchased for the outside of the first restaurant could only hold nine letters. They knew they wanted *pizza* in the name. With only four spaces left open, they came up with *hut*, which described the tiny building. The rest, as they say, is history!

Flag: The state seal is at the center of the flag on a field of dark blue. Above the seal is a sunflower resting on a bar of twisted gold. Below the seal is the word *Kansas*.

Seal: The Great Seal of Kansas is described in the act that authorized its use in 1861: "The east is represented by a rising sun in the right-hand corner of the seal; to the left of it, Commerce is represented by a river and a steamboat; in the foreground, agriculture is represented as the basis of future prosperity of the state by a settler's cabin and a man plowing with a pair of horses; beyond this is a train of ox-wagons going west; in the background is seen a herd of buffalo, retreating, pursued by two Indians on horseback; toward the top is the motto: 'Ad astra per aspera.' Beneath is a cluster of 34 stars. The circle is surrounded by the words *Great Seal of the State of Kansas January 29, 1861*."

Bread Basket of the World

Have you ever heard of Turkey Red Wheat? It's a type of wheat that is hearty enough to grow in the winter, brought to the United States by early Mennonite immigrants from Russia. Because of this unique wheat, Kansas thrived and eventually became known as the "Bread Basket of the World."

The Mennonites

The early Mennonites immigrated to the United States from a small village in South Russia, Alexanderwohl. In 1874, because of religious persecution, the 800 Mennonites boarded two ships and set sail for America. They settled in the Kansas prairie lands (Marion, McPherson and other smaller counties). The hearty wheat seeds they brought with them from southern Russia adapted well to conditions in Kansas.

The following project is a tribute to the Mennonites and reflects their unique influence on this country.

Notable Natives

Kirstie Alley (1951-), actress, Wichita

Ed Asner (1929-), actor, Kansas City

Robert Duane Ballard (1942-), underwater explorer, author, Wichita

Frank Ambrose Beach (1911-1988), biologist, academic writer, Emporia

Gwendolyn Elizabeth Brooks (1917-2000), poet, Pulitzer Prize-winning novelist, Topeka

Walter Percy Chrysler (1875-1940), auto manufacturer, Wamego

Charles Curtis (1860-1936), U.S. Vice President, Topeka

Bob Dole (1923-), U.S. senator, Republican presidential candidate, Russell

Amelia Earhart (1897-1937), aviatrix, Atchison

Gladys Anderson Emerson (1903-1984), biochemist, Caldwell

Melissa Etheridge (1961-), singer, Leavenworth

Gary Hart (1936-), politician, presidential candidate, Ottawa

Dennis Hopper (1936-), actor, Dodge City

Walter Johnson (1887-1946), baseball player, Humboldt

Buster Keaton (1895-1966), comedic actor, Piqua

Emmett Kelly (1898-1979), clown, Sedan

Craig Kilborn (1962-), talk show host, Kansas City

Harold Lloyd (1893-1971), comedic actor, Burchard

Edgar Lee Master (1869-1950), poet, Garnett

Hattie McDaniel (1895-1952), Oscar-winning actress, Wichita

Zasu Pitts (1989-1963), actress, Parsons

Jeff Probst (1961-), television show *Survivor* host, Wichita

Barry Sanders (1968-), football player, Wichita

Vivian Vance (1912-1979), actress who played "Vivian" on *I Love Lucy*, Cherryvale

William Allen White (1868-1944), editor, journalist, author, Emporia

Wheat Sheaf

This project requires heat.

Materials

* 1 cup salt
* 1 cup flour
* 1 cup water
* aluminum foil
* paper clip
* cookie sheet
* paintbrush
* varnish
* mixing bowl
* clay modeling tools
* rolling pin

Instructions

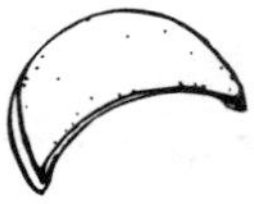

1. Mix the salt and flour together in a bowl. Drizzle in water.
2. Remove the dough from the bowl and knead for 5 to 8 minutes. (Figure 1)
3. Pull the dough into three parts. One third will be used to roll out flat, the second to roll into strips; and, the third to use as the wheat. (Figure 2)
4. Copy the half moon design on page 78. Cut out and set aside. (Figure 3)
5. Lightly flour a work surface. Roll the first third of dough 1/4" flat. Lay the paper half moon shape on top of the dough and cut around it. Carefully remove the half moon and place it on a sheet of aluminum foil. (Figure 4)
6. Slip a paper clip under the center of the half moon. (Figure 5)
7. Make wheat stalks by rolling out thin pieces of dough (about 5" long x 1/4"). Spread them out against the half moon shape. (Figure 6)
8. For the wheat, roll out 1/2" x 1/4" shapes. Make several and attach them to the wheat stalks. (Figure 7)

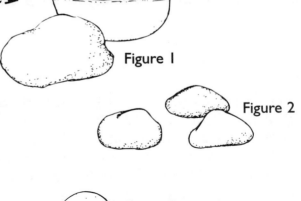

Figure 1

Figure 2

Figure 3

Figure 4

Figure 5

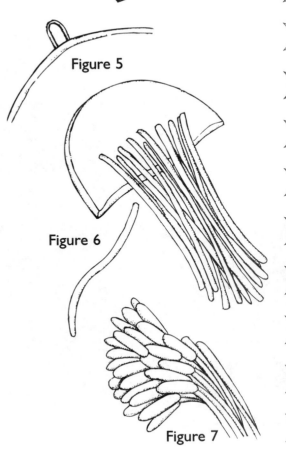

Figure 6

Figure 7

9. Flatten the wheat shapes with a knife and use a clay tool or knife to form into a wheat sheaf. Use water to soften any drying dough. (Figure 8)
10. Layer the additional sheaves on top of others while building up the three-dimensional form. (Figure 9)
11. Gently lift the foil and place the wheat sheet onto a cookie sheet. Heat oven to 250°F for a slow but consistent bake. The baking process could take up to 8 to 10 hours. Allow the sheaves to cool, then apply a light varnish or spray with hairspray.
12. Hang by the paper clip. If it breaks from the dough, attach it with epoxy or another strong glue. (Figure 10)

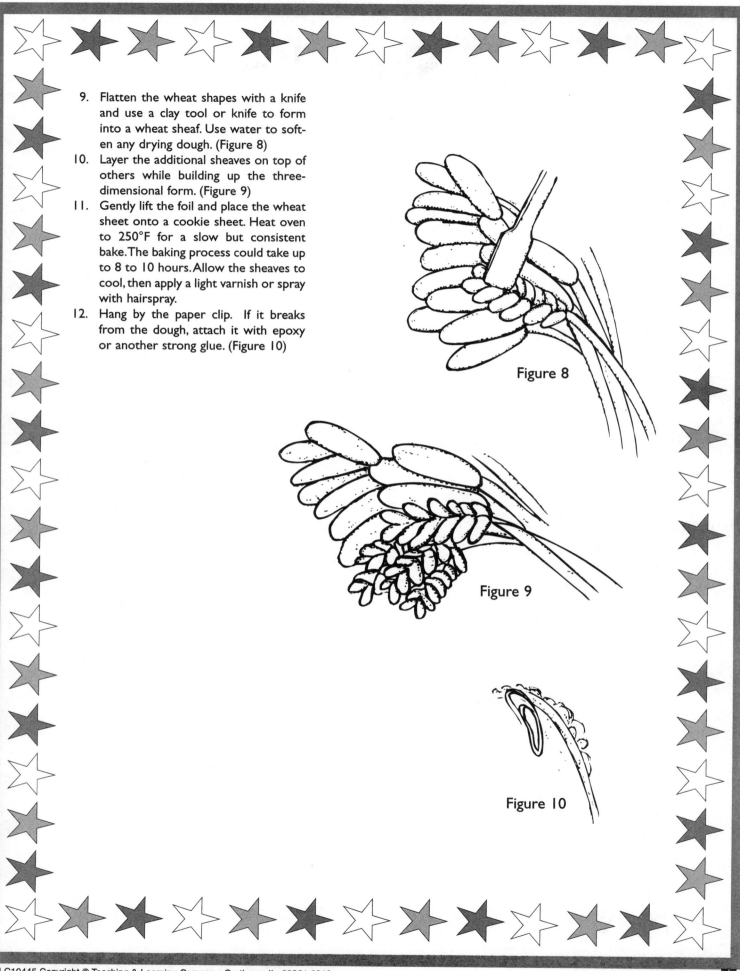

Figure 8

Figure 9

Figure 10

Name _____

Wheat Sheaf Designs

Fun Facts

Wild Animal: Gray Squirrel (Sciurus carolinensis)

Butterfly: Viceroy (Basilarchia archippus)

Bird: Cardinal (Cardinalis cardinalis)

Fish: Kentucky Bass (Micropterus punctulatus)

Flower: Goldenrod (Solidago)

Fossil: Brachiopod

Gem: Freshwater Pearl

Horse: Thoroughbred

Motto: "United We Stand, Divided We Fall"

Nickname: Bluegrass State

Song: "My Old Kentucky Home" by Stephen Collins Foster

Tree: Tulip Tree or Tulip Poplar (Liriodendron tulipifera)

Statehood: June 1, 1792; 15th state admitted to the Union

Population: (2000 estimate) 4,041,769

Area: 40,411 square miles of land and water; 37th largest state

Highest Point: Black Mountain; 4145 feet above sea level

Lowest Point: Mississippi River; 257 feet above sea level

Capital: Frankfort

Largest City: Louisville

Major Crop: Horses, cattle, tobacco, fruit, wheat, dairy products, hogs

Major Industry: Petroleum, natural gas, transportation equipment, food processing, tobacco products, textiles, coal, brooms, tourism

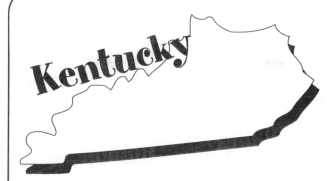

Name: The word <u>Kentucky</u> *comes from an Iroquois word that has been translated to mean several things—"dark and bloody ground," "meadowland" and "land of tomorrow."*

Did You Know?

The busiest day of the year for telephone calls is the day we set aside to honor our mothers. Every year on this special day, children all over America give cards and presents to their mothers. Those who are away from home call and send cards, flowers and gifts. Mother's Day, celebrated in America every May, was first observed by Mary S. Wilson in Henderson, Kentucky, in 1887. Julia Howe first suggested the special day in 1872, but it didn't become a national holiday until 1915 when President Woodrow Wilson signed a law officially proclaiming Mother's Day as a day of national observance.

The Kentucky State Seal is reproduced with permission from the Kentucky Secretary of State.

Seal: In the center of the circular seal are a statesman and a frontiersman shaking hands, with the words of the state motto, "United We Stand, Divided We Fall," on a ribbon under them. In the outside circle are sprays of goldenrod, the state flower, and the words *Commonwealth of Kentucky*.

Flag: The state seal is centered on a navy blue field surrounded by the words *Commonwealth of Kentucky*. Below the seal are sprays of goldenrod, the state flower.

Run for the Roses

Kentucky's mild climate, lush vegetation and bluegrass meadows have made it one of the most important states for horse breeding and racing. The Kentucky Derby is one of the most respected thoroughbred races in the United States. Held at Churchill Downs, this prestigious horse race was started in 1875 by Meriwether Lewis Clark, Jr. He had visited England's famous Epsom Derby and wanted to have a racetrack that rivaled it in Kentucky. The first Kentucky Derby was run on May 17, 1875. The horse who ran the 1½-mile course and crossed the finish line first was a thoroughbred named Aristides. For his hard work, Aristides was given an extra portion of alfalfa.

Traditions play an important role during the Derby. Colonel Clark began the festivities by having a Derby breakfast served the first day of the race. Another tradition is that as soon as the race is over, the winning horse's owner is invited to a private party given by the president of Churchill Downs. Sipping mint julep from a sterling silver cup decorated with a wreath of roses in the shape of the winning horse's shoe is another tradition. Since 1932, each winning horse has worn a blanket of red roses sewn together and a rose victory wreath around its neck.

Famous horses that have made history at the track include: Man of War, Sea Biscuit, Secretariat and Smarty Jones.

Notable Natives

Muhammad Ali (Cassius Marcellus Clay) (1942-), world heavyweight champion boxer, Louisville

Robert Anderson (1806-1871), soldier, near Louisville

Alben Barkley (1877-1956), U.S. Vice President, Graves City

Roy Bean (c.1825-1903), frontiersman, Mason County

Ned Beatty (1937-), actor, Louisville

James Gillespie Birney (1792-1857), abolitionist, publisher, Danville

Louis Brandeis (1856-1941), U.S. Supreme Court Justice, Louisville

John Cabell Breckinridge (1821-1875), U.S. Vice President, Lexington

William Wells Brown (c.1814-1884), abolitionist, novelist, near Lexington

Kentucky "Kit" Carson (1809-1868), pioneer scout, Madison County

George Clooney (1961-), actor, Lexington

Rosemary Clooney (1928-2002), singer, actress, Maysville

Billy Ray Cyrus (1961-), country singer, Flatwood

Jefferson Davis (1808-1889), president of the Confederate States of America, Christian County

Johnny Depp (1963-), actor, Owensboro

Irene Dunne (1898-1990), actress, Louisville

Don Everly (1937-), singer, Brownie

Simon Flexner (1863-1946), microbiologist, Louisville

Crystal Gayle (1951-), singer, Paintsville

D.W. Griffith (1875-1948), pioneering film director, Floydsfork

Lionel Hampton (1909-2002), jazz musician, Louisville

John Bell Hood (1831-1879), Confederate general, Owingsville

Naomi Judd (1946-), singer, Ashland

Wynonna Judd (1964-), singer, Ashland

Abraham Lincoln (1809-1865), 16th President (1861-1865), Hardin County now Larue

Loretta Lynn (1935-), singer, Butcher Hollow

Carry A. Nation (1846-1911), temperance leader, Garrard County

Patricia Neal (1926-), actress, Packard

Diane Sawyer (1945-), broadcast journalist, Glasgow

Hunter Thompson (1937-), journalist, writer, Louisville

Frederick Vinson (1890-1953), U.S. Supreme Court Chief Justice, Louisa

Robert Penn Warren (1905-1989), writer, poet, Guthrie

Dwight Yoakam (1956-), singer, Pikesville

Sean Young (1959-), actress, Louisville

Run for the Roses Paper Flowers

Materials

* large Styrofoam™ circle (at least 12")
* utility knife
* scissors
* ruler
* black felt-tip pen
* wire cutters

For each paper flower you will need:
* ¼ green pipe cleaner
* 3 pieces of red tissue paper
* florist tape

Optional
* 15 or more silk roses

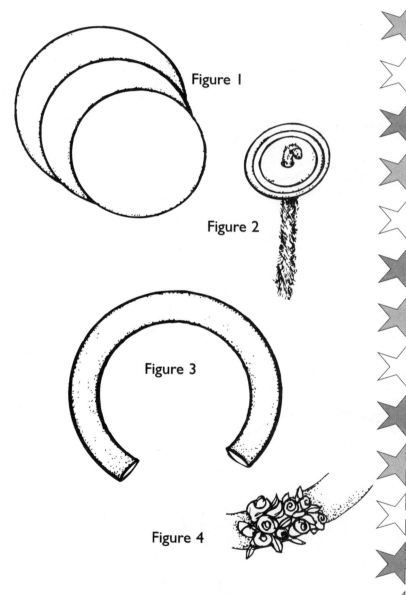

Figure 1

Figure 2

Figure 3

Figure 4

Instructions

1. Cut three pieces of tissue paper the same size as the circles on page 82.
2. Stack the tissue paper from largest to smallest. (Figure 1)
3. Push the pipe cleaner through the middle of the tissue paper and turn down its tip. Use florist tape to secure the flowers on the pipe cleaner stems. Make additional flowers this way and set them aside. The more you make, the better they will fill the Styrofoam™ base. (Figure 2)
4. Cut off one-third of the Styrofoam™ circle. (Figure 3)
5. Cut the silk roses at their bases with wire cutters. Glue the ends of the handmade flowers and silk flowers with glue. Push them into the Styrofoam™ and begin to build up all sides of the wreath. (Figure 4)

Paper Flower Patterns

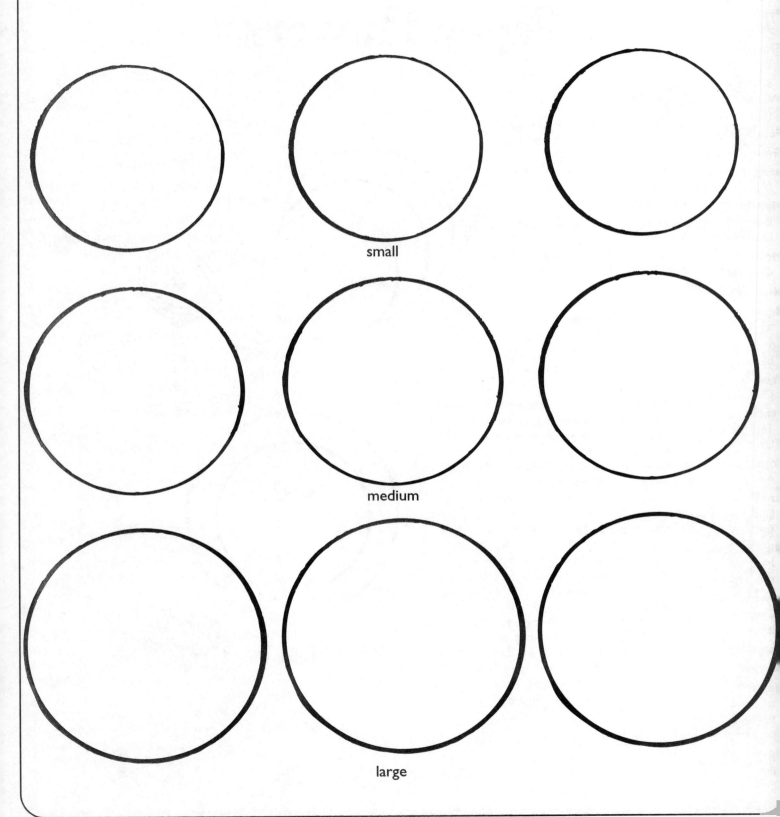

small

medium

large

Fun Facts

Amphibian: Green Tree Frog (Hyla cinerea)

Bird: Brown Pelican (Pelecanus occidentalis)

Crustacean: Crawfish (Procambarus clarkii)

Dog: Catahoula Leopard Dog

Freshwater Fish: White Perch (Pomoxis annularis)

Flower: Magnolia Tree Blossom (Magnolia grandiflora)

Wildflower: Louisiana Iris (Giganticaerulea)

Fossil: Petrified Palm Tree

Gem: Agate (Silicon dioxide)

Insect: Honeybee (Apis mellifera)

Mammal: Louisiana Black Bear (Ursus americanus luteolus)

Motto: "Union, Justice, and Confidence"

Nickname: Pelican State

Reptile: Alligator (Alligator mississippiensis)

Song: "Give Me Louisiana" by Doralice Fontane

Tree: Bald Cypress (Taxodium distichum)

Statehood: April 30, 1812; 18th state admitted to the Union

Population: (2000 estimate) 4,468,976

Area: 51,843 square miles of land and water; 31st largest state

Highest Point: Driskill Mountain; 535 feet above sea level

Lowest Point: at New Orleans; 8 feet below sea level

Capital: Baton Rouge

Largest City: New Orleans

Major Crop: Seafood, cotton, sweet potatoes, pecans, soybeans, cattle, sugarcane, poultry, eggs, rice

Major Industry: Chemical products, salt, oil, natural gas, coal products, food processing, paper products, tourism

Louisiana

Name: Sieur de Rene Robert Cavelier La Salle (1643-1687), a French explorer who explored the Mississippi River in the 1680s, claimed and named the lands in honor of King Louis XIV of France.

Did You Know?

One of the largest land deals in American history was the Louisiana Purchase. Over 828,000 square miles of land nearly doubled the size of the United States! Thomas Jefferson, our third President, authorized the purchase at a staggering cost of $15 million. The territory eventually became 13 states, one of which was Louisiana. The land was purchased from France, and Louisiana is rich in French history. Named after King Louis XIV of France, it is the only state in the Union with references to French law in its state law code.

Seal: The circular seal of Louisiana has a pelican, the state bird, in the center craning its long neck apparently to feed three baby pelicans in the nest. The babies are all facing upward to their mother. Above the pelicans are the words *Union* and *Justice*. Below is the word *Confidence*. In the outer ring of the seal are the words *State of Louisiana*.

Flag: The flag shows a mother pelican and her three babies in a nest on a field of blue. Underneath is a ribbon bearing the state motto: "Union, Justice and Confidence."

Mardi Gras

One of the greatest festivals in America is Mardi Gras. Though celebrated in European history since Ancient Roman days, it was considered a pagan holiday by early Christians. Instead of banning the holiday, they allowed the celebration days before Lent. Mardi Gras did not reach the North American continent until 1699 when French explorer, Iberville, launched an expedition up the Mississippi River. On March 3, he and his group of explorers camped on the west bank of the river, about 60 miles south of where New Orleans is located today. The site was named Point du Mardi Gras because the celebration was observed at that location. By the late 18th century, New Orleans was under French rule. The pre-Lenten festival and masked balls were the fashion of the day. When New Orleans came under Spanish rule, the festival was banned. In 1803, New Orleans and all of Louisiana came under the control of the United States. Mardi Gras was legalized about 24 years later.

Mardi Gras is rich with traditions and secrecy. The secret society, Comus, added beauty to Mardi Gras festivities by incorporating parades with unified float themes followed by extravagant balls. The king and queen of Mardi Gras have their identities guarded until the day of the parade.

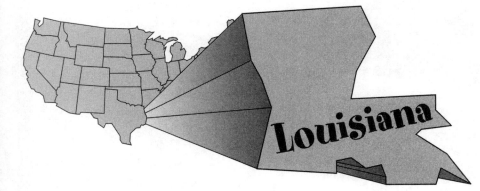

Notable Natives

Louis Armstrong (1901-1971), trumpet musician, singer, New Orleans

Sidney Joseph Bechet (1897-1959), jazz musician, New Orleans

Arna Wendell Bontemps (1902-1973), poet, writer, Alexandria

Terry Paxton Bradshaw (1948-), football player, television sportscaster, Shreveport

Truman Capote (1924-1984), writer, New Orleans

Kitty Carlisle (1910-), actress, New Orleans

Clyde Vernon Cessna (1879-1954), small aircraft manufacturer, Hawthorne

Clifton Chenier (1925-1987), zydeco accordionist, Opelousas

Van Cliburn (1934-), pianist, Shreveport

Harry Connick, Jr. (1967-), musician, New Orleans

Michael De Bakey (1908-), heart surgeon, Lake Charles

Johnny Dodds (1892-1940), jazz clarinetist, New Orleans

Fats Domino (1928-), musician, New Orleans

Louis Moreau Gottschalk (1829-1869), pianist, composer, New Orleans

Bryant Gumbel (1948-), television broadcaster, New Orleans

Buddy Guy (1936-), blues guitarist, singer, Lettsworth

Lillian Hellman (1907-1984), playwright, New Orleans

George Herriman (1880-1944), newspaper cartoonist, New Orleans

Al Hirt (1922-1999), trumpeter, New Orleans

Mahalia Jackson (1911-1972), gospel singer, New Orleans

Dorothy Lamour (1914-1996), actress, New Orleans

John Larroquette (1947-), actor, New Orleans

Jerry Lee Lewis (1935-), singer, Ferriday

Huey Pierce Long (1893-1935), politician, Winnfield

Branford Marsalis (1960-), musician, New Orleans

Wynton Marsalis (1961-), musician, New Orleans

Tim McGraw (1967-), country singer, Delhi

Jelly Roll Morton (1890-1941), jazz musician, New Orleans

Aaron Neville (1941-), singer, New Orleans

Randy Newman (1943-), singer, New Orleans

Cokie Roberts (1943-), television journalist, New Orleans

Britney Spears (1981-), pop singer, Kentwood

Edward Douglass White (1845-1915), U.S. Supreme Court Chief Justice, Lafourche Parish

Mardi Gras Mask

Materials

* miscellaneous beads, ribbons and glitter
* gold trim
* Styrofoam™ wig head
* 1/2" dowel, 24" long
* plastic wrap
* 2 cups flour
* 1/2 cup wallpaper paste
* acrylic paint (your choice of colors)
* 20 newspaper sheets
* water
* mixing bowl
* white glue
* permanent marker
* Gesso™ or latex paint

Instructions

1. Make a newspaper mash by tearing newspaper into small pieces and soaking it in water overnight.
2. Drain the excess water from the mash and put the pulp back in the bowl. Mix flour, water and wallpaper paste together with the newspaper to make a workable paste.
3. Cover the Styrofoam™ wig head with plastic wrap. Secure the head to the table with tape, holding the back of the head against the table. (Figure 1)
4. Mark the masked area with a permanent marker. (Figure 2)
5. Choose a face design for your mask from page 86.
6. Slather the papier-mâché onto the Styrofoam™ head. Build the face, exaggerating the features. Set aside and let it dry. (Figure 3)
7. Cut away the chin area of the mask. (Figure 5)
8. Sand any rough edges and paint. Coat with a layer of Gesso™ then paint according to your taste.
9. Glue glitter, ribbons and beads on the mask.
10. Tape and glue the dowel to the back of the mask. (Figure 6)
11. The mask should be used during Mardi Gras. Place a jester's hat on the top of the mask for the full effect!

Figure 1

Figure 2

Figure 3

Figure 4

Figure 5

Figure 6

Mardi Gras Face Designs for Masks

Typical Mardi Gras Masks

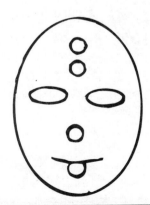 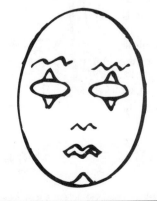 

Fun Facts

Animal: Moose (Alces alces)

Berry: Wild Blueberry (Vaccinium angustifolium aiton)

Bird: Chickadee (Parus atricapillus)

Cat: Maine Moon Cat

Fish: Landlocked Salmon (Salmo salar Sebago)

Flower: White Pinecone and Tassel (Pinus strobes, Linnaeus)

Fossil: Trimerophyte plant (Pertica quadrifaria)

Gem: Tourmaline (Complex Aluminum Borosilicate)

Herb: Wintergreen (Gaultheria procumbers)

Insect: Honeybee (Apis mellifera)

Motto: "Dirigo" (I lead.)

Nickname: Pine Tree State

Song: "State Song of Maine" by Roger Vinton Snow

Tree: White Pine (Pinus strobus)

Statehood: March 15, 1820; 23rd state admitted to the Union

Population: (2000 estimate) 1,274,923

Area: 35,387 square miles of land and water; 39th largest state

Highest Point: Katahdin Mountain; 5268 feet above sea level

Lowest Point: Atlantic coast, sea level

Capital: Augusta

Largest City: Portland

Major Crop: Seafood, poultry, eggs, vegetables, potatoes, dairy products, apples, cattle, blueberries

Major Industry: Paper, lumber and wood products, toothpicks, food processing, leather products, textiles, tourism

Maine

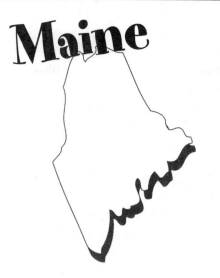

Name: There are two possible origins of the state's name. It may have been named after an ancient French province or after the "main"land, to distinguish it from the many coastal islands.

Did You Know?

Maine is famous for its lobsters, a delicacy food connoisseurs all over the country enjoy. Most of the lobsters eaten in the United States, almost 40 million pounds, come from Maine's coastal waters. Another delicacy that Maine is famous for is blueberries. Tasty in all sorts of desserts or just by themselves, nearly 100% of the wild blueberries eaten in the United States are grown in Maine. After you've eaten Maine lobster or blueberry pie, you may need a toothpick. There is a good chance that toothpick is from the same place. Nearly 90% of America's toothpicks are made in Maine!

Flag: The Maine state flag displays the state seal centered on a blue background.

Seal: The state seal shows a seaman resting on an anchor and a farmer resting on a scythe on either side of a shield. Inside the shield is a pine tree and a moose resting beneath it. Above the shield is a five-point star representing the North Star. Under the star is a ribbon with the state motto, "Dirigo." *Dirigo* translates to "I lead." The two men and the shield rest on a ribbon that bears the name of the state, *Maine.*

Maine's Salt Mills

Salt has been an important commodity throughout history, particularly for the early American colonies. The Gulf of Maine is where the majority of colonial salt works were developed. This area, formed by great ice flows that cut lakes, rivers and canyons underneath the surface of the water, provides a perfect environment for marine life. As a result, rich minerals also accumulated from dissolved minerals and sea life.

From the late 1600s to the War of 1812, salt works were a booming industry up and down the coast of Maine. Salt was highly prized for preserving meats, seasoning foods and for medicinal purposes. Salt was so important, in colonial days the term, *sitting above the salt*, meant you were an important person. Salt mills were placed close to the head of the table. "Sitting above the salt" was the owner of the house. Next to the owner were invited guests or dignitaries, also "above the salt." Lesser guests, women, children and indentured servants sat "below the salt." The further away one "sat from the salt" the lower their status in society.

Notable Natives

Ezra Abbott (1819-1894), biblical scholar, Jacksc

Jacob Abbott (1803-1879), clergyman, author, Hallowell

Benjamin Paul Akers (1825-1861), sculptor, Saccarappa

John Albion Andrew (1818-1867), abolitionist politician, Windham

Natalie Clifford Barney (1876-1972), poet, playwright, Bar Harbor

William Cranch Bond (1789-1859), astronomer Portland

Charles Farrar Browne (pseudonym Artemus War (1834-1867), humorist, Waterford

Dorothea Dix (1802-1887), civil rights reforme Hampden

Neal Dow (1804-1897), reformer politician, Portland

Geraldine Farrar (1882-1967), soprano opera singer, Melrose

John Ford (Sean Aloysius O'Fearna) (1895-1973) film director, Cape Elizabeth

Melville Fuller (1833-1910), U.S. Supreme Cou Chief Justice, Augusta

Frank Bunker Gilbreth (1868-1924), efficiency expert, engineer, Fairfield

Hannibal Hamlin (1809-1891), U.S. Vice President, politician, Paris Hill

Marsden Hartley (1877-1943), modern artist, Lewiston

Oliver Otis Howard (1830-1909), Civil War soldier, first president of Howard Universi Leeds

Stephen King (pseudonym Richard Bachman) (1947-), writer, Portland

Linda Lavin (1937-), actress, Portland

Henry Wadsworth Longfellow (1807-1882), poe Portland

Edna St. Vincent Millay (1892-1950), poet, Rockland

George Palmer Putnam (1814-1872), publisher, Brunswick

Joan Benoit Samuelson (1957-), Olympic gold medal runner, Cape

Elizabeth Margaret Chase Smith (1897-1995), politician, Skowhegan

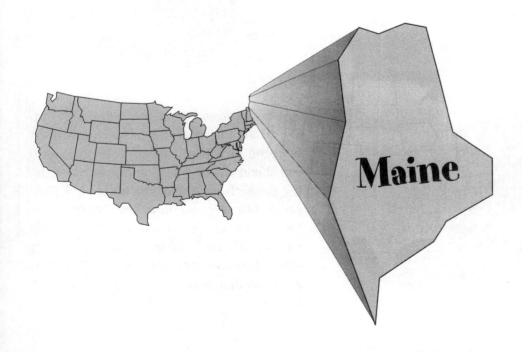

Colonial Salt Mill

This project requires heat.

Figure 1

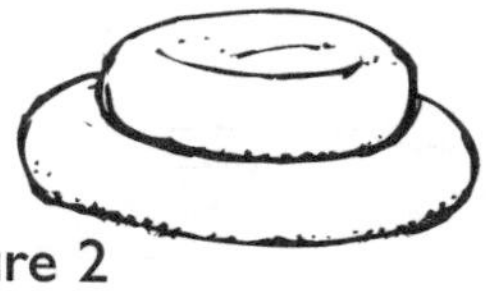

Materials

* 1/3 cup table salt
* 1 cup water
* spoon
* pan to boil water
* hot plate or stove
* self-hardening clay
* acrylic paints: white, brown or tan

Figure 2

Figure 3

Figure 4

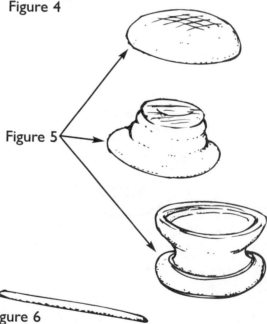

Figure 5

Instructions

1. Mix the salt and water together in a pan and soak for two days.
2. Set it on the stove and bring to a boil. Turn the heat down to a simmer. Allow the moisture to slowly evaporate as much as possible without burning. Stir with a spoon occasionally.
3. After 10 minutes, remove from heat. Salt should be slightly moist. Stir and set aside to dry naturally. Place in sun if necessary.
4. Choose a salt mill design from page 90.
5. Roll clay into 1/4" thick coils.
6. Shape the clay into a 3" circle to make the base of the salt mill. (Figure 1)
7. Build the mill by attaching a slightly smaller clay coil to the base. (Figure 2)
8. Drizzle water on the base and press the coils together by shaping. This is the top; set it aside. (Figure 3)
9. Following the same shape design, build a base using more coils. (Figure 4)
10. Attach the top to the base by scribing both sections. Add a little water to secure it. Add clay, if necessary. (Figure 5)
11. Roll out additional coils to make handles. (Figure 6)
12. Attach them by scribing into the clay and drizzling with water. Press and mold the handles onto the form. Allow them to dry. (Figure 7)
13. Paint and varnish the mill. When dry, place the dried salt into the mill. Pinch a bit of the fresh salt onto your food.

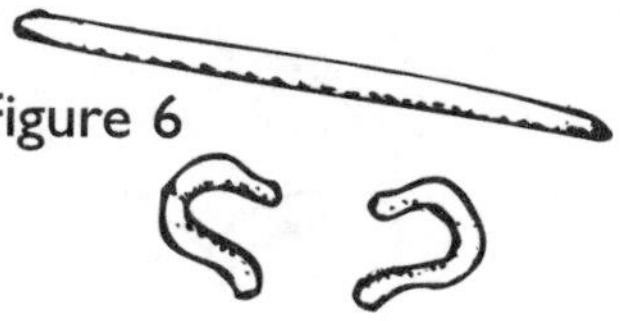

Figure 6

Figure 7

Colonial Salt Mill Designs

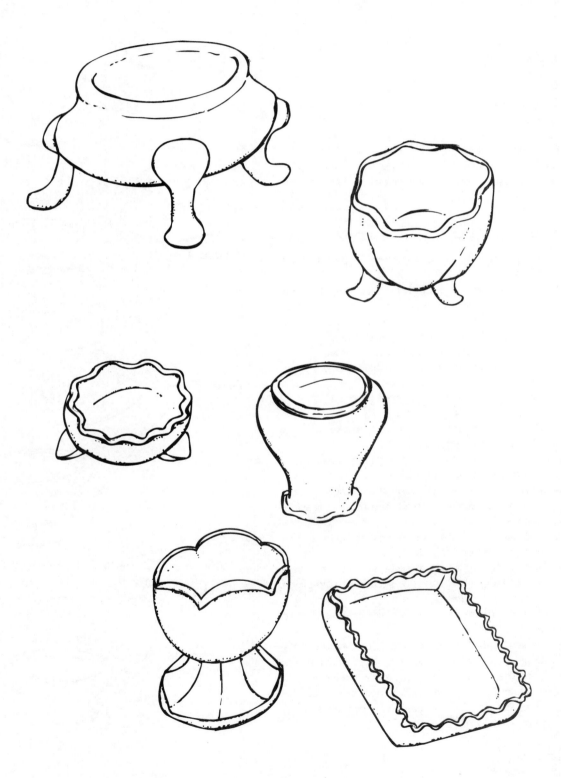

Fun Facts

Bird: Baltimore Oriole (Icterus galbula)

Cat: Calico Cat

Crustacean: Maryland Blue Crab (Callinectes sapidus Rathbun)

Dinosaur: Astrodon johnstoni (Astrodon means "star tooth")

Dog: Chesapeake Bay Retriever

Fish: Rockfish or Striped Bass (Morone saxatilis)

Flower: Black-Eyed Susan (Rudbeckia hirta)

Fossil: Extinct Snail (Ecphora gardnerae gardnerae)

Horse: Thoroughbred

Insect: Baltimore Checkerspot Butterfly (Euphydryas phaeton)

Motto: "Fatti maschii parole femine" (Strong deeds, gentle words or Manly deeds, womanly words)

Nickname: Old Line State

Reptile: Diamondback Terrapin (Malaclemys terrapin)

Song: "Maryland, My Maryland" by James Ryder Randall

Tree: White Oak (Quercus alba)

Statehood: April 28, 1788; 7th state admitted to the Union

Population: (2000 estimate) 5,296,486

Area: 12,407 square miles of land and water; 42nd largest state

Highest Point: Backbone Mountain; 3360 feet above sea level

Lowest Point: Bloody Point Hole; 174 below sea level

Capital: Annapolis

Largest City: Baltimore

Major Crop: Seafood—oysters, crabs, clams, fin fish; poultry; eggs; dairy products; cattle; soybeans

Major Industry: Food processing, computer products, electronic products, chemical products, transportation machinery, primary metals, cement production, sand, gravel, clay, tourism

Maryland

Name: Maryland is named after an English monarch, Queen Henrietta Maria, the wife of King Charles I of England. Charles was King of England from 1625 to 1649.

Did You Know?

During a 24-hour siege on a September night during the War of 1812, Francis Scott Key watched from aboard a ship in the harbor as the British bombarded Fort McHenry. He was not sure if the Americans would be able to withstand the barrage of over 1500 shells lobbed at the fort as well as a ground assault. But the next morning, through fog, smoke and mist, the American flag was still flying over the fort. The British had failed. Key was so moved at the sight of the flag that morning, he wrote a poem, "The Defense of McHenry." It became our national anthem.

Flag: The flag is divided into four quadrants. The first and fourth quarters of the flag are gold and black, the arms of George Calvert, first Lord Baltimore, founder of Maryland. The second and third quarters are red and white crosses bottony. Red and white were the family colors of Lord Baltimore's mother.

Seal: The circular state seal of Maryland has a shield in the center divided into four quadrants in the same design as the state flag. Next to the shield is a man with a shovel on one side, presumably representing mining. On the other side is a man holding a fish, symbolizing the importance of water and the fishing industry to Maryland. Above the shield is a crown. The entire scene is inside an ermine fur drape. The outer circle displays the Latin words *Scuto Bonae Volvntatis Tuae Coronasti Nos* and the year, 1632.

Antebellum

Antebellum, Maryland, was a rural farming region in the South where life was hard, especially for the slaves who lived there. However, Maryland was also a border state. It gained a reputation as one of the first regions with a strong, functioning Underground Railroad, in spite of its Southern sympathies.

The wood cut images for this project are taken from John Gruber's *Hagerstown Town and Country Almanac*. They depict the life of a farmer throughout the year. It is important to note that while slaves were the largest group of manual laborers on Maryland's farms and plantations, they were not depicted in these original *Town and Country Almanac* wood cuts.

Notable Natives

Spiro Agnew (1918-1996), U.S. Vice President, Baltimore

Benjamin Banneker (1731-1806), mathematician, Oella/Ellicott City

Kate Josephine Bateman (1842-1917), actress, Baltimore

Eubi Blake (1883-1983), composer, musician, Baltimore

Toni Braxton (1966-), singer, Severn

James Mallahan Cain, (1892-1977), novelist, Annapolis

Charles Carroll (1737-1832), signer of the Declaration of Independence, Annapolis

Samuel Chase (1741-1811), U.S. Supreme Court Justice, Somerset County

Martha Clarke (1944-), dancer, choreographer, Baltimore

Stephen Decatur (1779-1820), War of 1812 naval commander, Sinepuxent

John Dickinson (1732-1808), writer, Revolutionary War era politician, Talbot County

Frederick Douglass (Frederick Augustus Washington Bailey) (1817-1895), writer, abolitionist, Tuckahoe

Philip Glass (1937-), composer, Baltimore

Rose O'Neal Greenhow (1817-1864), Confederate spy, Port Tobacco

Ethel Harvey (1885-1965), embryologist, Baltimore

Billie Holiday (Eleanora Fagan) (1915-1959), jazz singer, Baltimore

Johns Hopkins (1795-1873 businessman, financier, Anne Arundel County

Spike Jonze (1969-), singer, Rockville

Francis Scott Key (1780-1843), "The Star-Spangled Banner" author, Carroll County

Thurgood Marshall (1908-1993), U.S. Supreme Court Justice, Baltimor

H.L. Mencken (1880-1956 journalist, critic, Baltimore

Edward Norton (1969-), actor, Columbia

Jameson Parker (1947-), actor, Baltimore

Charles Willson Peale (1741-1827), painter, Queen Annes County

Babe Ruth (George Herm Ruth) (1895-1948), bas ball player, Baltimore

Upton Sinclair (1878-196 writer, Baltimore

Jada Pinkett Smith (1971-actress, Baltimore

Roger B. Taney (1777-186 U.S. Supreme Court Chief Justice, Calvert County

Harriet Tubman (1820-1913), active in the Underground Railroa Dorchester County

Leon Uris (1924-), writ Baltimore

John Waters (1946-), fil director, Baltimore

Montel Williams (1956-talk show host, Baltimore

Frank Zappa (1940-199 singer, Baltimore

Wood Cut Display

Materials

* 12 pieces of 3" x 3½" plywood
* wire cutters
* round nose pliers
* hook and eye hooks
* masking tape
* white glue
* 3 sheets of manila colored heavy card stock
* scissors
* sawtooth hanger

Figure 1

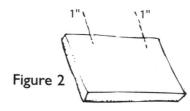

Figure 2

Instructions

1. Copy the Antebellum wood cut designs on page 94.
2. Cut ¼" around each wood cut design. (Figure 1)
3. Glue each wood cut design to a wood panel and let it dry.
4. Arrange the wood in order of months, numbering them lightly on the back.
5. Set aside the January wood panel.
6. Flip the wood panels over. Measure in 1" on both sides of the top edge. (Figure 2)
7. Carefully screw an eye hook at the 1" edge. Do the same to the other end. Attach hooks to the top and bottom of each wood panel. (Figure 3)
8. The wooden panels should attach evenly to each other. Make sure you've measured the 1" mark properly on each one. (Figure 4)
9. Attach the wooden panels together. (Figure 5)
10. Attach a sawtooth hanger to the back of the January panel. Attach the hook and eye hooks to the bottom edge. (Figure 6)
11. Attach the month of January to the February panel. Hang the 12-part display.

Figure 3

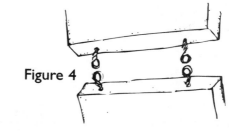

Figure 4

Figure 5

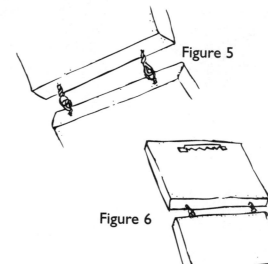

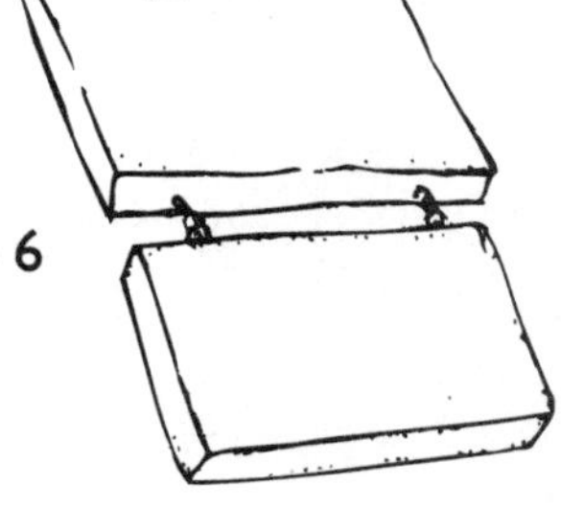

Figure 6

Name _____

Antebellum Wood Cut Designs

John Gruber's <u>Hagerstown Town and Country Almanac</u> Wood Cuts

January

February

March

April

May

June

July

August

September

October

November

December

Massachusetts

Name: Like so many other states in the Union, Massachusetts has its origin in the Native American language. _Massachusetts_ is a Native American word that means "large hill place."

Did You Know?

Hardly anything tastes better than chocolate chip cookies right out of the oven and a cold glass of milk. The chocolate chip cookie recipe was first created in Whitman, Massachusetts, in 1930 by Ruth Wakefield.

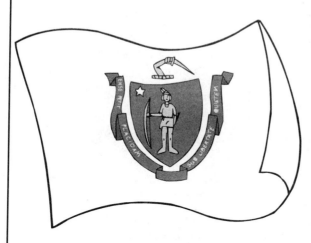

Flag: The flag is white with the state coat of arms in the center.

Seal: The circular state seal shows a shield with a lone Native American holding a bow in one hand and arrows pointing down to represent peace in the other. In the upper left-hand corner of the shield is a five-point star symbolizing the state as one of the original 13 colonies. Above the shield is a raised arm holding a sword. Below the shield and on both sides is a ribbon that bears the state's motto: "Ense petit placidam sub libertate quietem." Around the seal are the words _Sigillum Reipublicae Massachusettensis._

The Real Story of Paul Revere

On the evening of April 18, 1775, Paul Revere was instructed to ride to Lexington, Massachusetts, to warn Samuel Adams and John Hancock that British troops were marching to arrest them and uncover a cache of arms hidden by the colonists. The Sons of Liberty pre-arranged a signal to designate how the British were to enter the region: One lantern hung in the bell-tower of the Church of Christ in Boston would indicate that troops were marching overland. Two lanterns would show the troops were coming by sea to the Charles River.

On his way to Lexington, Revere sounded the alarm across the countryside, stopping at each house to warn that the British were coming. At midnight, he finally reached the house where Adams and Hancock were staying. A sentry guarding the house insisted that Revere stop making such a racket when he tried to wake them. Revere was furious. "Noise!" he cried. "You'll have noise enough before long. The regulars are coming out!" Adams and Hancock wasted no time in finding another hiding place.

Paul Revere's Lantern

Lanterns were an important light source in colonial history and were used to signal that the British were coming!

Massachusetts

Notable Natives

John Adams (1735-1826), 2nd President (1797-1801), Braintree

John Quincy Adams (1767-1848), 6th President (1825-1829), Braintree

Samuel Adams (1722-1803), American Revolutionary War patriot, Boston

Susan B. Anthony (1820-1906), suffragist, Adams

Clara Barton (1821-1912), founder of the American Red Cross, Oxford

George Herbert Walker Bush (1924-), 41st President (1989-1993), Milton

William Cullen Bryant (1794-1878), poet, Cummington

John Chapman (Johnny Appleseed) (1774-1845), apple tree planter, pioneer, Leonminster

John Singleton Copley (1738-1815), portrait artist, Boston

e.e. cummings (1894-1962), poet, Cambridge

Matt Damon (1970-), actor, Cambridge

Bette Davis (1908-1989), actress, Lowell

Cecil B. DeMille (1881-1959), film producer, director, Ashfield

Emily Dickinson (1830-1886), poet, Amherst

Ralph Waldo Emerson (1803-1882), writer, poet, Boston

Benjamin Franklin (1706-1790), patriot, scientist, publisher, Boston

Theodore Seuss Geisel (Dr. Seuss) (1904-1991), author, illustrator, Springfield

John Hancock (1737-1793), American Revolutionary War patriot, Braintree

Nathaniel Hawthorne (1804-1864), novelist, short story writer, Salem

Oliver Wendell Holmes, Jr. (1841-1935), U.S. Supreme Court Justice, Boston

Winslow Homer (1836-1910), painter, Boston

Elias Howe (1819-1867), inventor of the sewing machine, Spence

John Fitzgerald Kennedy (1917-1963), 35th President (1961-1963), Brookline

Matt LeBlanc (1967-), actor, Newton

Cotton Mather (1662-1728), clergyman, Boston

Samuel F.B. Morse (1791-1872), inventor of the telegraph, Charlestown

Leonard Nimoy (1931-), actor, Boston

Conan O'Brien (1963-), talk sho host, Brookline

Mathew Perry (1969-), actor, Williamstown

Edgar Allan Poe (1809-1849), sho story writer, poet, Boston

Paul Revere (1735-1818), Americ Revolutionary War patriot, Boston

Louis Henry Sullivan (1856-1924 architect of the first skyscraper, Boston

James Taylor (1948-), singer, Boston

Henry David Thoreau (1817-186 writer, poet, Concord

Uma Thurman (1970-), actress Boston

James McNeill Whistler (1834-1903), watercolor and oil painter, Lowell

Eli Whitney (1765-1825), invente of the cotton gin, Westboro

Paul Revere's Lantern

Adult supervision required with this project.

Materials

* large tin can, clean with tip removed
* thin aluminum sheet or aluminum flashing equal in circumference to the tin can, plus two inches
* soldering flux
* tin cutters
* protective gloves
* pliers
* measuring tape
* compass
* tape
* goggles
* hammer
* penny nail
* fine wire
* soldering mat
* wire cutters
* candle
* plank of wood

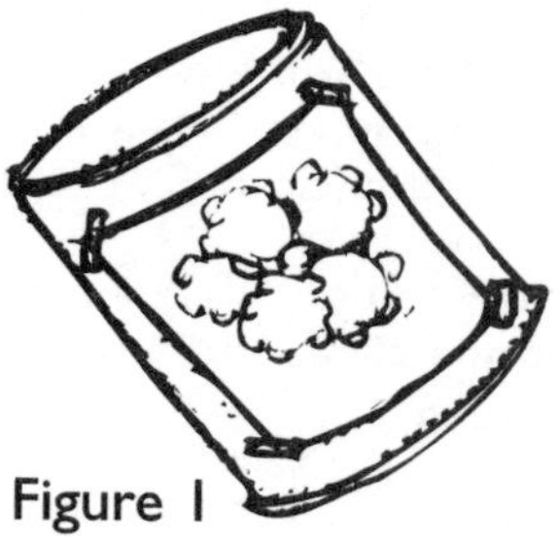

Figure 1

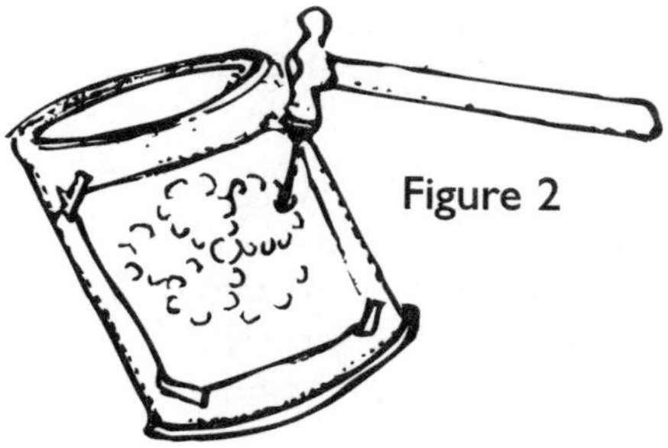

Figure 2

Figure 3

Instructions

Wear gloves while handling all tin and soldering items and goggles when soldering.

1. Fill the can with water and freeze it overnight.

2. Copy the lantern design on page 99 and tape it on the side of the can. (Figure 1)

3. Carefully hammer holes on the design with a nail. (Figure 2)

4. Then cut out a rectangle doorway on the undecorated side of the can with the tin cutters. (Figure 3)

5. Turn over the cut edges with pliers to make the can smooth and safe. (Figure 4)

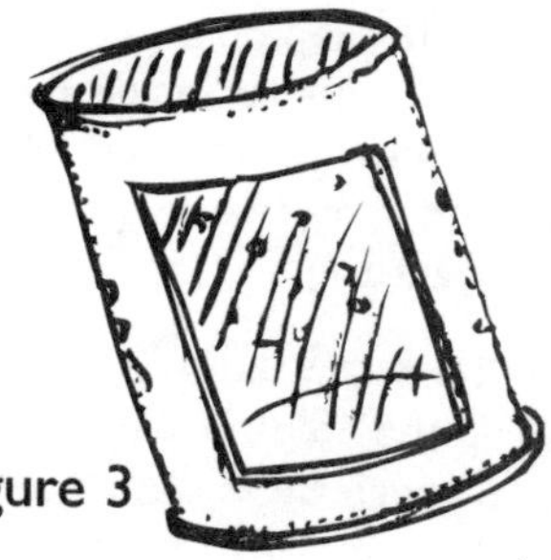

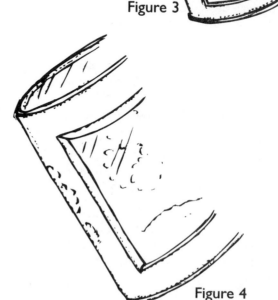

Figure 4

6. To make the lid, measure the top of the can with a measuring tape. Add an additional 1/2". Mark a line that length on the aluminum. Place a compass on the center of the line and draw a circle. Cut it out carefully. (Figure 5)

7. Hammer small nail holes about 1/2" in from the curved edge of the lid circle. (Figure 6)

8. Lay the lid on a pile of newspapers and hammer holes at the center and along 1/4" of the circle as shown, using a large nail. Fold in the rough edges and hammer them down. Cut away the shaded area. (Figure 7)

9. Cut a strip of aluminum 3/4" x 1/4" wider than the diameter of the candle you will use. Cut the circle about 1/4" from one line of holes to the center of the circle. Hammer 1/4" edge down to remove the sharp edges. (Figure 8)

10. Set the can on a soldering mat. Place the candle holder inside the center bottom of the can and carefully solder. (Make sure you wear gloves and goggles.) (Figure 9)

11. Curve the lid into a cone shape, lining up the holes. Use pliers to lace thin wire through the holes as shown. Solder the wire in place and cut off the extras. (Figure 10)

12. Tape the lid on the can and turn it upside down. Solder the lid to the can. Make sure each solder joint is thick and strong. (Figure 11) Remove the tape.

13. Curve additional wire into a loop and pass it through the top cone of the lantern top. Tie it together with pliers and solder it for safety. This is the lantern handle. (Figure 12)

14. Place a candle inside the completed lantern and light it. Do not leave lit and unattended, and never place it on a flammable surface.

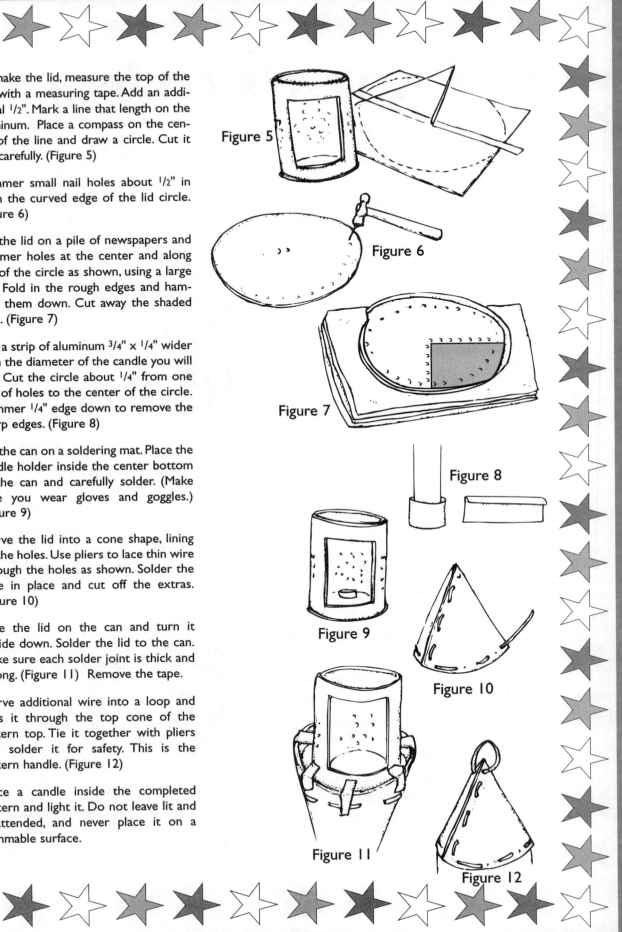

Figure 5

Figure 6

Figure 7

Figure 8

Figure 9

Figure 10

Figure 11

Figure 12

Paul Revere's Lantern Design

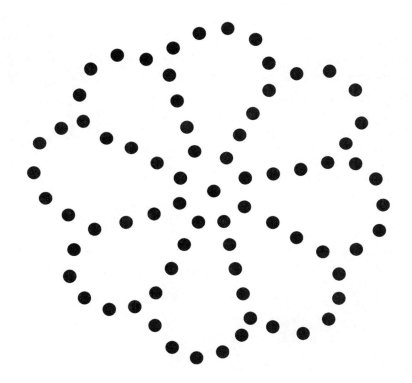

Fun Facts

Bird: American Robin (Turdus migratorius)

Fish: Brook Trout (Salvelinus fontinalis)

Flower: Apple Blossom (Pyrus coronaria)

Wildflower: Dwarf Lake Iris (Iris lacustris)

Fossil: Mastodon (Mammut americanum)

Gem: Isle Royal Greenstone (Chlorastrolite)

Game Mammal: White-Tailed Deer (Odocileus virginianus)

Motto: "Si quaeris peninsulam amoenam, circumspice" (If you seek a pleasant peninsula, look about you.)

Nicknames: Wolverine State, Great Lakes State

Reptile: Painted Turtle (Chysemys picta)

Stone: Petoskey Stone (Hexagonia pericarnata)

Song: "Michigan, My Michigan" by Douglas M. Malloch

Tree: White Pine (Pinus strobus)

Statehood: January 26, 1837; 26th state admitted to the Union

Population: (2000 estimate) 9,938,444

Area: 96,810 square miles of land and water; 11th largest state

Highest Point: Mt. Arvon; 1980 above sea level

Lowest Point: Lake Erie Shore; 572 feet above sea level

Capital: Lansing

Largest City: Detroit

Major Crops: Dairy products, apples, grapes, blueberries, pears, cattle, vegetables, hogs, corn, soybeans, sugar beets

Major Industry: Motor vehicle manufacturing, car part production, machinery, fabricated metal products, food products, cereal production, chemical products, iron and steel production, tourism, recreation

Michigan

Name: Native Americans know as the Chippewa lived by what is now called the Great Lakes. They referred to Lake Michigan as _michigama_ which means "great water." The state got its name from the great water.

Did You Know?

The world's first soda pop was ginger ale, invented by accident. James Vernor, a pharmacist in Detroit, was trying to create a new drink. He made a batch and stored it in an oak cask. Then the Civil War erupted and James was called to serve as a soldier. When he returned four years later, he checked the drink he had brewed. It had a delicious ginger taste, and Vernor's ginger ale was born.

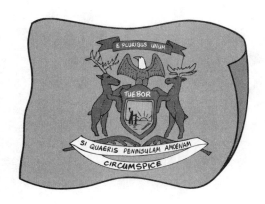

Flag: The flag has a deep blue background with the state seal, minus the outer ring, at the center of it.

Coat of Arms: The state coat of arms has a shield at its center. On the shield is a man with a raised hand holding a gun. The sun is rising over a lake with a peninsula in the background. The gun the man holds represents Michiganers' ability to fight for their rights. His raised hand symbolizes their wish for peace. The Latin word on the shield, _Tuebor_, means "I will defend." On the sides of the shield are an elk and a moose, two animals native to the state. They stand on a ribbon containing the state motto: "Si Quaeris Peninsulam Amoenam Circumspice," which means, "If you seek a pleasant peninsula, look about you." Above the shield is an eagle which represents the United States of America. Above the eagle is a ribbon with the Latin words _E Pluribus Unum_, which mean, "From many comes one."

Windmills

Michigan is considered to be the Windmill Capital of the United States. In the mid-19th and early 20th centuries several Michigan companies in Lansing, Plymouth and Kalamazoo applied their trade to developing windmills for the burgeoning country. It is still common to see windmills across the horizon in rural Michigan.

These wonderful icons of the Midwest helped farmers and ranchers move water to their animals and crops. Windmills were also important to the newly developed railroads. They were built along tracks to help steam-powered locomotives replenish their water supplies. Other windmills were designed to grind grain—wheat, corn and buckwheat—grown on the prairies. Some windmills were up to 30 feet high.

Most windmills or windpumps are used to pump water from underground springs to dry locations. This technology developed the agricultural industry and the spread of townships throughout the state of Michigan. Today industrial windmills, called wind turbines are used for generating electricity.

Notable Natives

Nelson Algren (1909-1981), novelist, Detroit

Leonard Bacon (1801-1881), Congregationalist clergyman, antislavery editor, Detroit

Liberty Hyde Bailey (1858-1954), botanist, researcher, South Haven

George David Birkoff (1884-1944), mathematician, Overisel

William Edward Boeing (1881-1956), aircraft manufacturer, Detroit

Olympia Brown (1835-1926), suffragist, Prairie Ronde

Ralph Bunche (1904-1971), statesman, Nobel Prize winner, Detroit

Ellen Burstyn (Edna Rae Gillooly) (1932-), actress, Detroit

Dean Cain (1966-), actor, Mt. Clemens

Bruce Catton (1899-1978), Pulitzer Prize-winning historian, Petoskey

Francis Ford Coppola (1939-), film director, Detroit

Clyde Lorrain Cowan, Jr. (1919-1974), physicist, Detroit

Heber Doust Curtis (1872-1942), astronomer, Muskegon

Pam Dawber (1951-), actress, Farmington Hills

Thomas E. Dewey (1902-1971), politician, two-time Republican presidential candidate, Owosso

Richard Ellmann (1918-1987), biographer, professor, Detroit

Edna Ferber (1885-1968), Pulitzer Prize-winning writer, Kalamazoo

Mary Frances Kennedy Fisher (1908-1992), cookbook writer, Albion

Henry Ford (1863-1947), car manufacturer, founder of the Ford Motor Co., Dearborn

Barry Gordy, Jr. (1929-), record executive, music producer, Detroit

Bill Haley (1925-1981), pioneering rock 'n' roll musician, Highland Park

Julie Harris (1925-), actress, Grosse Pointe Park

Earvin "Magic" Johnson (1959-), basketball player, coach, Lansing

Casey Kasem (1932-), radio personality, disc jockey, Detroit

Ring Lardner (1885-1933), short story writer, journalist, Niles

Charles A. Lindbergh (1902-1974), aviator, Detroit

Madonna (Madonna Ciccone) (1958-), singer, Bay City

Dick Martin (1922-), comedian, co-host of *Laugh In*, Detroit

Ed McMahon (1923-), talk show co-host, Detroit

John Mitchell (1913-1988), U.S. Attorney General, Detroit

Michael Moore (1945-), author, documentary film producer, director, Flint

Gilda Radner (1946-1989), comedienne, original cast of *Saturday Night Live*, Detroit

Della Reese (1931-), actress, Detroit

Smokey Robinson (1940-), singer, Detroit

Diana Ross (1944-), singer, Detroit

Steven Seagal (1951-), actor, Lansing

Tom Selleck (1945-), actor, Detroit

Potter Stewart (1915-1985), U.S. Supreme Court Justice, Jackson

Danny Thomas (1912-1991), actor, Deerfield

Marlo Thomas (1938-), actress, Deerfield

Lily Tomlin (1939-), actress, Detroit

Stevie Wonder (1950-), musician, singer, Saginaw

Wind Wheel

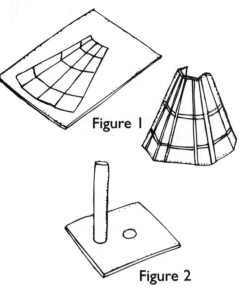
Figure 1

Materials

* straw
* paper towel tube
* white glue
* scissors
* 1 1/16" x 8" x 12" balsawood sheet
* 1 brass fastener
* manila folder
* wooden dowel, 1/4" thick x 15" long
* utility knife
* tape
* red and silver paint or markers

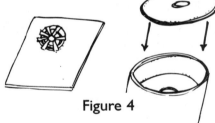
Figure 2

Figure 3

Instructions

1. Copy the windmill designs on page 103. Color the wind wheel red and the wind base silver.
2. Glue the main windmill base pattern to the manila folder. Cut out. Fold where indicated and glue. (Figure 1)
3. Stand the paper towel tube on a small piece of the manila folder, draw a circle around it and cut out. Draw a second circle 1/4" bigger around the first circle and cut out. (Figure 2)
4. Cut a small hole in the center of the two manila circles big enough for the dowel to fit through. (Figure 3)
5. Glue the windmill wheel design to the remaining piece of the manila folder. Cut it out and set it aside.
6. Tape and glue one manila circle inside the paper towel tube and the other over the end of the tube. Slip the windmill base over the tube. (Figure 4)
7. Drill a hole in the dowel. Fasten the windmill wheel to the dowel with the brass fastener. (Figure 5)
8. Put dowel down into the paper towel tube. Allow to dry. (Figure 6)

Figure 4

Figure 5

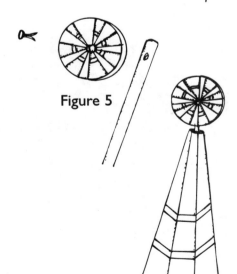
Figure 6

Windmill Designs

Windmill Wheel

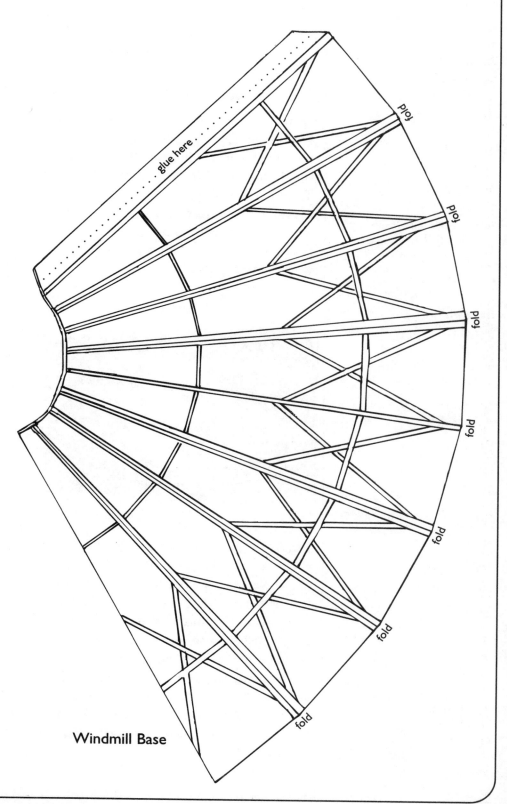

glue here · · · · · · · · · ·

fold

fold

fold

fold

fold

fold

fold

Windmill Base

Fun Facts

Bird: Common Loon (Gavia immer)

Butterfly: Monarch (Danaus plexippus)

Fish: Walleye (Stizostedion vitreum)

Flower: Pink and White Lady Slipper (Cypripedium reginae)

Gem: Lake Superior Agate

Grain: Wild Rice (Zizania aquatica or Zizania palusttris)

Motto: "L'Etoile du nord" (The star of the north)

Mushroom: Morel (Morchella esculenta)

Nicknames: North Star State, Land of 10,000 Lakes

Song: "Hail! Minnesota" by Truman E. Rickard and Arthur E. Upson

Tree: Norway Pine or Red Pine (Pinus resinosa)

Statehood: May 11, 1858; 32nd state admitted to the Union

Population: (2000 estimate) 4,919,479

Area: 86,943 square miles of land and water; 12th largest state

Highest Point: Eagle Mountain; 2301 feet above sea level

Lowest Point: Lake Superior Shore; 602 feet above sea level

Capital: St. Paul

Largest City: Minneapolis

Major Crop: Dairy products—milk, butter; sugar beets; corn; soybeans; alfalfa; oats; green peas; hogs; barley; wheat; wild rice; potatoes; cattle; turkeys

Major Industry: Machinery, food processing, printing and publishing, fabricated metal products, electrical equipment, iron ore production, tourism, recreation

Minnesota

Did You Know?

Frank C. Mars, who founded the M&M/Mars Candy Company, lived with his wife and family in Minneapolis for a time in the 1920s. Though his company began in Tacoma, Washington, it eventually was moved to New Jersey. One of their most famous candy bars, the Milky Way™, was first produced in Minnesota in 1923. It was an instant success.

Flag: The flag is a field of royal blue with the state seal in the center. Three dates are woven into a wreath made of the state flower surrounding the seal: 1858, when Minnesota became a state; 1819, when Fort Snelling was established and 1893, when the flag was adopted. Nineteen stars surround the flower wreath, representing Minnesota as the 19th state to become a state after the original 13. The largest star symbolizes Minnesota and the North Star.

Name: <u>Minnesota</u> was a word the Native American Dakota tribe used to describe the river that runs through the state. It meant "cloudy" or "sky-tinted" water.

Seal: The circular state seal shows the words *The Great Seal of the State of Minnesota,* and the date, *1858* surrounding a scene of a rising sun, pine trees and a waterfall. A Native American holding a spear is riding a horse as a pioneer plows a field in the foreground. At the top of the scene is a ribbon which bears the state motto in French, "L'Etoile du nord."

Paul Bunyan & Babe

Paul Bunyan is the best-known folk hero of Minnesota. His legend reflects a time when America was young with an abundance of wilderness in the Great Lakes area. His mythic strength was symbolic of the men who built the Midwest. His legend was originally told by lumberjacks around evening campfires. The legend grew to include impossible feats: Paul pulled trees up from the earth with his hands and scooped out Lake Superior. The footprints of his boy helper formed Minnesota's lakes! The tall tales of Paul Bunyan grew larger and larger, and today exemplifies the American ideal that anything is possible regardless of hardships.

Legends about Paul Bunyan include:

* When Paul Bunyan was born, it took five storks to deliver him. He weighed over 80 pounds at birth and his little baby voice sounded like a bass drum and buzz saw.

* As a baby, he could eat over 40 pounds of porridge.

* He rescued a calf named Babe from drowning during the Blue Storm winter. That is why Babe is blue. She grew 24 axe handles tall and could eat 30 bales of hay for a snack.

* Paul liked to work with the Seven Axemen, each of them over six feet tall and weighing over 350 pounds. Their arms worked like chainsaws as they cut down timber. During the winter they grew beards so long they wrapped them around their bodies like blankets on cold winter nights.

Notable Natives

Loni Anderson (1946-), actress, St. Paul

La Verne Andrews (1915-1967), singer, one of the Andrews Sisters, Minneapolis

Maxene Andrews (1918-1995), singer, one of the Andrews Sisters, Minneapolis

Patti Andrews (1920-), singer, one of the Andrews Sisters, Minneapolis

James Arness (1923-), actor, Minneapolis

Patty Berg (1918-), golfer, Minneapolis

Jessie Shirley Bernard (1903-1996), sociologist, writer, Minneapolis

Robert Elwood Bly (1926-), poet, writer, editor, Madison

Warren Burger (1907-1995), U.S. Supreme Court Chief Justice, St. Paul

Arthur Walter Burks (1915-), computer scientist, Duluth

Ethan Coen (1957-), film producer, screenwriter, St. Louis Park

Joel Coen (1954-), film director, screenwriter, St. Louis Park

William O. Douglas (1898-1980), U.S. Supreme Court Justice, Maine

Julia Duffy (1951-), actress, Minneapolis

Bob Dylan (Robert Allen Zimmerman) (1941-), singer, Duluth

F. Scott Fitzgerald (1896-1940), writer, St. Paul

Judy Garland (Frances Gumm) (1922-1969), singer, actress, Grand Rapids

J. Paul Getty (1892-1976), oil magnate, art collector, Minneapolis

Terry Vance Gilliam (1940-), director, animator, Medicine Lake

Duane Hanson (1925-1996), sculptor, Alexandria

Milton Lasell Humason (1891-1972), astronomer, Dodge Center

Garrison Keillor (1942-), radio personality, humorist, author, Anoka

Jessica Lange (1949-), actress, Cloquet

Sinclair Lewis (1885-1951), Nobel Prize-winning writer, Sauk Center

John Madden (1936-), sportscaster, Austin

Roger Maris (1935-1985), baseball player, Hibbing

E.G. Marshall (1910-1998), actor, Owatonna

Charles Horace Mayo (1865-1939), surgeon, Rochester

Eugene McCarthy (1916-), U.S. senator, presidential candidate, Watkins

Walter F. Mondale (1928-), U.S. Vice President and presidential candidate, Celyon

"Prince" (Rogers Nelson) (1959-), singer, Minneapolis

Marion Ross (1928-), actress, Albert Lea

Jane Russell (1921-), actress, Bemidji

Winona Ryder (1971-), actress, Winona

Charles Monroe Schulz (1922-2000), creator of the Peanuts comic strip, Minneapolis

Cheryl Tiegs (1947-), super model, Breckenridge

Jesse Ventura (1951-), wrestler, Minnesota governor, Minneapolis

Paul Bunyan & Babe

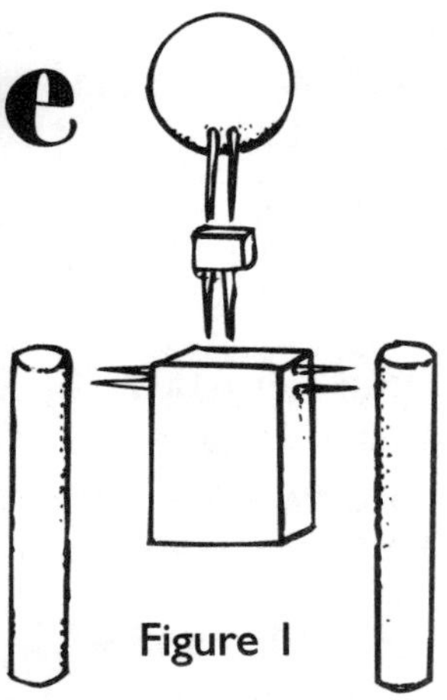

Materials

* 3" Styrofoam™ ball (head)
* 1" x 1" Styrofoam™ cylinder (neck)
* 4" x 3" x 1½" Styrofoam™ rectangle (trunk)
* 4—1" x 6" Styrofoam™ cylinders (arms and legs)
* 1—6" x 6" x ½" Styrofoam™ square (base)
* 10 large sheets of newspaper
* 1 cup white glue
* wooden toothpicks
* paints: red, white, tan (or white, red and yellow mixed), dark blue, black
* medium felt-tip pen
* medium-sized basin and water

Materials for Babe

* 2—3" x 6" x ½" Styrofoam™ rectangles (base and body)
* 4—4" x ¼" Styrofoam™ cylinders (legs)
* tagboard or card stock

Instructions for Paul Bunyan

1. Rip newsprint into small pieces and soak in basin of water overnight.
2. Squeeze out excess water and mix pulp with white glue to make papier-mâché.
3. Copy the Paul Bunyan design on page 109 and use it as a guide for your papier-mâché model.
4. Connect foam head, neck, trunk and legs with toothpicks and glue. (Figure 1)
5. Place figure on base with toothpicks and glue. (Figure 2)
6. Cover all Styrofoam™ pieces with papier-mâché. (Figure 3)
7. Define and shape the body. Let it dry.
8. Paint the figure following the Paul Bunyan guide on page 109. Draw the face with felt-tip pen. (Figure 4)

Figure 1

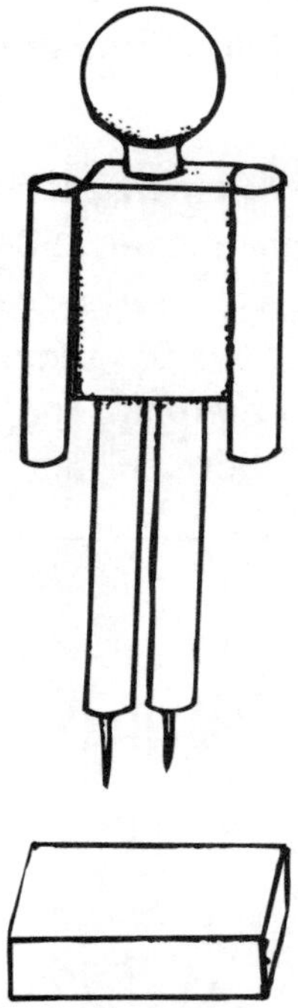

Figure 2

Figure 3

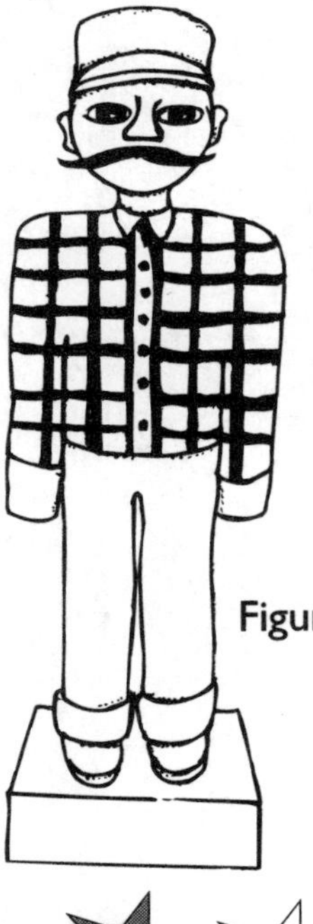

Figure 4

Instructions for Babe

1. Cut one of the large Styrofoam™ rectangles into two smaller pieces for the head. Cut one of the smaller pieces in half again for the neck. Attach Babe's body pieces together with toothpicks and glue. (Figure 5)
2. Add an additional toothpick to tail area and let it dry. (Figure 6)
3. Cut ears and horns out of tagboard or card stock following the patterns on page 108. Fold and glue.
4. Make papier-mâché by following the directions on page 106. Use the Babe designs on page 108 as a guide.
5. Glue the ears and horns onto the body and secure with 1/2" toothpick. Let dry and cover with papier-mâché. (Figure 7)
6. Once Babe has dried, paint with light blue paint. Draw on a face with marker and stand her next to Paul Bunyan.

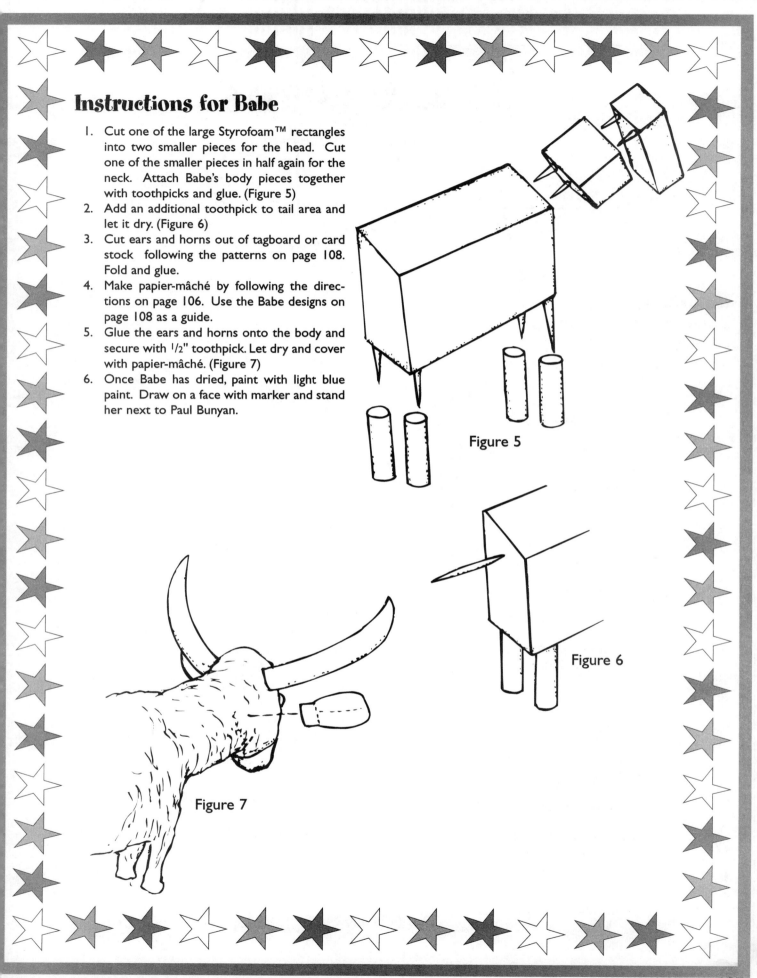

Figure 5

Figure 6

Figure 7

Babe Designs

Color according to the color key.

Color Key
a. brown
b. white
c. red

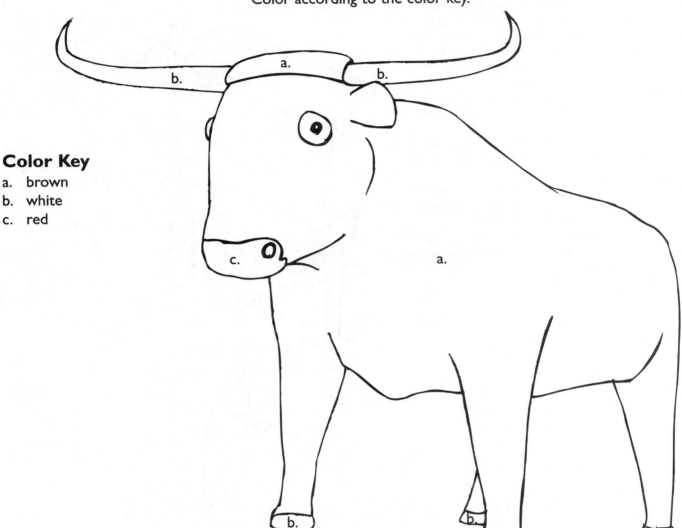

Horns (fold and glue)

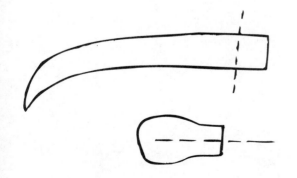

Ears (fold and glue)

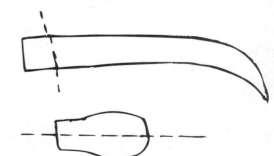

Paul Bunyan

Color according to the color key.

Color Key

a. red
b. white
c. tan
d. dark blue
e. black
f. light blue

a. all shirt squares red

b. all shirt vertical stripes white

f. all shirt horizontal stripes light blue

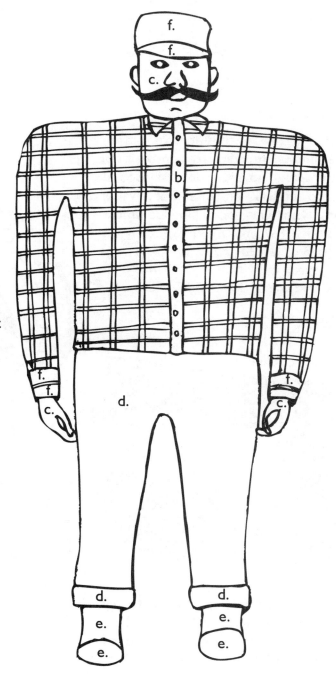

Fun Facts

Bird: Mockingbird (Mimus polyglottos)

Butterfly: Spicebrush Swallowtail (Battus philenor)

Fish: Largemouth or Black Bass (Micropterus salmoides)

Flower: Magnolia Blossom (Magnolia grandiflora)

Fossil: Prehistoric Whale (Basilosaurus cetoides)

Insect: Honeybee (Apis mellifera)

Land Mammals: White-Tailed Deer (Odocoileus virginianus), Red Fox (Vulpes vulpes)

Water Mammal: Bottlenosed Dolphin (Tursiops truncates)

Motto: "Virtute et armis" (By valor and arms)

Nickname: Magnolia State

Shell: Oyster Shell (Crassostrea virginica)

Song: "Go, Mississippi" by Houston Davis

Stone: Petrified Wood

Waterfowl: Wood Duck (Aix sponsa)

Tree: Magnolia (Magnolia grandiflora)

Statehood: December 10, 1817; 20th state admitted to the Union

Population: (2000 estimate) 2,844,658

Area: 48,434 square miles of land and water; 32nd largest state

Highest Point: Woodall Mountain; 806 feet above sea level

Lowest Point: Gulf coast; sea level

Capital: Jackson

Largest City: Jackson

Major Crop: Cotton, peanuts, pecans, poultry, eggs, cattle, pond-raised catfish, soybeans, dairy products, rice

Major Industry: Textiles and apparel, lumber and wood products, food processing, furniture manufacturing, electrical machinery, transportation equipment

110

Mississippi

Name: Mississippi's name may have come from two different words from two separate Native American peoples. The state name probably comes from the Chippewa word, mici zibi which means "great river" or "gathering-in of all waters." Some believe, however, that Mississippi has its origins in an Algonquin word, messip.

Did You Know?

Wheaties™ has a tradition of putting popular and talented athletes on the front of their cereal boxes. The first football player to appear on one was Walter Payton, who was born in Columbia, Mississippi. Payton, who played for the Chicago Bears, held the record for most rushing yards in National Football League history. He was nicknamed "Sweetness."

Seal: The seal consists of a shield on an eagle with wings spread. In its right talon is a palm branch and in the left a bundle of arrows. The words *The Great Seal of the State of Mississippi* are in the outer circle.

Flag: The flag is made up of three stripes of equal width—blue, white and red. In the upper left corner of a field of red is a blue X with 13 five-point stars on it to represent the 13 original states.

Huckleberry Finn Travels the Mississippi

The sultry days and nights of Mississippi conjure up unique characters in American literature. Mark Twain created such characters in 1884, in his book *The Adventures of Huckleberry Finn*, the most controversial book of its day. The Mississippi River and the southern towns that lined its shores were the backdrop to this story. The main characters, Huckleberry Finn and a runaway slave named Jim, escape from their abusive lives and find the peace they crave on the Mississippi River. So long as Huck and Jim travel down river on the raft, honesty prevails, but whenever they touch shore, the lies and greed of society overtake them.

The Adventures of Huckleberry Finn is a satire on religion and morals, greed and prejudice of southern society during the 1800s. But the Mississippi River remained a constant reminder of peace and safe haven for anyone, regardless of race.

Make a literary bag that celebrates the Mississippi River's greatest literary character, Huckleberry Finn.

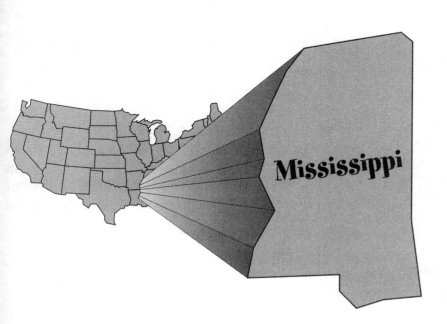

Mississippi

Notable Natives

Ralph Boston (1939-), Olympic gold-medal jumper, Laurel

Big Bill Broonzy (1893-1958), blues musician, Scott

Jimmy Buffet (1946-), singer, Pascagoula

Craig Claibone (1920-2000), food critic, cookbook author, Sunflower

Sam Cooke (1931-1964); soul, gospel and blues singer, Clarksdale

Bo Diddley (Elias Bates) (1928-), guitarist, McComb

Medgar Evers (1925-1963), civil rights leader, Decatur

William Cuthbert Faulkner (1897-1962), Nobel Prize-winning writer, Oxford

Shelby Foote (1916-), historian, writer, Greenville

Fannie Lou Hamer (1918-1977), civil rights activist, Montgomery County

Jim Henson (1936-1990), puppeteer, Greenville

Faith Hill (1967-), singer, Jackson

John Lee Hooker (1920-2001), blues singer, guitarist, Clarksdale

Howlin' Wolf (Chester Arthur Burnett) (1910-1976), blues musician, West Point

James Earl Jones (1931-), actor, Arkabutla

B.B. King (1925-), guitarist, Itta Bena

Diane Ladd (1932-), actress, Meridian

Walter Payton (1954-1999), football player, Columbia

Elvis Presley (1935-1977), singer, actor, Tupelo

Charley Pride (1938-), country singer, Sledge

Leontyne Price (1927-), opera singer, Laurel

Jerry Rice (1962-), football player, Starkville

LeAnn Rimes (1982-), country singer, Flowood

Eric Roberts (1956-), actor, Biloxi

Conway Twitty (1933-1993), country singer, Friars Point

Sela Ward (1956-), actress, Meridian

Muddy Waters (McKinley Morganfield) (1915-1983), blues singer, Rolling Fork

Eudora Welty (1909-2001), Pulitzer Prize-winning writer, Jackson

Tennessee Williams (Thomas Lanier) (1911-1983), Pulitzer Prize-winning playwright, Columbus

Oprah Winfrey (1954-), television talk show host, Kosciusko

Richard Wright (1908-1960), writer, Natchez

Tammy Wynette (1942-1998), country singer, Tupelo

Literary Bag

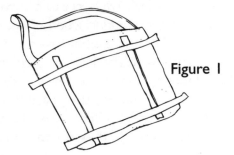

Figure 1

Materials

* canvas bag (or paper bag)
* acrylic paints for material bag (regular acrylic or tempera paints for paper bag) Fabric paints are preferable for this project.
* cosmetic sponges
* freezer paper
* 2" painter's tape
* paper towels
* cutting board
* transfer paper or carbon paper
* permanent black marker
* iron
* blotting cloth
* ball-point pen
* 1/2" tape

Figure 2

Instructions

1. Lay canvas bag flat. Use tape to mark off a 6" square at the center. (Figure 1)
2. Slip the freezer paper and cutting board or other hard surface inside the bag to keep paint from seeping through. (Figure 2)
3. Coat the taped square area with white textile or acrylic paint to seal the cloth. Let it dry.
4. Sponge a rainbow of mixed paints with the cosmetic sponge.
5. Copy the picture of Huckleberry Finn on page 113. Tape it to the painted square panel. (Figure 3)
6. Slip carbon or transfer paper under the picture. Go over it with ball-point pen to make an impression against the canvas. Pull the picture off. Go over the outline with permanent marker. (Figure 4)
7. Lightly sponge white paint on Huck's face on the canvas bag to highlight it. Paint the rest of the picture. (Figure 5)
8. If any black lines are painted out, redraw them when the paint has dried.
9. Remove the freezer paper and hard surface from inside the bag when the paint has dried for 24 hours.

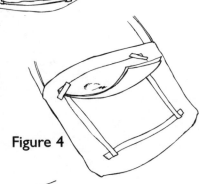

Figure 3

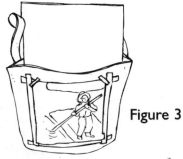

Figure 4

Figure 5

Name _____

Huckleberry Finn

Fun Facts

Animal: Missouri Mule

Aquatic Animal: Paddlefish (Polyodon spathula)

Bird: Bluebird (Sialia sialis)

Fish: Channel Catfish (Ictalurus punctatus)

Flower: White Hawthorn Blossom (crateagus)

Fossil: Crinoid (Delocrinus missouriensis)

Horse: Missouri Fox Trotting Horse

Insect: Honeybee (Apis mellifera)

Mineral: Galena (Lead sulfide)

Motto: "Salus Populi Suprema Lex Esto" (Let the welfare of the people be the supreme law)

Nickname: Show Me State

Rock: Mozarkite

Song: "Missouri Waltz" by J.R. Shannon

Tree: Flowering Dogwood (Cornus florida)

Tree/Nut: Eastern Black Walnut (Juglans nigra)

Statehood: August 10, 1821; 24th state admitted to the Union

Population: (2000 estimate) 5,595,211

Area: 69,709 square miles of land and water; 21st largest state

Highest Point: Taum Sauk Mountain; 1772 feet above sea level

Lowest Point: Saint Francis River; 230 feet above sea level

Capital: Jefferson City

Largest City: Kansas City

Major Crops: Cattle, soybeans, sorghum, rice, hay, hogs, dairy products, corn, poultry, eggs

Major Industry: Tourism; travel; food processing; beverage production; chemical products; electrical equipment; car part production; fabricated metal products; mining—iron ore, zinc

114

Missouri

Did You Know?

7-Up® soda pop was invented by Charles Leiper Grigg, owner of the Howdy Corporation of St. Louis. The lemon-lime drink was invented in 1929, but it was originally called "Bib-Label Lithiated Lemon-Lime Soda."

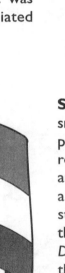

Flag: The state flag has three horizontal stripes of red, white and blue symbolizing valor, purity, vigilance and justice. In the center of the flag is the Missouri coat of arms, circled by a blue band containing 24 five-point stars representing Missouri as the 24th state admitted to the Union.

Seal: In the center of the circular seal is a smaller circle cut into three parts. One part is the United States coat of arms representing the federal government; on another is a grizzly bear and on the third a crescent moon symbolizing that the state's fortunes are on the rise. Around the circle are the words: _United We Stand Divided We Fall_. Standing on the sides of the circular shield are two grizzly bears, indicative of the strength of Missouri and the bravery of its citizens. The bears are atop a scroll bearing the Missouri state motto: "Salus Populi Suprema Lex Esto." Under that is the date, in Roman numerals, _MDCCCXX, 1820_, the year Missouri began its state functions. Between the bears is a helmet to represent the state's sovereignty. Above that in a cloud, representing the problems Missouri had becoming a state, are 24 five-point stars. The largest star, symbolizing Missouri, is directly above the helmet.

Jefferson Peace Medal

The Lewis and Clark journey across the North American continent was actually the dream of President Thomas Jefferson. It happened after the United States acquired Louisiana territory from France. Jefferson convinced Congress to fund a mission of exploration of the new territory through the Northwest Passage to the Pacific. The Northwest Passage was believed to be a link between the Atlantic and Pacific oceans that would allow direct trade across the continent. Since they would encounter native peoples on their expedition, Jefferson had several Peace Medals made for Lewis and Clark to give to tribal chiefs. It was to be a mission of discovery and peace.

After much preparation, Lewis and Clark gathered their supplies, gifts and Peace Medals and headed to their first winter camp, north of St. Louis, Missouri. They named the location, Camp Wood. There they made final preparations and trained 45 volunteers for the expedition up the Missouri River.

In August 1804, Lewis and Clark met with the first of many Native American groups along the shores of the Missouri River and invited the leaders to a council at their camp where they gave out the first peace medals.

Notable Natives

Robert Altman (1925-), film director, Kansas City

Maya Angelou (1928-), writer, poet, St. Louis

Burt Bacharach (1928-), songwriter, Kansas City

Josephine Baker (1906-1975), singer, dancer, St. Louis

Yogi Berra (1925-), baseball player, St. Louis

Chuck Berry (1926-), singer, St. Louis

Linda Blair (1959-), actress, St. Louis

Omar Nelson Bradley (1893-1981), five-star general, Clark

William Burroughs (1914-1997), writer, St. Louis

George Washington Carver (c. 1860-1943), agricultural chemist, Diamond Grove

Calamity Jane (Martha Jane Burke) (1852-1903), frontierswoman, Princeton

Samuel Langhorne Clemens (pen name Mark Twain) (1835-1910), writer, Florida

Walter Cronkite (1916-), television newscaster, journalist, St. Joseph

Sheryl Crow (1962-), singer, Kennett

T.S. Eliot (1888-1965), Nobel Prize-winning poet, St. Louis

Eminem (1972-), singer, St. Joseph

Eugene Field (1850-1895), writer, poet, St. Louis

Redd Foxx (1922-1991), actor, comedian, St. Louis

James Fulbright (1905-1995), U.S. senator, Sumner

John Goodman (1952-), actor, Affton

Betty Grable (1916-1973), actress, St. Louis

Jean Harlow (Harlean Carpenter) (1911-1937), actress, Kansas City

Edwin Hubble (1889-1953), astronomer, Marshfield

James Langston Hughes (1902-1967), poet, fiction writer, Joplin

John Huston (1906-1987), film director, Nevada

Don Johnson (1949-), actor, Flatt Creek

Kevin Kline (1947-), actor, St. Louis

Rush Limbaugh (1951-), radio personality, Cape Girardeau

Geraldine Page (1924-1987), actress, Kirksville

John J. "Black Jack" Pershing (1860-1948), World War I hero, general, Linn County

Vincent Price (1911-1993), actor, St. Louis

Doris Roberts (1929-), actress, St. Louis

Ginger Rogers (Virginia McMath) (1911-1995), dancer, actress, Independence

Casey Stengel (1890-1975), baseball player, Kansas City

Harry S Truman (1884-1972), 33rd President (1945-1953), Lamar

Dick Van Dyke (1925-), actor, West Plains

Dennis Weaver (1924-), actor, Joplin

Roy Wilkins (1901-1981), civil rights leader, St. Louis

Jane Wyman (Sarah Jane Fulks) (1914-), actress, St. Joseph

Thomas Jefferson Peace Medal

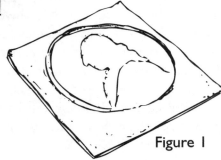

Figure 1

Materials

* 4" to 6" shallow plastic bowl
* fine-tip permanent marker (black or brown)
* 1/2 cup plaster of Paris
* water
* mixing stick
* gold spray paint
* leather string
* X-acto™ knife
* petroleum jelly
* toothpick
* 2 clear plastic lids from a potato chip can
* tape
* metal file or sandpaper
* long plastic straw
* hole punch
* carbon paper

Figure 2

Instructions

1. Copy the Peace Medal designs on page 118 and lay a plastic lid on the front part of it. Reduce or enlarge it to fit the bottom of the plastic bowl.
2. Go over the outlines with a permanent marker. (Figure 1)
3. Cut around the design on the plastic to make a mold and set it aside. Continue the same process with the back of the Peace Medal design.
4. Place both plastic molds together and punch a hole through them. (Figure 2)
5. Flip the back of the mold over so it is upside down. Smear petroleum jelly over it. Place the design at the bottom of the plastic bowl with the petroleum jelly-covered side facing up. (Figure 3)
6. Smear petroleum jelly around the straw and slip it upright into the medal's hole. (Figure 4)

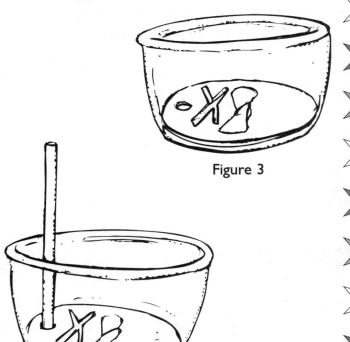

Figure 3

Figure 4

7. Smear petroleum jelly on the bottom of the front portion of the Peace Medal. Put it on the tip of the straw right side up as shown. Make sure it does not slip down until ready. (Figure 5)

8. Mix plaster and pour it into the bowl, carefully covering the Peace Medal mold at the bottom. (Figure 6)

9. Quickly slip the top medal mold down the straw and into the plaster before it hardens. Lightly press it to make a significant imprint on the plaster. Allow it to set. (Figure 7)

10. When the plaster has hardened, pop the entire medal out of the bowl. Carefully pull the plastic off both sides. (Figure 8)

11. Sand down any bumps.

12. Cover your work surface with paper, then spray gold paint on one side of the medal and let it dry. Paint the other side and let it dry.

13. Tape the paper copy of the front of the medal over the plaster copy. Slip carbon paper under the design and go over the lines. Remove the carbon paper and paper copy. Ink the lines in with black or brown permanent marker. Do the same for the back side. (Figure 9)

14. Thread leather string through the hole in the medal and tie a knot for a hanger. (Figure 10)

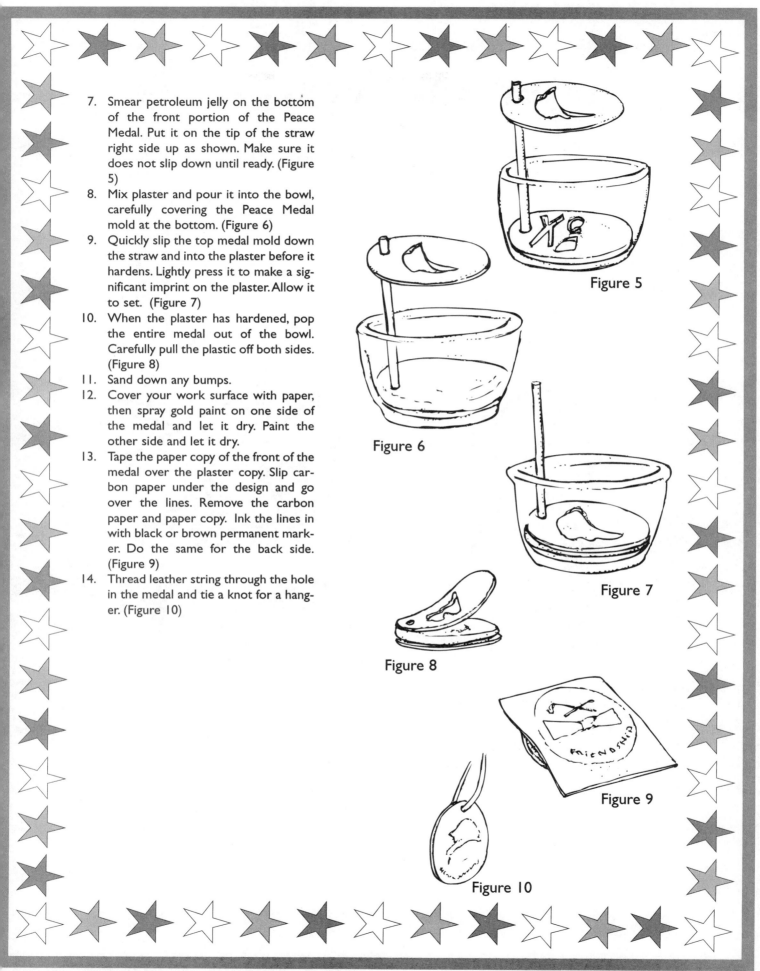

Figure 5

Figure 6

Figure 7

Figure 8

Figure 9

Figure 10

Jefferson Peace Medal

Thomas Jefferson

(front)

Peace Medal

(back)

Animal: Grizzly Bear (Ursus arctos horribilis)

Bird: Western Meadowlark (Sturnella neglecta)

Butterfly: Mourning Cloak (Nymphalis antiopa)

Fish: Blackspotted (West slope), Cutthroat Trout (Salmo clarki)

Flower: Bitterroot (Lewisia redevia)

Fossil: Maiasaura pebble-sorum

Gem: Montana Sapphire (Aluminum Oxide)

Grass: Bluebunch Wheatgrass (Agropyron spicatum-pursh)

Motto: "Oro y Plata" (Gold and Silver)

Nickname: Treasure State

Song: "Montana" by Charles C. Cohen

Tree: Ponderosa Pine (Pinus pondersa)

Statehood: November 8, 1889; 41st state admitted to the Union

Population: (2000 estimate) 902,125

Area: 147,046 square miles of land and water; 4th largest state

Highest Point: Granite Peak; 12,799 feet above sea level

Lowest Point: Kootenai River; 1800 feet above sea level

Capital: Helena

Largest City: Billings

Major Crops: Cattle, sheep, flaxseed, rye, oats, wheat, barley, sugar beets, potatoes, hay

Major Industry: Mining—copper, lead, silver, coal, zinc; lumber and wood products; tourism

Montana

Did You Know?

On April 6, 1983, the governor of Montana signed a bill into law that named the grizzly bear as the state animal. The selection of the grizzly is unique because more than 55,000 schoolchildren all across the state participated in the process. They campaigned for the animal they thought should be picked, making bumper stickers, posters and speeches, and handing out campaign buttons promoting their animal of choice. Elections were held in 425 Montana schools. The grizzly bear won, beating the elk by a two-to-one margin. Many students were impressed with the physical size of the grizzly—it can weigh up to 1000 pounds and measure eight feet tall. Its size does not mean that it is slow—the grizzly can run nearly 35 miles per hour. State legislators agreed with the schoolchildren and chose the grizzly bear as Montana's state animal.

Name: Montana is named for one of its geographic features—its mountains. <u>Montana</u> is a Latin word that means "mountainous."

Flag: The word *Montana* stretches across three-quarters of the top of the blue banner, with the state seal centered underneath.

Seal: The circular seal depicts a rising sun shedding light on some of Montana's beautiful scenery, including mountains, forests and the Great Falls of the Missouri River. In the foreground, representing mining and farming are a pick, shovel and plow. A ribbon bears the state motto, "Oro y Plata."

Stegosaurus Fossils

Imagine finding dinosaur bones in your backyard! That's what happened to a ranching family just outside Great Falls, Montana. They had been digging a retaining wall on their ranch when they discovered the first Stegosaurus ever found in Montana. Since 2003, a team of scientists and amateur paleontologists have been slowly unearthing this Stegosaurus.

Though the Stegosaurus found in Great Falls is one of the rarest dinosaurs in North America, many other dinosaur species have been found in northeastern and eastern Montana. Some lucky, person might one day find a bone sticking out of the ground that leads to the discovery of a completely new species!

Notable Natives

Raymond Perry Ahlquist (1914-1983), pharmacologist, Missoula

Zoe Akins (1886-1958), Pulitzer Prize-winning dramatist, Humansville

Dana Carvey (1955-), comedian, actor, Missoula

Gary Cooper (1901-1961) actor, Helena

Patrick Duffy (1949-), actor, Townsend

Chet Huntley (1911-1974), pioneering television journalist, Cardwell

Phil D. Jackson (1945-), basketball player, coach Deer Lodge

Myrna Loy (1905-1993), actress, Helena

David Lynch (1946-), film maker, Missoula

Jeannette Rankin (1880-1973), first woman elected to the U.S. Congress

Martha Raye (1916-1994), actress, Butte

Montana

Stegosaurus Fossils

This project requires heat.

Materials

* 1 sheet heavy card stock
* 1¼ cups flour
* 1½ cups coffee grounds
* ¼ cup cold coffee
* ¾ cup salt
* aluminum foil
* cookie sheet
* oven
* mixing bowl
* dull plastic knife

Instructions

1. Copy the stegosaurus fossil design on page 122 onto heavy card stock.
2. Cover the cookie sheet with aluminum foil.
3. Mix flour, salt, coffee grounds and coffee into a dough. Spread the dough out into an irregular flat shape on the foil. Keep the form approximately ½" thick, 6" wide and 9" long. (Figure 1)
4. Cut out the paper Stegosaurus shapes and place them on the top of the dough in their proper positions. (Figure 2)
5. Press the paper shapes firmly into the dough, leaving impressions in the dough. (Figure 3)
6. Pull the paper shapes off and use the plastic knife to lightly form any impressions that are not clear. (Figure 4)
7. Set the dough in a preheated oven at 300°F. Check the piece every half hour until it is hard to the touch.

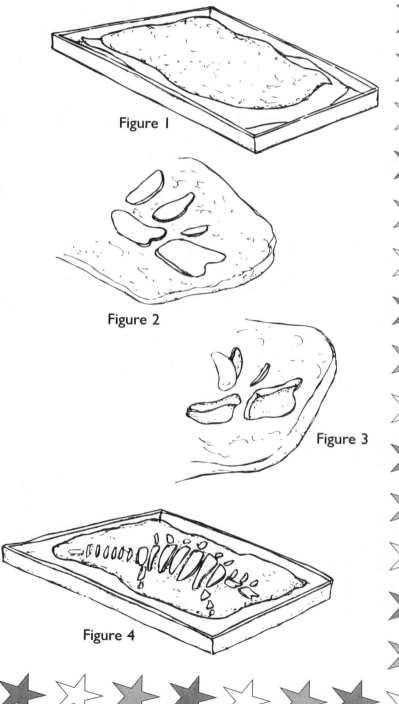

Figure 1

Figure 2

Figure 3

Figure 4

Stegosaurus Fossil

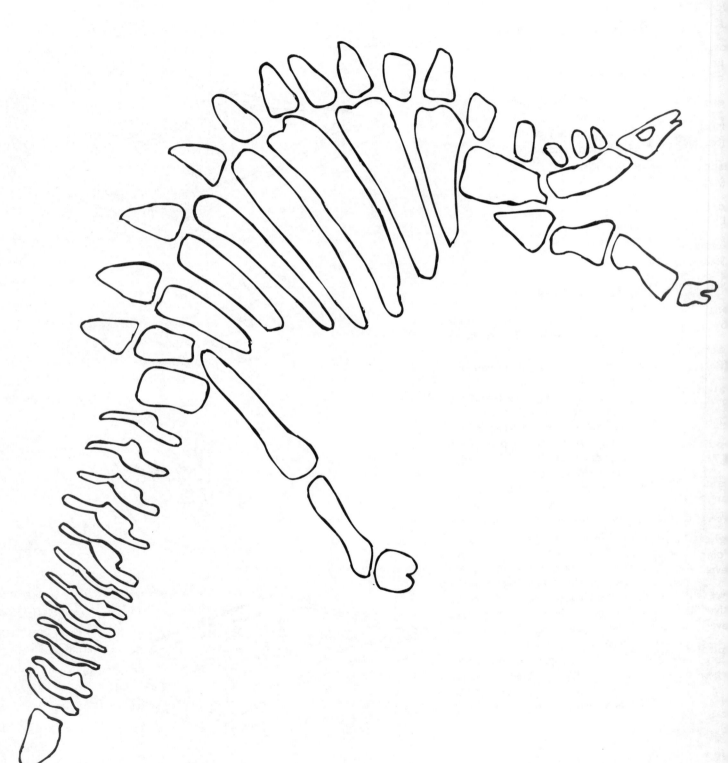

Fun Facts

Animal: White-Tailed Deer (Odocoileus virginianus)

Bird: Western Meadowlark (Sturnella neglecta)

Fish: Channel Catfish (Ictalurus punctatus)

Flower: Goldenrod (Solidago serontina)

Fossil: Mammoth (Elephas primigenius or Elephas columbi)

Gem: Blue Chalcedony

Grass: Little Bluestem (Schizachyrium scoparium)

Insect: Honeybee (Apis mellifera)

Motto: "Equality Before the Law"

Nicknames: Cornhusker State, Tree Planters' State

Rock: Prairie Agate

Song: "Beautiful Nebraska" by Jim Fras

Tree: Cottonwood (Populus deltoids)

Statehood: March 1, 1867; 37th state admitted to the Union

Population: (2000 estimate) 1,711,263

Area: 77,358 square miles of land and water; 16th largest state

Highest Point: Panorama Point; 5424 feet above sea level

Lowest Point: Missouri River; 480 feet above sea level

Capital: Lincoln

Largest City: Omaha

Major Crops: Cattle, sorghum, corn, hogs, soybeans, wheat

Major Industry: Food processing, car accessories, farm machinery, pharmaceuticals, electrical equipment, printing and publishing

Nebraska

Name: _Nebraska_ is an Omaha or Oto word. Both tribes lived on the plains where Nebraska now is. The word means "broad water" or "flat river" which they used to describe the Platte River which crosses the state and empties into the Missouri River.

Did You Know?

The governor of Nebraska named Kool-Aid™ the official state soft drink on May 21, 1998, because Kool-Aid™ was invented in Nebraska. In 1927, an enterprising young man, Edwin E. Perkins, developed the tasty drink by creating a mix of dry ingredients, that would turn into a refreshing drink when mixed with water for hot Nebraska summers. He packaged his new drink in wax paper packages in six flavors—raspberry, cherry, grape, lemon, orange and root beer. Strawberry flavored Kool-Aid™ was added to the line later. Mr. Perkin's favorite flavor was raspberry; what's yours?

Seal: On the circular seal is a steamboat going up the Missouri River; a smith with a hammer and anvil, representing mechanical arts; a settler's cabin, sheaves of wheat and stalks of growing corn to represent agriculture; and a train heading towards the Rocky Mountains to the west. At the top of the circle is the motto: "Equality Before the Law." That circle is surrounded by another with the words _Great Seal of the State of Nebraska, March 1st, 1867._

Arbor Day

Nebraska was once a treeless territory of plains, but J. Sterling Morton changed that. In 1854, Morton and his family left their Detroit home for the new Nebraska Territory. He and his fellow pioneers missed having trees around them as they had in their home states. But there were also practical reasons for having trees on the prairie. They would help protect pioneers from the hot sun and act as windbreaks across the desolate plains. And trees would be an excellent source for building homes.

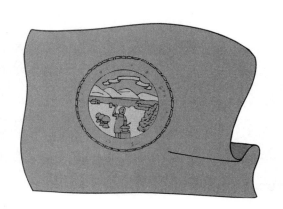

Flag: The state seal is centered on a field of national blue.

123

How Arbor Day Began

J. Sterling Morton was a journalist and soon became the editor of Nebraska's first newspaper, which he used to give voice to his ideas about planting trees. Many agreed, and soon individuals and civic organizations caught the idea of planting trees on the prairie.

On January 4, 1872, Morton proposed the first tree-planting holiday for April 10, 1872. Prizes would be given to those who planted the greatest number of trees that day. It is estimated that over one million trees were planted that first Arbor Day.

Accounts from the *Nebraska City News*, April 1885, state that the city celebrated Arbor Day with a grand parade and a speech by Morton. Schoolchildren from various grades met to plant trees. Labels were made to indicate the grade and the time each was planted. Over 1000 students formed a line from the beginning of the parade to the city's Opera House. They carried banners and waited for Morton to make his speech about trees and civic duty.

In 1885, Arbor Day became an official legal holiday on April 22— J. Sterling Morton's birthday. He was the father of Arbor Day.

Seed Packets for Arbor Day

Many trees drop their own seeds. Before they are collected by animals or blown away, collect your tree's seeds and trade them with friends. On Arbor Day you can find a designated area to plant your seeds. By doing this you will help to promote the beauty and importance of all trees.

Keep your seeds in the seed packets you make until the day you trade and plant them. The impression on your envelope will help you identify which tree your seeds will grow into.

Nebraska

Notable Natives

Grace Abbott (1878-1939), author, social reformer, director, Grand Island

Grover Cleveland "Pete" Alexander (1887-1950), baseball player, Elba

Adele Astaire (Adele Austerlitz) (1898-1981), dancer, singer, Omaha

Fred Astaire (Frederick Austerlitz) (1899-1987), dancer, actor, Omaha

George Wells Beadle (1903-1989), Nobel Prize-winning geneticist, Wahoo

Marlon Brando (1924-2004), Oscar-winning actor, Omaha

Warren Buffett (1930-), investor, one of the world's wealthiest people, Omaha

Dick Cavett (1936-), television actor, talk show host, Gibbon

Dick Cheney (1941-), Vice President, Lincoln

Montgomery Clift (1920-1966), actor, Omaha

James Coburn (1928-2002), actor, Laurel

John Ray Dunning (1907-1975), physicist, Shelby

Harold Eugene Edgerton (1903-1990), electrical engineer, Fremont

Val Logsdon Fitch (1923-), Nobel Prize-winning physicist, Merriman

Henry Fonda (1905-1982), Oscar-winning actor, Grand Island

Gerald Rudolf Ford (Leslie King, Jr.) (1913-), 38th President (1974-1977), Omaha

Jay Wright Forrester (1918-), computer engineer, Anselmo

Bob Gibson (1935-), baseball player, Omaha

Howard Hanson (1896-1981), composer, Wahoo

Marg Helgenberger (1958-), actress, Fremont

L. Ron Hubbard (1911-1986), founder of the Church of Scientology, Tilden

David Janssen (1930-1980), actor, Naponee

Swoosie Kurtz (1944-), actress, Omaha

Malcom X (Malcom Little) (1925-1965), civil rights activist, Omaha

Martin Emil Marty (1928-), church historian, scholar, West Point

Nick Nolte (1941-), actor, Omaha

Red Cloud (Sioux name—Mahpiua Luta) (1822-1909), Native American rights leader

Robert Taylor (1911-1969), actor, Filley

Paul Williams (1940-), singer, songwriter, Omaha

Paula Zahn (1956-), television journali Omaha

Darryl Zanuck (1902 1979), film produ Wahoo

Seed Packets

Materials

* white paper
* white glue
* crayons or markers
* small envelope (per design)

Instructions

1. Gather seeds from a tree (or its pod) and set them aside.
2. Copy the leaf design on page 126 that most closely matches the tree your seeds are from.
3. Color and cut out the design. (Figure 1)
4. Glue the colored leaf design on a white envelope. Place your seeds in the envelope and write the name of the tree under the design. (Figure 2)
5. Share your seeds with friends or give them as gifts. Set them aside for Arbor Day. Do the world a favor by planting trees.

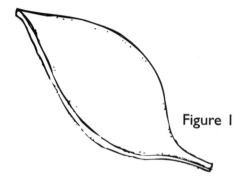

Figure 1

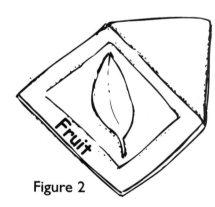

Figure 2

Leaf Designs

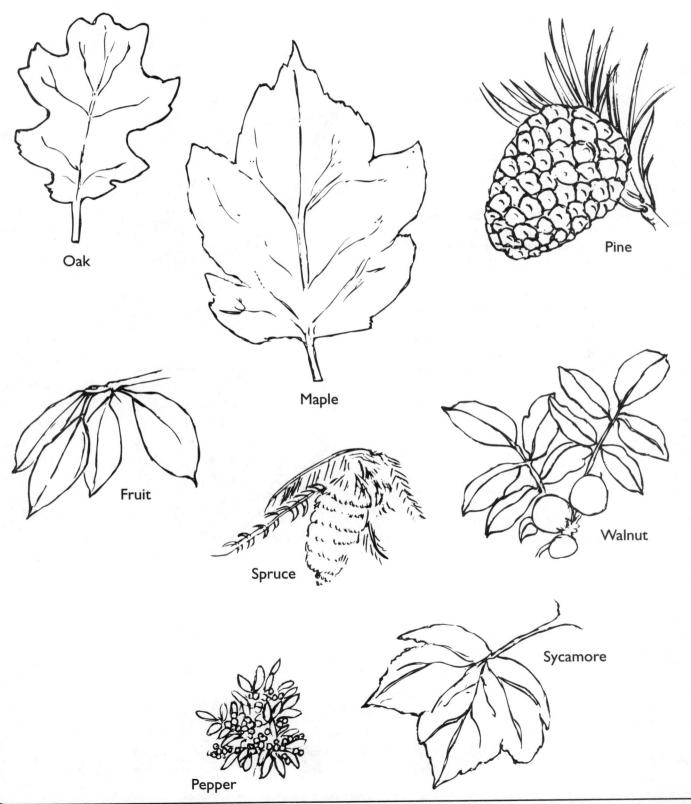

Oak

Maple

Pine

Fruit

Spruce

Walnut

Sycamore

Pepper

Fun Facts

Animal: Desert Bighorn or Nelson Sheep (Ovis canadensis nelsoni)

Bird: Mountain Bluebird (Sialia currucoides)

Fish: Lahontan Cutthroat Trout (Salmo clarki henshawi)

Flower: Sagebrush (Artemisia tridentata)

Fossil: Ichthyosaur (Shonisaurus popularis)

Gem: Virgin Valley Black Fire Opal

Semi-Precious Gem: Turquoise

Grass: Indian Ricegrass (Oryzopsis hymenoides)

Motto: "All for Our Country"

Nicknames: Silver State, Sagebrush State

Reptile: Desert Tortoise (Gopherus agassizii)

Rock: Sandstone

Song: "Home Means Nevada" by Bertha Raffetto

Trees: Single-Leaf Piñon (Pinus monophylla), Bristlecone Pine (Pinus aristata)

Statehood: October 31, 1864; 36th state admitted to the Union

Population: (2000 estimate) 1,998,257

Area: 110,567 square miles of land and water; 7th largest state

Highest Point: Boundary Peak; 13,143 feet above sea level

Lowest Point: Colorado River; 470 feet above sea level

Capital: Carson City

Largest City: Las Vegas

Major Crops: Cattle, barley, wheat, hay, dairy products, potatoes

Major Industry: Tourism; mining—gold, copper, lead, silver, zinc, mercury, tungsten; machine manufacturing; specialty printing; seismic equipment; food processing; electrical equipment

Nevada

Name: *Nevada* is a Spanish word which means "snow clad," referring to the snow-topped mountains.

Did You Know?

The largest single building project using tax payers' money in United States history is Hoover Dam. Completed in 1935, it is a massive 6,600,000-ton concrete structure, built in Black Canyon on the Colorado River. There is enough concrete in Hoover Dam to pave a 16-foot wide highway from New York to San Francisco! At the height of its construction, over 5000 people were working on the dam. Nearly 70 years after the dam was completed, it is still supplying electricity to Las Vegas and surrounding areas.

Flag: The state flag is cobalt blue. In the upper left corner, two sprays of sagebrush form a half-wreath design. Finishing the circle is a golden scroll with the words *Battle Born* in black. Below the scroll is a five-point silver star. Beneath the star is the state name, *Nevada*, in gold letters.

Seal: The circular state seal shows a mountainous scene with a rising sun. At the base of the mountains is a locomotive with smoke gently rising from its smoke stack as the train goes over a trestle. Mining and industry are represented by a miner and wagon. In the foreground is a plow representing agriculture. Below the plow in a ribbon is the state motto: "All for Our Country." In the outer ring of the seal are the words: *The Great Seal of the State of Nevada.*

Basque Arbourglyphs

Over 9000 feet up in the mountainous elevations of Nevada stand glorious Aspen trees. But just as beautiful are the remarkable Arbourglyphs carved into the trees by lonely Basque sheepherders. Emigrating from their homeland in the Pyrenees Mountains in the mid-1800s because of the limited land available, the Basque applied their familiar shepherding trade after the California Gold Rush and Nevada's Silver Rush did not deliver the riches they sought.

The sheepherders lived among cougars, bears and coyotes while tending their sheep. As they sat alone, contemplating the inspiring beauty of their surroundings, they created a story that historians are clamoring to save today. Arbourglyphs are not simple carvings, but important documents with names and messages found nowhere else. Out of tens of thousands of the Arbourglyphs, 75 percent are becoming extinct. They are almost the only records of the human beings who wandered the mountains so long ago. The Basque carvings were a messaging system but also a remedy for loneliness and boredom. Messages translated from the original language include statements ("it's nice to be in the shade") to love poems. The Aspens hold names, places, birth dates, hometowns, poems, drawings and religious symbols that give us insight into the lives of those who carved them.

Create your own Arbourglyphs without an Aspen tree. You will gain a better understanding of the lives of people who traveled the highlands with their sheep and how they were able to communicate with each other. The carvings have lasted for more than a hundred years.

Notable Natives

Andre Agassi (1970-), tennis player, Las Vegas

Helen Delich Bentley (1923-), newspaperwoman, congresswoman, Ruth

Abby Dalton (1932-), actress, Las Vegas

Molissa Fenley (1954-), dancer, choreographer, Las Vegas

Jack Kramer (1921-), tennis player, Las Vegas

Thelma Catherine Patricia Ryan Nixon (1912-1993), First Lady, Ely

Harry Reid (1939-), U.S. senator, Searchlight

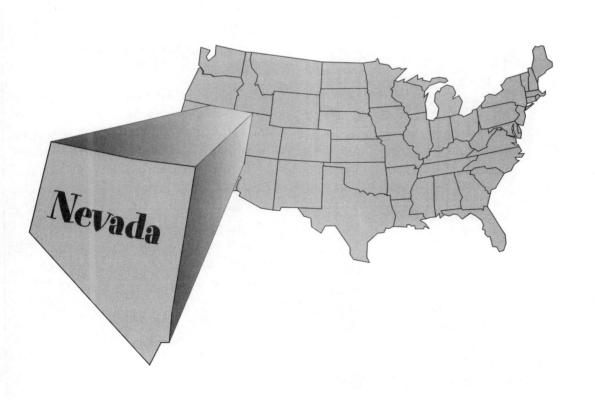

Basque Arbourglyphs

Materials

* 8½" x 11" rice paper that has strands of cotton, leaves and/or wood shavings
* craft knife
* silicone adhesive
* spray sealer
* pencils and pencil eraser
* 8½" x 11" card stock
* toothpick
* water sprayer
* white glue
* wooden boards

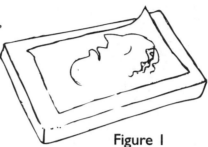

Figure 1

Instructions

1. Enlarge the designs from page 130 on card stock and cut them out.
2. Use white glue to attach each design to a wooden board. Let it dry. (Figure 1)
3. Follow the interior and exterior lines with silicone adhesive and let it dry. (Figure 2)
4. Lay rice paper over the dried silicone adhesive and lightly dampen it with water.
5. Press the paper down around the silicone impressions. Use an eraser to stretch some of the paper's fiber out. Let it dry. (Figure 3)
6. Turn the paper impression over to see an image similar to those found in the high Sierras of Nevada made by Basque sheepherders.

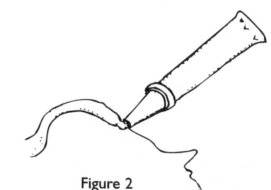

Figure 2

Figure 3

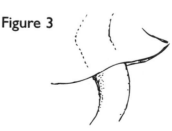

Basque Arbourglyph Designs

Fun Facts

Amphibian: Spotted Newt (Notophthalmus viridescens)

Animal: White-Tailed Deer (Odocoileus virginianus)

Bird: Purple Finch (Carpodacus purpureus)

Butterfly: Karner Blue (Lycaeides melissa)

Saltwater Game Fish: Rockfish or Striped Bass (Morone saxatilis)

Freshwater Fish: Brook Trout (Salvelinus fontinalis)

Flower: Purple Lilac (Syringa vulgaris)

Wildflower: Pink Lady's Slipper (Cypripedium acaule)

Gem: Smoky Quartz

Insect: Ladybug (Coccinella novemnotata)

Mineral: Beryl

Motto: "Live free or die"

Nickname: Granite State

Song: "Old New Hampshire" by John F. Holmes

Tree: Paper Birch (Betula papyrifera)

Statehood: June 21, 1788; 9th state admitted to the Union

Population: (2000 estimate) 1,235,786

Area: 9351 square miles of land and water; 46th largest state

Highest Point: Mt. Washington; 6288 feet above sea level

Lowest Point: Atlantic coast; sea level

Capital: Concord

Largest City: Manchester

Major Crops: Dairy products, truck vegetables, cattle, corn, potatoes, hay, apples, poultry, eggs

Major Industry: Machinery, pulp and paper products, rubber and plastic products, stone and clay products, tourism

New Hampshire

Name: New Hampshire is the only state in the Union named after a county! That's right, Captain John Mason named it in 1629 after Hampshire County in England where he grew up.

Did You Know?

One of the best-tasting treats is syrup on hot pancakes. New Hampshire is famous for the maple syrup produced there. But don't waste the syrup on your French toast or pancakes because it takes nearly 40 gallons of sap from a maple tree to make just one gallon of maple syrup.

Flag: The state flag bears the state seal in the center of a field of blue. Surrounding the seal is a wreath of laurel leaves and nine five-point stars, representing New Hampshire's order of admission.

Seal: The circular seal of New Hampshire displays the frigate *Raleigh* on stocks. Behind the ship is a rising sun. The ship is encircled by a laurel wreath. In the outer circle of the seal are the words, *Seal of the State of New Hampshire*, and the date, *1776*.

Puritan Markers

Puritan gravestones provide us with some extravagant records. These are not dreary or frightening works of art but tributes to life and statements of the Puritan spirit and their beliefs in the afterlife. These gravestones are still found in old church yards, telling a history of people brave enough to help forge our nation. To the Puritans, death was the source of their greatest rewards. Therefore, the gravestone was a centerpiece of celebration. These designs evoke a new reverence for the past, representing the Puritan courage as well as the afterlife.

Notable Natives

Charles Greely Abbot (1872-1973), astrophysicist, Wilton

Thomas Bailey Aldrich (1836-1907), poet, novelist, Portsmouth

Hosea Ballou (1771-1852), clergyman, newspaper editor, Richmond

Amy Marcy Beach (1867-1944), pianist, composer, Henniker

Laura Dewey Bridgman (1829-1889), teacher of children with disabilities, Hanover

Benjamin Franklin Butler (1818-1893), Civil War general, politician, Deerfield

Lewis Cass (1782-1866), politician, Exeter

Salmon Portland Chase (1808-1873), U.S. Secretary of the Treasury, U.S. Supreme Court Chief Justice, Cornish

James Freeman Clark (1810-1888), theologian, author, Hanover

Charles Anderson Dana (1819-1897), newspaper editor, Hinsdale

John Adams Dix (1798-1879), Civil War general, politician, Boscawen

Samuel Gardner Drake (1798-1875), publisher, historian, Pittsfield

Mary Morse Eddy (1821-1910), founder of the Christian Science Church, Bow

William Pitt Fessenden (1806-1869), U.S. senator, politician, Boscawen

Daniel Chester French (1850-1931), sculptor, Exeter

Horace Greeley (1811-1872), journalist, politician, Amherst

Sarah Joseph Hale (1788-1879), editor, writer, Newport

Charles Francis Hall (182 1871), explorer, Rochester

John Irving (1942-), writer, Exeter

Alan Shepard (1923-1998 astronaut, East Derry

Harlan F. Stone (1872-1946), U.S. Supreme Court Chief Justice, Chesterfield

Daniel Webster (1782-1852), U.S. senator, statesman, Salisbury

Joseph Worcester (1784-1865), lexicographer, Bedford

Franklin Pierce (1804-1869) 14th President (1853-1857), Hillsbor

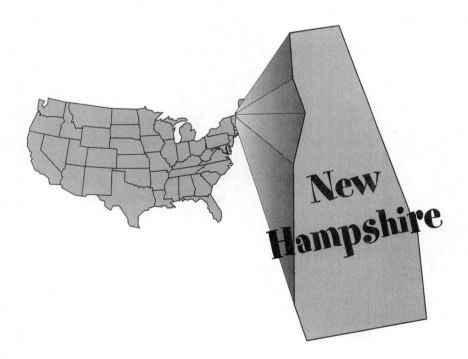

New Hampshire

Puritan Markers

Materials

* rectangular plastic food storage box, approximately 6" x 10"
* water
* 1/4" weather stripping tape
* 5" x 9" wood block
* paper
* 4 cups plaster of Paris
* white glue
* basin or low pan
* acrylic paints: black, white
* sponge
* utility knife

Figure 1

Figure 2

Instructions

1. Mix plaster with water and pour into the plastic food container. (The plaster should be at least 1/2" high). Set aside to dry.

2. Choose a design from page 134. Enlarge it to fit on the wood block.

3. Glue the design on the wood block and set it aside. (Figure 1)

4. Roll thin stripping tape out and peel off the under-paper, outlining the design glued to the block to make a stamp. (Figure 2)

5. Carefully pop the plaster out of its container when it's dry. (Figure 3)

6. Mix paint colors into a light gray. Sponge the paint with light splashes of black to make a faux finish of granite on the plaster. Let it dry. (Figure 4)

7. Pour black paint into a basin. Press your stamp, stripping tape side down, into the paint. Try to get as much paint as possible on the tape. Press the stamp on a piece of paper to test it. When satisfied, move the stamp to the plaster slab and carefully press it down. Pull it up carefully and let it dry. (Figure 5)

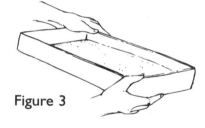

Figure 3

Figure 4

Figure 5

Puritan Marker Designs

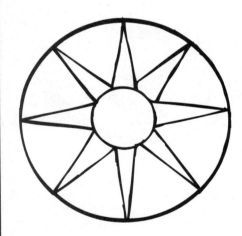

Fun Facts

nimal: Horse
(Equus caballus)

rd: Eastern Goldfinch
(Carduelis tristis)

nosaur: Hadrosaurus
oulkii

sh: Brook Trout
(Salvelinus fontinalis)

ower: Common Meadow
Violet (Viola sororia)

uit: Blueberry

sect: Honeybee
(Apis mellifera)

otto: "Liberty and
Prosperity"

ckname: Garden State

ell: Knobbed Whelk
(Busycon carica gmelin)

ng: "I'm from New Jersey"
y Red Mascara

ee: Red Oak (Quercus
orealis maxima)

emorial Tree: Flowering
Dogwood (Cornus florida)

atehood: December 18,
787; 3rd state admitted to
he Union

pulation: (2000 estimate)
,414,350

ea: 8,722 square miles of
nd and water; 47th largest
tate

ghest Point: High Point;
803 feet above sea level

west Point: Atlantic coast;
ea level

pital: Trenton

gest City: Newark

jor Crops: Horses,
egetables, cranberries,
lueberries, peaches, nuts,
eafood, dairy products

jor Industry: Chemical
roducts, oil refinery, phar-
aceuticals, machinery,
ectrical equipment and
ods, food processing,
xtiles and apparel, printing
d publishing, tourism

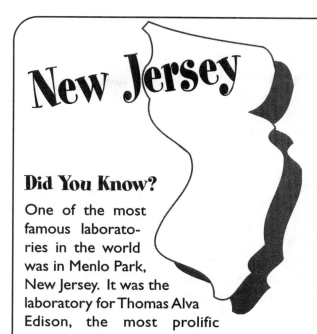

New Jersey

Did You Know?

One of the most famous laborato-ries in the world was in Menlo Park, New Jersey. It was the laboratory for Thomas Alva Edison, the most prolific inventor in American history. He invented important items such as: the light bulb, motion pictures, the phonograph and hundreds of others. Edison, never one to brag, chalked up his success more to hard work than intelligence. He said: "Genius is one percent inspiration and ninety-nine percent perspiration."

Flag: The flag has the state coat of arms in the center of a buff-colored field. The buff color was chosen by George Washington.

Seal: The circular seal shows a shield with three plows on it, representing the importance of agriculture and the state's farming tradition. Directly above the shield is a helmet which represents the state as a sovereign government. Above the helmet is a horse's head. A woman stands on each side of the shield. Liberty,

Name: Like a few other states, New Jersey is named for another place. New Jersey was named after England's Isle of Jersey by the Duke of York in 1664. The Duke had granted a land patent to Sir George Carteret and John Berkeley for the area to be called "Novia Caesaria," Latin for <u>New Jersey</u>.

the woman on the left holds a staff with has the liberty cap on top of it. The woman on the right is Ceres, the Roman goddess of grain. She holds a cornucopia full of a bountiful harvest. Below the shield is a scroll with the state motto: "Liberty and Prosperity," and the year of American independence, 1776.

Pirate Treasure

In the late 17th and 18th centuries pirates and privateers infested the New Jersey shoreline. Many colonists did business with pirates and privateers. In fact, some wealthy colonists gained fortunes by investing in various expeditions. Others bought plundered goods from pirates and resold them on the black market. Pirates were tolerated and even encouraged by some, but their actions were illegal. Privateers, however, were sanctioned by the British government.

The True Story of Captain Kidd

Captain Kidd commanded privateer ships for the Royal Navy, establishing himself as a wealthy colonist with high political connections in New Jersey. As a royally sanctioned privateer, Kidd was encouraged to seize and capture French ships as well as pirate ships on the high seas. He split all goods with the British government and financial backers.

Captain Kidd's favorite hunting grounds were the Red Sea and the Caribbean where ships loaded with silk and gold traveled back and forth from Asia to Europe. Though many pirates sailed these waters, Kidd rarely focussed on them. He preferred instead to plunder French ships. When his crew grew tired of chasing French ships that offered them few riches, a mutiny broke out and Captain Kidd killed his gunner with a blow to the head. From then on, Kidd chased every ship, regardless of its origin.

The ship, *Quedah Merchant*, was from India and carried vast riches in gold, spices and silk. Kidd followed it from the Indian Ocean to the Caribbean Sea. When he captured the ship, he split the cargo with his crew. Then he learned that he was wanted by the British government as a pirate. Loot in hand, Captain Kidd purchased a small sloop and sailed to the New Jersey shore. He dropped anchor off the coast of Monmonth County with the intention of restoring his reputation as a privateer. He hid his treasures off the coast of New Jersey. When Captain Kidd reached Boston, he was arrested and sent to England to be tried as a pirate and murderer by the British Admiralty. He was hanged on May 23, 1701. His body then tarred, bound in chains and hung over the Thames River in London as a warning to all pirates to never cross the fine line from privateer to pirate.

Some people believe Captain Kidd's buried treasure is still waiting to be discovered off the New Jersey coast. Spanish gold pieces have been found on some nearby islands. Tales have been told of Captain Kidd's treasures hidden in the creeks near Sandy Hook, Money Island, Raritan Bay, Cliffwood Beach, Matawan Creek and Treasure Lake. The true location of Captain Kidd's treasure remains a mystery.

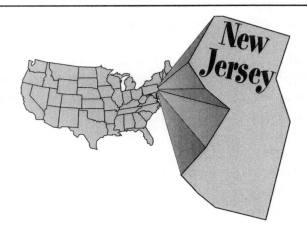

New Jersey

Notable Natives

Bud Abbott (1895-1974), comedic actor, Asbury Park

Edwin "Buzz" Aldrin (1930-), astronaut, Montclair

Jason Alexander (1959-), actor, Newark

William "Count" Basie (1904-1984), band leader, Red Bank

Clint Black (1962-), country singer, Long Branch

Judy Blume (1938-), writer, Elizabeth

William Brennan (1906-1997), U.S. Supreme Court Justice, Newark

Aaron Burr (1756-1836), U.S. Vice President, Newark

Mary Chapin Carpenter (1958-), singer, Princeton

Grover Cleveland (1837-1908), 22nd President (1885-1889), 24th President (1893-1897), Caldwell

James Fenimore Cooper (1789-1851), writer, Burlington

David Copperfield (1956-), magician, Metuchen

Lou Costello (1906-1959), comedic actor, Paterson

Stephen Crane (1871-1900), writer, Newark

Sandra Dee (1942-2005), actress, Bayonne

Michael Douglas (1944-), actor, New Brunswick

Connie Francis (Concetta Rosa Maria Franconero) (1938-), singer, Newark

James Gandolfini (1961-), actor, Westwood

William Frederick Halsey, Jr. (1884-1959), fleet admiral, Elizabeth

Ed Harris (1950-), actor, Tenafly

Lauryn Hill (1975-), rapper, South Orange

Whitney Houston (1963-), singer, Newark

Ice-T (1958-), rapper, Newark

Jon Bon Jovi (John Franci Bongiovi, Jr.) (1962-) musician, Sayreville

Nathan Lane (1956-), actor, Jersey City

Jerry Lewis (1926-), comedian, Newark

Judith Light (1949-), actress, Trenton

Norman Mailer (1923- Pulitzer Prize-winnin writer, Long Branch

Mary McCormack (1969-), actress, Plainsfield

Bette Midler (1945-), actress, singer, come enne, Paterson

Bebe Neuwirth (1958- actress, dancer, Newark

Jack Nicholson (1937- Oscar-winning actor Neptune

Dorothy Parker (1893-1967), poet, short story writer, West E

Joe Pesci (1943-), acto Newark

Zebulon Montgomery Pi (1779-1813), explore Lamberton

Queen Latifah (1970- singer, Newark

Tara Reid (1975-), actress, Wyckoff

Antonin Scalia (1936- U.S. Supreme Court Justice, Trenton

Norman Schwarzkopf (1934-), general, Trenton

Paul Simon (1941-), singer, Newark

Frank Sinatra (1915-1998), singer, actor, Hoboken

Kevin Spacey (1959-), actor, South Orange

Bruce Springsteen (1949- musician, Freehold

Meryl Streep (1949-), actress, Summit

John Travolta (1954-), actor, Englewood

Dionne Warwick (1940- singer, East Orange

Captain Kidd's Treasure

This project requires heat.

Materials

* small index card box made of wood, cardboard or tin
* newspaper strips
* mixing bowl
* papier-mâché mix of 1 cup flour and 1/4 cup water
* acrylic paints: brown, red, gold
* brush
* epoxy glue
* glass nuggets of assorted colors (found in craft stores)
* Shrink Art™ plastic sheets
* thin copper, brass and aluminum foil sheets—36 gauge (found in craft stores)
* scissors
* 4 leather strips 1/2" wide x 10" long
* fine-point permanent marker
* cookie sheet
* aluminum foil

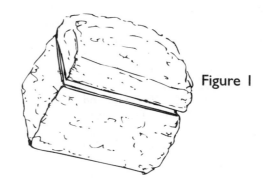

Figure 1

Figure 2

Instructions

1. Make a papier-mâché mix of flour and water. Rip newspaper into strips. Slip them into the papier-mâché mix, then lay them over the index box. Cover the entire box until it looks like a miniature treasure chest. (Be careful not to seal the lid closed!) Cover the inside by the same process and let it dry. (Figure 1)
2. Paint the exterior of the chest brown and the interior red. Let it dry.
3. Glue two leather strips over the top of the chest and let hang loose over the front. Glue leather strips over the bottom with the top and bottom strips meeting to tie together. (Figure 2)
4. Glue on the jewel-like glass nuggets to decorate and set it aside. (Figure 3)
5. Copy the coin designs on page 139. Lay the Shrink Art™ sheet on the coin designs. Tape it down and draw their images onto the Shrink Art™ with permanent marker. Make as many coins as you like. (Figure 4)

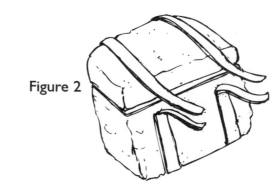

Figure 3

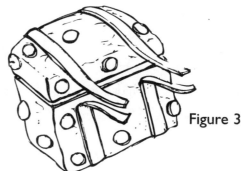

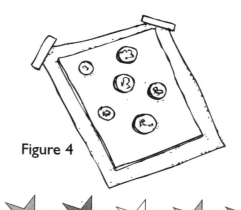

Figure 4

6. Cut the coins from the Shrink Art™ sheet and set them on a piece of foil on a cookie sheet. Follow the directions for the Shrink Art™. Place them in the oven and heat according to the directions on the Shrink Art™ sheet. Make sure the coins do not curl up. (Figure 5)

7. Lay the completed Shrink Art™ coins on sheets of various metals (thin copper, brass, aluminum foil). Tape them in place and draw around each coin. Cut the metal and set it aside. Do this for all the coins. (Figure 6)

8. Mix epoxy glue and slather it on the copper rounds. Set the Shrink Art™ coins faceup on the glued copper. Wipe off extra glue. Set aside to dry. Repeat this process for all the coins. (Figure 7)

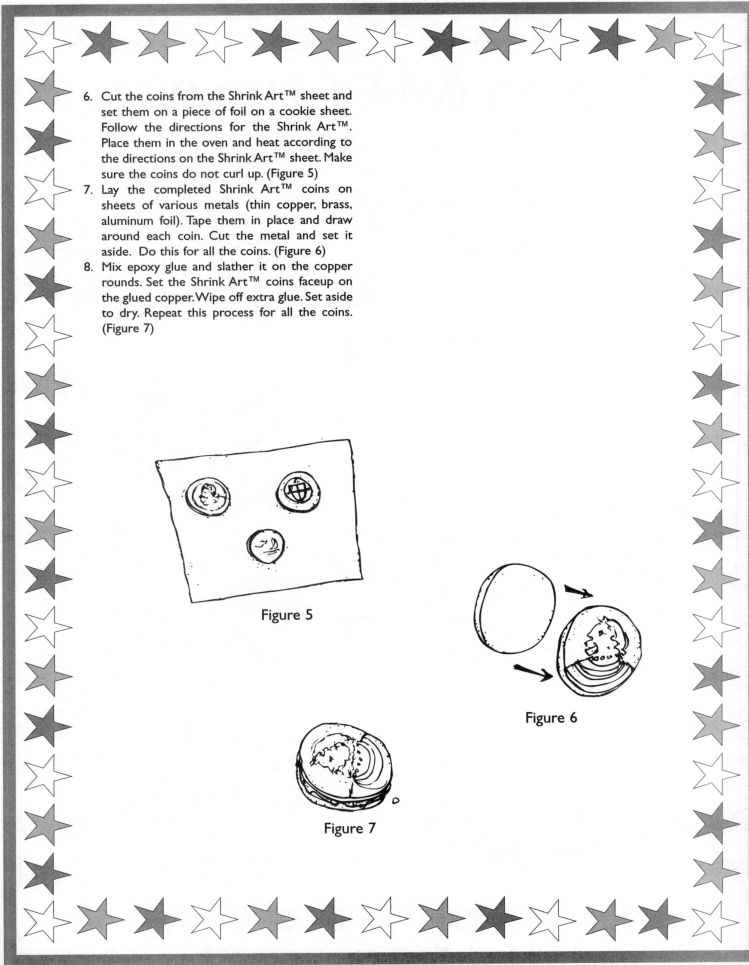

Figure 5

Figure 6

Figure 7

Captain Kidd's Treasure

Gold Coins of Great Britain
James I minted between 1619 and 1625

Charles II (1600-1685)
Maundy Silver Fourpence

Gold Coins of India's Mughal Empire
Aurangzeb (1658-1707)

Gold Coins of Italy (Naples)
Phillip II (1556-1598)

Gold Coins of Spain
Ferdinand and Isabella (1476-1516)
gold double excelente

Fun Facts

Animal: Black Bear
(Ursus americanus)

Bird: Roadrunner
(Geococcyx californianus)

Fish: Rio Grande Cutthroat
Trout (Oncorhynchus clarki
virginalis)

Flower: Yucca Flower
(Yucca glauca)

Fossil: Hollow-Form Dinosaur
(Coelophysis bauri)

Grass: Blue Gramma Grass
(Bouteloua gracillis)

Insect: Tarantula Hawk Wasp
(Pepsis formosa)

Motto: "Crescit Eundo"
(It grows as it goes)

Nickname: Land of
Enchament

Song: "O, Fair New Mexico"
by Elizabeth Garrett

Tree: Piñon Pine
(Pinus edulis)

Statehood: January 6, 1912;
47th state admitted to the
Union

Population: (2000 estimate)
1,819,046

Area: 121,593 square miles
of land and water;
5th largest state

Highest Point: Wheeler
Peak; 13,161 feet above sea
level

Lowest Point: Red Bluff
Lake; 2817 feet above sea
level

Capital: Santa Fe

Largest City: Albuquerque

Major Crops: Cattle, sheep,
dairy products, hay,
sorghum, peanuts, cotton,
pecans, onions, chilies

Major Industry: Energy
research and development;
electrical equipment; petroleum and coal products;
food processing; printing
and publishing; stone; glass
and clay products; mining—
copper, lead, silver, zinc,
uranium, potassium; tourism

New Mexico

Name: "New" Mexico, the area north and west of the Rio Grande River, was named by Spanish explorers during the 1500s.

Did You Know?

Smokey Bear is the symbol of National Fire Safety. When a blazing fire raged in the Lincoln National Forest in New Mexico, firefighters went in to stop the forest fire and keep it from spreading with water hoses, chemicals and even shovels. When a tiny, black bear cub was found huddled in a tree, scared and trapped by fire all around him, he became the symbol of fire safety. Smokey is well known and recognized all over the United States today. Thirteen years later, in honor of that little bear cub who lost his home in a forest fire, New Mexico made the black bear their official state animal!

itself is a circle from which four rays of four points radiate. Four is a sacred number to the Zia, symbolic of the four directions, the four seasons, the four times of day (sunrise, noon, evening and night) and the four stages of life (childhood, youth adulthood and old age).

Seal: The circular seal shows an American eagle with wings outstretched over the Mexican brown eagle which has a snake in its beak and a cactus in its talons. This represents the change of sovereignty of the territory from Mexico to the United States in 1846. A ribbon with the state motto, "Crescit Eundo," is displayed below the scene.

Flag: The flag displays an ancient Zia Pueblo red sun design on a field of bright yellow. The red and yellow colors represent Queen Isabel of Castile. The sun

140

Carlsbad Caverns

Beneath the Chihuahuan Desert in southeastern New Mexico, is one of nature's great monuments—Carlsbad Caverns. Once a Permian Age reef, it is now a network of 800 limestone caves filled with breathtaking geological formations. The nation's deepest and third longest caves are found there. Because of its beauty and diversity, the site was designated a National Monument on October 25, 1923, and a World Heritage Site on December 6, 1997.

The Creation of the Great Caverns of Carlsbad

Carlsbad Caverns' current form is the result of many separate environmental changes that took place over millions of years. During this time a 400-mile-long horseshoe-shaped reef was created in an inland sea made up of the mineral calcite, deposited by simple sea creatures. Over time the sea evaporated and the reef was buried under massive amounts of gypsum, salt and other minerals. Eventually erosion uncovered the buried reef. Acidic rainwater seeped into cracks and caused the limestone to dissolve creating hollows that slowly formed the large chambers of Carlsbad. Meanwhile, hydrogen sulfide gas from the development of deep underground gas and oil deposits migrated toward the surface of the reef. The gases dissolved into the groundwater and formed a mild sulfuric acid, which also helped carve out the vast underground chambers.

Cavern Decorations

The caverns are adorned with stalactites and stalagmites, created drop by drop over 500,000 years, from mineral-laden water. The process started as falling rain and absorbed carbon dioxide from the atmosphere. The mild acid rain soaked into the ground and moved downward. It dissolved the rock below and carried it as the mineral, calcite, finally forming droplets on the ceilings of the underground caverns. Each drop deposited calcite crystals. When water dripped from the ceiling, stalactites formed. Where water fell to the floor, stalagmites and columns formed. Other unusual structures include cave pearls, layers of calcite built up around tiny objects and lily pads, formed on the surface of pools. Dams also formed where water flowed slowly across the cave floor.

The most important caverns:

* Green Lake Room—contains a small green pool

* King's Palace—considered the most ornate of all the chambers

* Queen's Chamber—noted for its translucent formations in rose and pinkish shades

* Papoose Room—very small chamber with a low ceiling and low hanging stalactites

* Sword of Damocles—with formations that hang from the ceiling like daggers

Mineral Formations

Cave formations grow from chemical components in different combinations. Following is a way to make your own formations.

Notable Natives

Jeff Bezos (1964-), founder of Amazon.com, Albuquerque

Edward Uhler Condon (1902-1974), theoretical physicist, Alamogordo

John Denver (1943-1997), singer, Roswell

William Hanna (1910-2001), Oscar-winning animator of *The Flintstones*, Melrose

Neil Patrick Harris (1973-), actor, Albuquerque

Conrad Hilton (1887-1979), hotel chain founder, San Antonio

William Henry "Bill" Mauldin (1921-2003), political cartoonist, Mountain Park

Demi Moore (1962-), actress, Roswell

Freddie Prinze, Jr. (1976-), actor, Albuquerque

Al Unser (1939-) four-time Indy 500 winner, Albuquerque

Bobby Unser (1934-) three-time Indy 500 winner, Albuquerque

Mineral Formations

This project requires heat.

Materials

* saucepan
* stove or other heat source
* shallow saucer
* spoon
* water
* thread
* pencil
* alum (ask your pharmacist)
* jars (preferably baby food jars)
* ice water

Figure 1

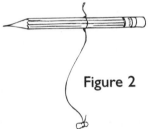

Figure 2

Instructions

1. Pour water in a saucepan and stir in approximately 2 ounces of alum for every cup of water.
2. Heat the alum/water solution and dissolve ingredients without boiling.
3. Remove from heat and stir in more alum until completely dissolved. Allow it to cool.
4. Pour 1/4 cup of the solution into the shallow saucer, storing the rest in a clean covered jar for later use. Wait a few days and watch as the water evaporates and tiny crystals form. (Figure 1)
5. Tie a piece of thread around a small crystal; tie the other end to the middle of a pencil. (Figure 2)
6. Pour the stored solution into a clean jar.
7. Center the pencil over the jar with the thread and small crystal in the solution. Make sure the crystal is thoroughly saturated. Keep it floating undisturbed in the solution for a few days as it continues to grow. Do not let the crystal touch the glass. (Figure 3)
8. Cover the jar with a paper towel and set it aside. (Covering the jar will slow the evaporation process and the crystal will grow larger.) If other crystals form, remove them from the jar since the main crystal will not grow if touching smaller crystals. (Figure 4)
9. Once the crystal has stopped growing it can be removed. Do not handle the crystal while it is growing or it will break apart.

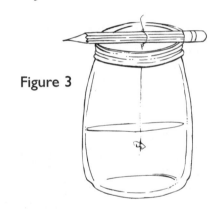

Figure 3

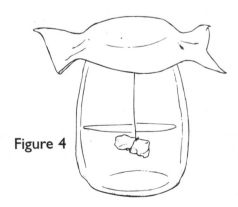

Figure 4

Fun Facts

Animal: Beaver (Castor canadensis)

Bird: Bluebird (Sialia sialis)

Fish: Brook Trout (Salvelinus fontinalis)

Flower: Rose (Rosa)

Fossil: Sea Scorpion (Eurypterus remipes)

Fruit: Apple (Malus pumila)

Gem: Garnet (Almadine garnet)

Insect: Ladybug (Coccinella novemnotata)

Motto: "Excelsior" (Ever upward)

Nickname: Empire State

Shell: Bay Scallop (Argopecten irradians)

Song: "I Love New York" by Steve Karmen

Tree: Sugar Maple (Acer saccharum)

Statehood: July 26, 1788; 11th state admitted to the Union

Population: (2000 estimate) 18,976,457

Area: 54,475 square miles of land and water; 27th largest state

Highest Point: Mt. Marcy; 5,344 feet above sea level

Lowest Point: Atlantic coast; sea level

Capital: Albany

Largest City: New York City

Major Crops: Dairy products, cattle and other livestock, corn, poultry, vegetables, apples

Major Industry: Shipping, apparel manufacturing, banking, printing and publishing, scientific instruments, electrical equipment, machinery, chemical products, travel, tourism

New York

Name: King Charles II of England, who reigned from 1649 to 1685, granted a large tract of land known as New Netherlands to his brother, the Duke of York. New York was named after the Duke.

Did You Know?

An all-time favorite dessert was invented in New York by Peter Cooper. He obtained a patent for manufacturing a gelatin treat in 1845, but it wasn't named Jell-O™ for another 50 years. A cough syrup medicine manufacturer bought the secret to making the treat. His wife, May Wait, named it Jell-O™. The very first four delicious flavors were strawberry, raspberry, orange and lemon.

Flag: The flag consists of a dark blue field with the state coat of arms in the middle.

Seal: On the circular seal is a large shield depicting a mountain range with a bright golden sun rising behind it. In the foreground are a ship and a sloop sailing on a river, bordered by a grassy shore. On each side of the shield is a woman. The woman on the left represents liberty. She holds a staff with a Phrygian cap on it and at her feet lies a royal crown, symbolizing the break with English monarchy. The

The New York State Seal is reproduced with permission from the New York Secretary of State.

woman on the right represents justice. She is blindfolded, holding scales in one hand and a sword in the other. Above the shield is the Earth with an American eagle on top of it. Below the shield is a scroll with the state motto, "Excelsior" on it.

The History That Created the Story of Sleepy Hollow

The Hudson River Valley was claimed as a Dutch territory in 1609 by Henry Hudson and settled by the Dutch by the early 1620s. The earliest inhabitants had been Weckquaesgeek Indians. Though England later controlled the region, the Dutch and Native Americans remained. During the Revolutionary War, much of this area remained neutral territory, often raided by both armies.

The Legend of Sleepy Hollow by Nathaniel Hawthorne

Nathaniel Hawthorne wrote *The Legend of Sleepy Hollow* about a sleepy Dutch village in the Hudson River Valley terrorized by a headless horseman. *The Legend of Sleepy Hollow* is an American literature classic and reflects the historical significance of the area.

The characters in the book are Ichabod Crane; the beautiful Katrina Van Tassel and Brom Bones, Katrina's suitor. One early autumn evening, Ichabod goes to a party at the Van Tassel's. After an evening of eating and dancing, the guests tell eerie legends about strange screeches and cries heard near the great tree where Major John Andre, a British spy, was captured. The sobs of a woman who died a terrible death in a winter storm, they say, can also be heard. She is destined to forever walk the countryside weeping.

The Headless Horseman, a demon Hessian, causes the most panic in the community. He follows dark paths and keeps his horse tethered in the graveyard of the Old Dutch church. The Headless Horseman chases his victims and slices off their heads with his sword. Brom Bones claims to have escaped death after crossing the church bridge, then seeing the Headless Horseman vanish with a flash.

After the Revoutionary War, Tarrytown flourished as a major shipping and trade center, and palatial mansions dotted the area. The village of North Tarrytown officially changed its name to Sleepy Hollow in 1996.

144

Notable Natives

Alan Alda (Alphonso D'Abruzzo) (1936-), actor in *M.A.S.H.*, New York City

Woody Allen (Allan Stewart Konigsberg) (1935-), screenwriter, actor, Brooklyn

Christina Aguilera (1980-), pop singer, Staten Island

Lauren Bacall (Betty Perske) (1924-), Tony-winning stage actress, New York City

Alec Baldwin (1958-), actor, Massapequa

Lucille Ball (1911-1989), "Lucy" in *I Love Lucy* television show, Jamestown

Anne Bancroft (Anna Louisa Italiano) (1931-), Oscar-winning actress, New York City

Angela Bassett (1958-), actress, Harlem

Humphrey Bogart (1899-1957), actor, New York City

James Cagney (1899-1986), actor, New York City

Jennifer Capriati (1976-), tennis player, New York City

Phoebe Cates (1963-), actress, New York City

Tom Cruise (1962-), actor, Syracuse

Tony Curtis (Bernard Schwartz) (1925-), actor, New York City

Claire Danes (1979-), actress, New York City

Sammy Davis, Jr. (1925-1990), actor, singer, New York City

Agnes de Mille (1905-1993), choreographer, New York City

Robert DeNiro (1943-), actor, New York City

Kirk Douglas (Issur Danielovich) (1916-), actor, Amsterdam

Julia Louis Dreyfus (1961-), actress, New York City

George Eastman (1854-1932), inventor of the box camera and rolled film, Waterville

Millard Fillmore (1800-1874), 13th President (1850-1853), Cayugo County

Henry Louis "Lou" Gehrig (1903-1941), baseball player, New York City

George Gershwin (Jacob Gershvin) (1898-1937), composer, Brooklyn

Mel Gibson (1956-), actor, Oscar-winning film director, Peekskill

Jackie Gleason (1916-1987), actor, Brooklyn

Susan Hayward (Edythe Marrenner) (1917-1975), Oscar-winning actress, New York City

Rita Hayworth (Margarita Carmen Cansino) (1918-1987), dancer, actress, New York City

Edward Hopper (1882-1967), painter, Nyack

Julia Ward Howe (1819-1910), poet, suffragette, New York City

Charles Evans Hughes (1862-1948), U.S. Supreme Court Chief Justice, Glens Falls

Washington Irving (1783-1859), write New York City

John Jay (1745-1829), statesman, first U.S. Supreme Court Chief Justice, New York City

Billy Joel (1949-), singer, songwriter, Bronx

Michael Jeffrey Jordan (1963-), basketball player, Brooklyn

Vince Lombardi (1913-1970), football coach, New York City

Jennifer Lopez (1970-), pop singer, actress, Bronx

Groucho Marx (Julius Henry Marx) (1895-1977), comedian, actor, New York City

Herman Melville (1819-1891), poet, short story writer, novelist, New York City

Ogden Nash (1902-1971), poet, Rye

Rosie O'Donnell (1962-), comedic actress, talk show host, Commac

Norman Rockwell (1894-1978), illustrator, New York City

Anna Eleanor Roosevelt (1884-1962), First Lady, humanitarian, New York City

Franklin Roosevelt (1882-1945), 32nd President (1933-1945), Hyde Par

Theodore Roosevelt (1858-1919), 26th President (1901-1909), New York City

Jonas Salk (1914-1995), polio researcher, New York City

Barbra Streisand (1942-), singer, New York City

Martin Van Buren (1782-1862), 8th President (1837-1841), Kinderhook

Walt Whitman (1819-1992), poet, West Hills

Jack-O'-Lantern Box

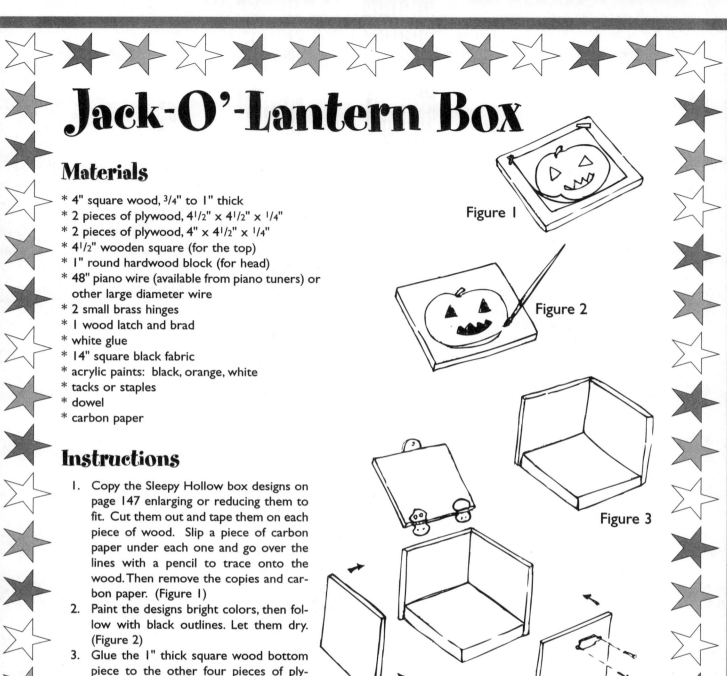

Figure 1

Figure 2

Figure 3

Figure 4

Figure 5

Materials

* 4" square wood, 3/4" to 1" thick
* 2 pieces of plywood, 4½" x 4½" x ¼"
* 2 pieces of plywood, 4" x 4½" x ¼"
* 4½" wooden square (for the top)
* 1" round hardwood block (for head)
* 48" piano wire (available from piano tuners) or other large diameter wire
* 2 small brass hinges
* 1 wood latch and brad
* white glue
* 14" square black fabric
* acrylic paints: black, orange, white
* tacks or staples
* dowel
* carbon paper

Instructions

1. Copy the Sleepy Hollow box designs on page 147 enlarging or reducing them to fit. Cut them out and tape them on each piece of wood. Slip a piece of carbon paper under each one and go over the lines with a pencil to trace onto the wood. Then remove the copies and carbon paper. (Figure 1)

2. Paint the designs bright colors, then follow with black outlines. Let them dry. (Figure 2)

3. Glue the 1" thick square wood bottom piece to the other four pieces of plywood. Let them dry. (Figure 3)

4. Attach the hinge to the backside of the top piece and the latch to the front. Press the hinge nails down if they stick out. (Figure 4)

5. Coil wire around a 1" or 1¼" diameter dowel. (Figure 5)

6. Wrap the wire around the dowel about 13 times. The larger the diameter, the fewer the coils. Bend the end of the wire near the end to make a straight piece about 2¼" long. Leave a hook at the top for the pumpkin's head. Cut off excess wire. (Figure 6)

7. Staple or tack the coil to the middle of the bottom of the box. (Figure 7)
8. Draw a pumpkin face on the round hardwood block. Paint the pumpkin's head orange. (Figure 8)
9. Hold the fabric in the middle and cut a small hole in it for the wire to poke out. Slip the fabric over the wire. (Figure 9)
10. Drill a small hole in the bottom center of the wooden pumpkin head. Place the head on the wire facing forward. (Figure 10)
11. Pull up the fabric and glue it to the pumpkin head. (Figure 11)
12. Gently push the head down and latch the top of the box closed. When you open it, the coil will pop the pumpkin head out.

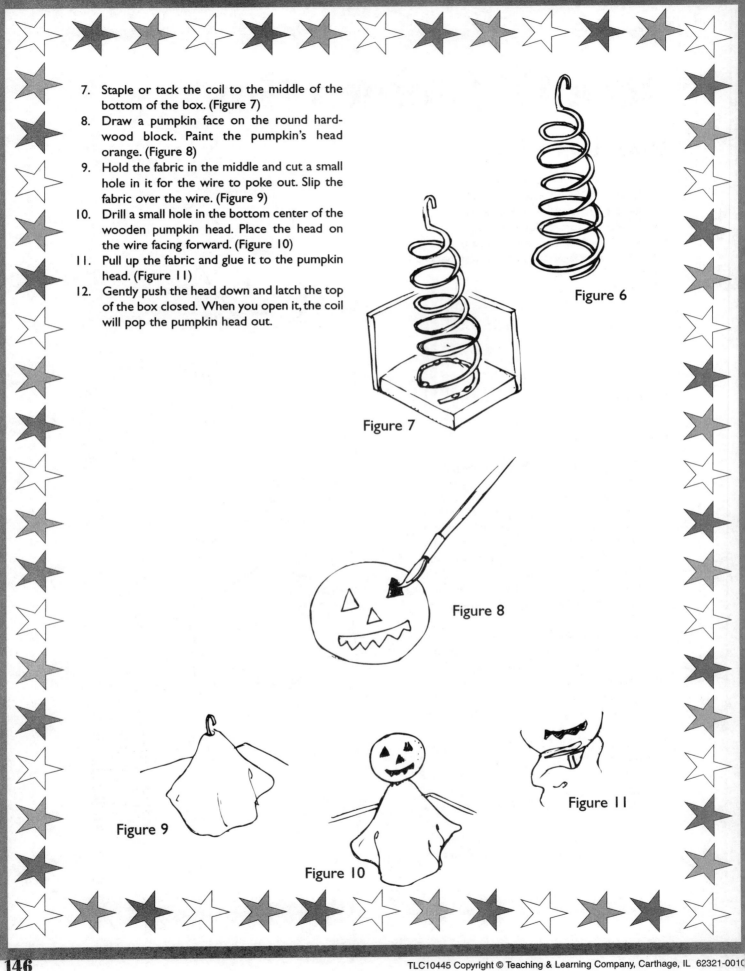

Figure 6

Figure 7

Figure 8

Figure 9

Figure 10

Figure 11

Sleepy Hollow Box Designs

Fun Facts

Blue Berry: Blueberry (Vaccinium)

Red Berry: Strawberry (Fragaria)

Bird: Cardinal (Cardinalis cardinalis)

Dog: Plott Hound

Fish: Channel Bass

Flower: Flowering Dogwood (Cornus florida)

Wildflower: Carolina Lily (Lilium michauxii)

Fruit: Scuppernong Grape (Vitis rotundifloria)

Gem: Emerald

Insect: Honeybee (Apis mellifera)

Mammal: Gray Squirrel (Sciurus carolinensis)

Motto: "Esse Quam Videri" (To be, rather than to seem)

Nicknames: Old North State, Tar Heel State

Reptile: Eastern Box Turtle (Terrapene carolina)

Rock: Granite

Shell: Scotch Bonnet (Phalium granulatum)

Song: "The Old North State" by William Gaston

Tree: Longleaf Pine (Pinus palustris)

Vegetable: Sweet Potato

Statehood: November 21, 1789; 12th state admitted to the Union

Population: (2000 estimate) 8,049,313

Area: 53,821 square miles of land and water; 28th largest state

Highest Point: Mt. Mitchell; 6684 feet above sea level

Lowest Point: Atlantic coast; sea level

Capital: Raleigh

Largest City: Charlotte

Major Crops: Poultry and eggs, corn, cotton, tobacco, hay, hogs, cattle, soybeans, peanuts

Major Industry: Tobacco products, furniture manufacturing, paper products, textile goods, chemical products, electrical equipment, machinery, tourism and recreation

North Carolina

Did You Know?

The home of Pepsi-Cola™ is New Bern, North Carolina. In 1898 a pharmacist named Caleb Bradham created a soft drink which he named Pepsi to serve his customers. The drink became so popular he could hardly keep up with all the orders he got for it.

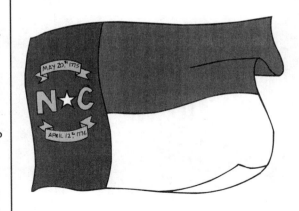

Flag: The rectangular flag of North Carolina is divided into three sections—a blue union, and two horizontal bars of equal length, the upper bar red and the lower bar white. In the middle of the union is a five-point white star, the letter "N" on the left, the letter "C" on the right. Above the star is a gold ribbon containing the date May 20th, 1775, the date of the Mecklenburg Declaration of Independence. Below the star is a gold-colored ribbon containing the date, April 12th, 1776, commemorating the date of the Halifax Resolves.

Name: *Like many U.S. states, North Carolina is named after an English monarch. King Charles I of England gave a large tract of land to Sir Robert Heath in 1619. The land was to be called the province of Carolana.* Carolana *is the Latin word for "Charles." In 1710, King Charles II of England granted land rights to others and divided Carolina into North and South.*

Seal: The circular seal shows two women. Liberty is standing and holding a staff with a liberty cap in one hand and a scroll with the word *Constitution* on it in the other. Seated and looking at the goddess Liberty, is Plenty, holding three heads of grain in one hand and an overflowing cornucopia in the other. The dates May 20, 1775, and April 12, 1776, are above and below the scene respectively. Around the circle are the words: *The Great Seal of the State of North Carolina* and the state motto, "Esse Quam Videri."

The Graveyard of the Atlantic

The coast of North Carolina is notoriously dangerous and rocky. Over 600 shipwrecks pepper the ocean floor and a string of small barrier islands also causes ships to fall prey to craggy rocks. One of the most interesting wrecks found was a sunken German U-boat during World War II, the only Nazi boat to come so close to U.S. shores. It was discovered prowling the coast by U.S. Navy vessels less than 20 miles off the coast of Nags Head. Today it lies 100 feet below the surface of the ocean.

Notable Natives

Romare Bearden (1914-1988), artist, Charlotte

Braxton Bragg (1817-1876), Confederate Civil War general, Warrenton

David Brinkley (1920-2003), television newscaster, television news pioneer, Wilmington

Betsy Cromer Byars (1928-), Newbery Medal-winning children's author, Charlotte

Joseph "Uncle Joe" Gurney Cannon (1836-1926) U.S. Speaker of the House, Guilford County

John William Coltrane (1926-1967), jazz musician, composer, Hamlet

Howard Cosell (1920-1995), sportscaster, Winston-Salem

John Augustine Daly (1838-1899), playwright, Plymouth

Elizabeth Hanford Dole (1936-), U.S. senator, Salisbury

Sam Ervin (1896-1985), U.S. senator, Morgantown

Roberta Flack (1939-), singer, Black Mountain

Ava Gardner (Lucy Johnson) (1922-1990), actress, Smithfield

Richard Gatling (1818-1903), inventor of a rapid-fire revolving gun, Money's Neck

Billy Graham (1918-), evangelist, Charlotte

Andy Griffith (1926-), television actor best known for *The Andy Griffith Show*, Mount Airy

Charles Gwathmey (1938-), architect, Charlotte

Jesse Helms (1921-), politician, U.S. senator, Monroe

Jackee (1956-), actress, Winston-Salem

Andrew Johnson (1808-1875), 17th President (1865-1869), Raleigh

Charles Kuralt (1934-1997), television journalist, Wilmington

Dolley Payne Madison (1768-1849), First Lady, Guilford County

Leonidas Polk (1806-1864), Confederate Civil War general, Raleigh

Ronnie Milsap (1933-), country singer, Robbinsville

Thelonious Monk (1917-1982), jazz pianist, Rocky Mount

Julianne Moore (1960-), actress, Fort Bragg

Edward R. Murrow (Egbert Roscoe Murrow) (1908-1965), Emmy-winning journalist, Pole Creek

Richard Petty (1937-), seven-time NASCAR champion auto racer, Level Cross

James Knox Polk (1795-1849), 11th President (1845-1849), Mecklenburg County

William Sydney Porter (O. Henry) (1862-1910), short story writer, Greensboro

Soupy Sales (1926-), comedian, Franklinton

Earl Eugene Scruggs (1924-), bluegrass musician, Flint Hill

Randy Travis (1959-), country singer, musician, Marshville

Ship in a Bottle

This project requires heat.

Materials

* clear bottle with cork (contents removed and cleaned out)
* plastic Shrink Art™ (found in craft stores)
* scissors
* black fine-point permanent marker
* permanent markers (fine or medium point)
* oven
* cookie sheets
* aluminum foil
* silicone adhesive
* drafting tape
* metal clothes hanger
* wire cutters

Figure 1

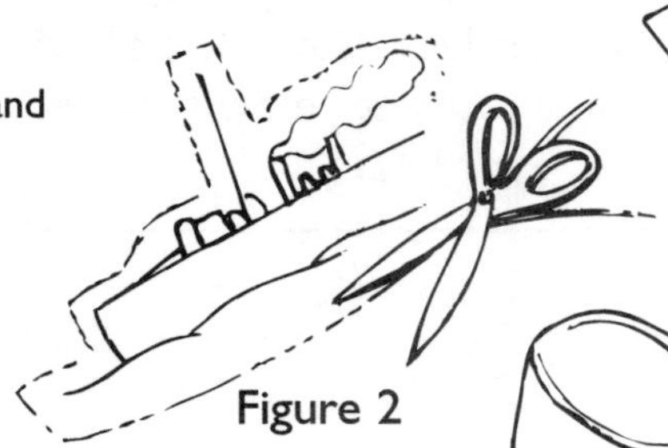

Figure 2

Figure 3

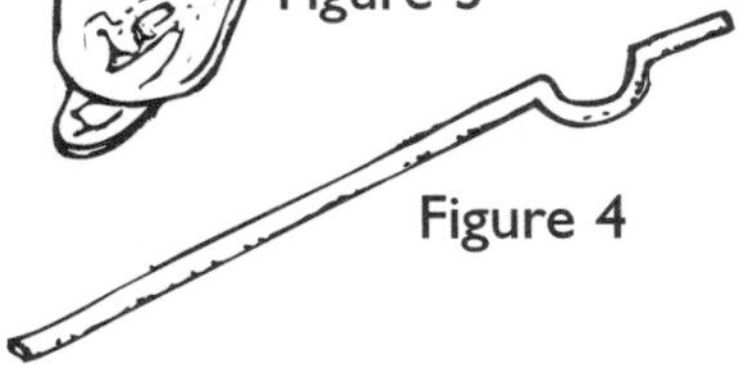

Figure 4

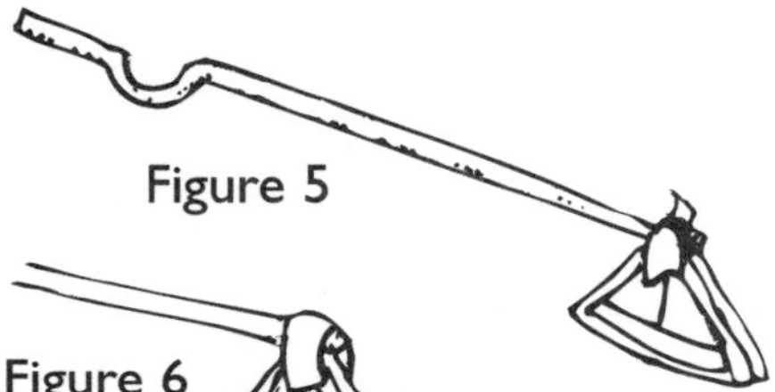

Figure 5

Figure 6

Figure 7

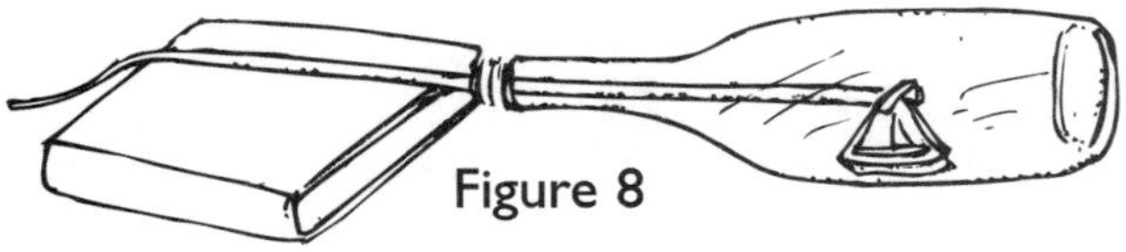

Instructions

1. Choose a ship design on page 151 and copy it. You may want to create an Armada of various ships to represent the variety of ships still resting on the coast of North Carolina.
2. Lay a clear plastic Shrink Art™ sheet on the ship designs and copy the lines carefully with a fine-point black permanent marker. (Figure 1)
3. Cut the ship design from the Shrink Art™ leaving a 1/8" border. Handle by the edges only. (Figure 2)
4. Preheat the oven and follow directions on the Shrink Art™ package.
5. Once the Shrink Art™ has properly melted and shrunk, quickly remove it from the oven and place a glass on it. Press down and hold for a moment to keep the image from curling. (Figure 3)
6. Cut the clothes hanger with wire cutters to make a pointer. (Figure 4)
7. Lightly tape the plastic ship on the top edge of the pointer. (Figure 5)
8. Add silicone adhesive in pea-size shapes to the bottom of the ship. (Figure 6)
9. Slip the ship through the bottle mouth and set it upright in the middle of the bottle. (Figure 7)
10. Keep your hand still once you have placed the ship upright in the bottle. Brace the pointer with something so it does not move until the adhesive dries. (Figure 8)
11. When it is dry, flick the pointer and tape off the ship and pull the pointer out. Seal the bottle with the cork. (Figure 9)

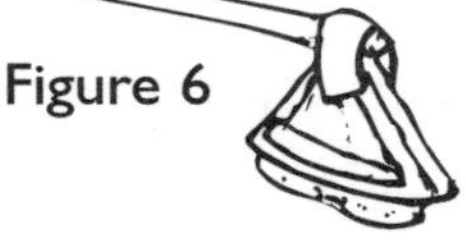

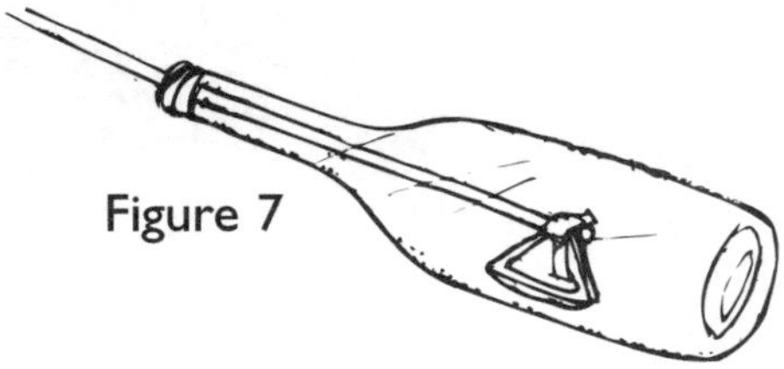

Figure 8

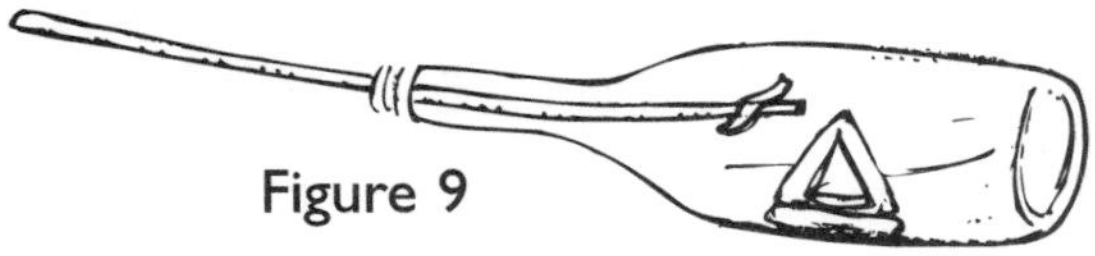

Figure 9

Ship Designs of Wreckages Found on North Carolina Coast

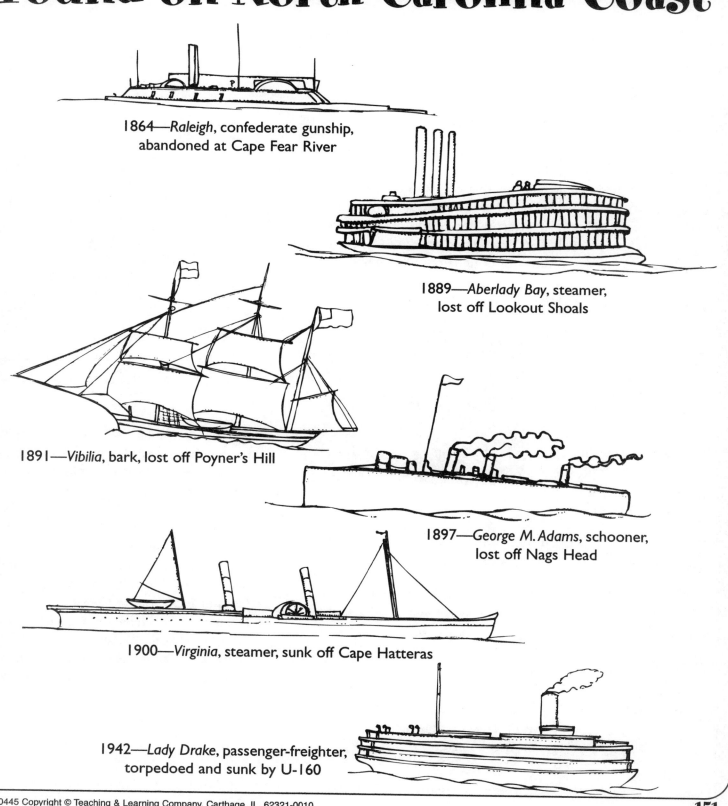

1864—*Raleigh*, confederate gunship,
abandoned at Cape Fear River

1889—*Aberlady Bay*, steamer,
lost off Lookout Shoals

1891—*Vibilia*, bark, lost off Poyner's Hill

1897—*George M. Adams*, schooner,
lost off Nags Head

1900—*Virginia*, steamer, sunk off Cape Hatteras

1942—*Lady Drake*, passenger-freighter,
torpedoed and sunk by U-160

Fun Facts

Bird: Western Meadowlark (Sturnella neglecta)

Equine: Nokota Horse

Fish: Northern Pike (Esox lucius)

Flower: Wild Prairie Rose, (Rosa blanda or Rosa arkansana)

Fossil: Teredo Petrified Wood

Grass: Western Wheatgrass (Agropyron smithii)

Motto: "Liberty and Union, Now and Forever, One and Inseparable"

Nicknames: Peace Garden State, Flickertail State

Song: "North Dakota Hymn" by James W. Foley

Tree: American Elm (Ulmus americana)

Statehood: November 2, 1889; 39th state admitted to the Union

Population: (2000 estimate) 642,200

Area: 70,704 square miles of land and water; 19th largest state in the Union

Highest Point: White Butte; 3506 feet above sea level

Lowest Point: Red River; 750 feet above sea level

Capital: Bismarck

Largest City: Fargo

Major Crops: Wheat, flaxseed, beans, cattle, hogs, sheep, barley, sunflowers, milk, honey, sugar beets

Major Industry: Food processing; quarry production—sand, gravel, clay; machinery; mining; oil and natural gas; tourism

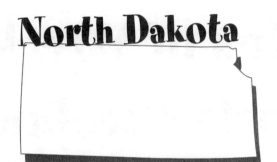

North Dakota

Name: Like many U.S. states, North Dakota takes its name from a Native American word. Dakota is a Sioux word which means "ally" or "friend." North comes from the fact that of the two states named Dakota, North Dakota is farthest north.

Did You Know?

In a nod to the dairy industry in North Dakota, the state legislature designated milk as the official state drink in 1983. While North Dakota is not the biggest milk producer of the 50 states, its nearly 40,000 cows do produce hundreds of millions of pounds of milk each year.

Flag: On a field of dark blue is an American eagle with its wings spread, holding an olive branch and a bundle of arrows in its talons. The words *One nation made up of many states* are inscribed on a ribbon the eagle holds in its beak. The shield on the eagle's breast has 13 red and white stripes, representing the original states. The fan design above the eagle represents the birth of the nation. The name *North Dakota* appears on a red scroll below the eagle.

Seal: The circular seal shows a tree in an open field surrounded by three bundles of wheat; on the right a plow, anvil and sledge; on the left a bow crossed with three arrows and a Native American on horseback pursuing a buffalo toward the setting sun. Above the tree is a half circle of 42 stars, with the motto above them, a quote from Daniel Webster: "Liberty and Union Now and Forever, One and Inseparable." The words *Great Seal* and *State of North Dakota* and the dates *October 1st* and *1889* surround the seal. October 1, 1889, is the date the state's constitution was approved.

Sacagawea and Baby Pomp's Cradleboard

A young Shoshone woman, Sacagawea, who guided Lewis and Clark and their Corps of Discovery to the Pacific and back, is celebrated as a heroine today. At age 12 she was captured by Hidatsa warriors and taken to what we now call North Dakota. She lived with the Hidatsa until she was sold or gambled away to the French Canadian trapper, Toussaint Charbonneau. She was 16 years old when she first met Lewis and Clark in 1804. Without her skills and abilities, the Corps might not have survived. Sacagawea translated for Lewis and Clark with local Native Americans, helped them acquire horses for their journey, dug roots and other foods for the starving party in winter, showed the men how to make leather clothes to replace their rotting fabrics and taught them how to make moccasins to save their feet from painful prickly pear needles on the prairie floor. When the party's canoe capsized in a river, Sacagawea helped save some of the important documents we still refer to today.

The explorers considered Sacagawea a good and gentle spirit. She traveled 4356 miles on foot, carrying a cradleboard with an infant on her back!

Notable Natives

Warren Minor Christopher (1925-), diplomat, Scranton

Angie Dickinson (1931-), actress, Kulm

William Gass (1924-), novelist, Fargo

Louis L'Amour (Louis Dearborn LaMoore) (1908-1988), writer, Jamestown

Peggy Lee (1920-2002), singer, Jamestown

Eric Sevareid (1912-1992), television journalist, commentator, Velva

Ann Sothern (1909-2001), actress, Valley City

Lawrence Welk (1903-1992), band leader, television variety show host, Strasburg

North Dakota

Baby Pomp's Cradleboard

Materials

* 2 pieces of 19" x 30" corrugated cardboard
* utility knife
* spray glue
* white glue
* 3 pieces of 36" x 42" faux leather fabric or tan-colored cloth
* ribbon
* acrylic paints
* awl
* leather string or thick tan-colored string
* blue chalk
* straight pins
* newspapers
* needle and thread

Instructions

1. Lay one piece of cardboard on top of the other and glue them together. Let dry. (Figure 1)
2. Looking at the cradleboard pattern on page 156, cut out a similar shape from the cardboard, large at the top tapering down to the bottom. (Figure 2)
3. Lay newspaper down on your work space and place the fabric on it. Place the cradleboard shape on the fabric. Draw around the cradleboard shape with blue chalk. Allow an extra inch for a border. Cut two pieces of cloth to fit the front and back sides. (Figure 3)
4. Spray-glue the top of the cardboard cradleboard shape and lay the cloth carefully on it. Smooth out any wrinkles. (Figure 4)
5. For the shoulder straps, use strips of cloth 4" wide and 36" to 42" long. Fold the strips lengthwise and sew the edges. (Figure 5)
6. Carefully pull the cloth inside out to hide the sewn seam and hem the ends. (Figure 6)
7. Flip the cradleboard over and lay one shoulder strap 6" down the back, with equal amounts at the top and bottom. Staple and glue it along the 6". (Figure 7)

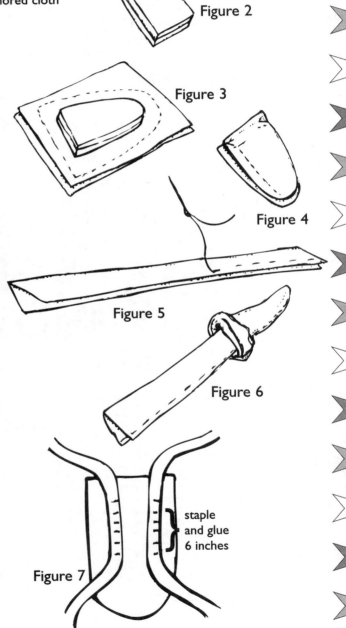

Figure 1

Figure 2

Figure 3

Figure 4

Figure 5

Figure 6

Figure 7

staple and glue 6 inches

8. Glue and staple the other strap to the board the same way.

9. Carefully align fabric on top of the cradleboard. Cut four vertical slits on the cloth top and bottom for the shoulder straps to slip through.

10. Pull the straps through the fabric slits.

11. Carefully spray-glue the back of the cradleboard cloth and press it down in position.

12. Use the third piece of fabric for the baby pouch. Cut a fabric triangle to cover the middle and bottom of the cradleboard. Staple the edges to the side. (Figures 8a and 8b)

13. Shove newspaper inside the baby pouch and mark a series of holes in a "V" shape down the middle of the pouch as shown. Use an awl to punch holes in the fabric for lacing. Lace string through the holes. (Figures 9a and 9b)

14. Glue and staple down all the edges of the fabric on the cradleboard. Trim any pieces that hang over the side.

15. Cut cloth into 2" wide strips. Glue them to the edges of the cradleboard in a fringe. Paint the edges with your favorite colors to represent beading. (Figure 10)

16. Place a small doll in the cradleboard.

17. Tie the cradleboard to your back.

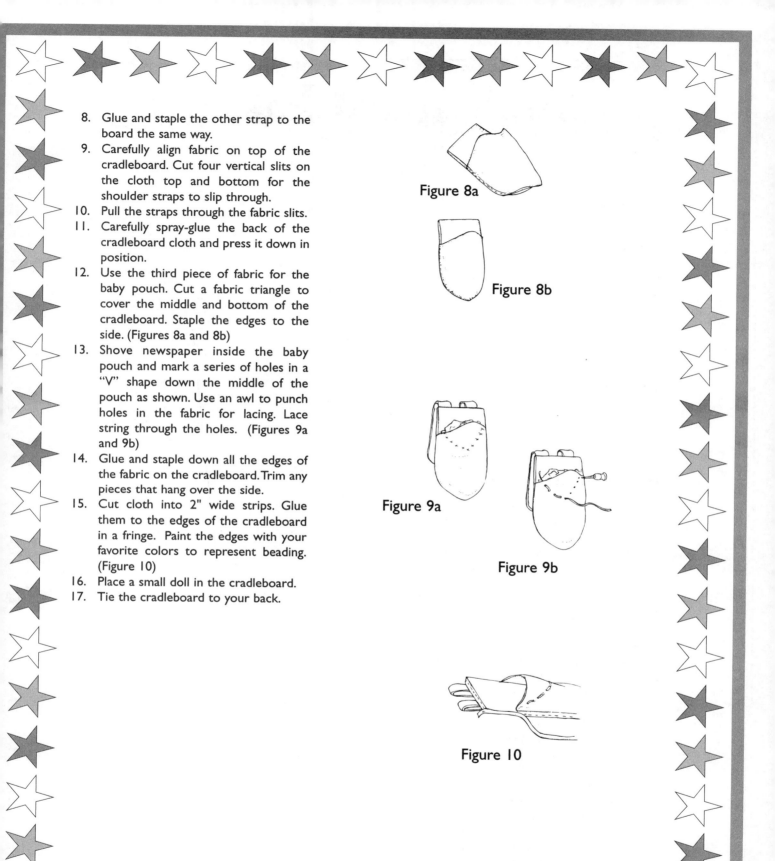

Figure 8a

Figure 8b

Figure 9a

Figure 9b

Figure 10

Name _____

Cradleboard Pattern

[An]imal: White-Tailed Deer
(Odocoileus virginianus)

[Bir]d: Cardinal
(Cardinalis cardinalis)

[Flo]wer: Scarlet Carnation
(Dianthus caryophyllus)

[Wi]ldflower: White Trillium
(Trillium grandiflorum)

[Fos]sil: Trilobite

[Ge]m: Flint

[Ins]ect: Ladybug
(Coccinella novemnotata)

[Mo]tto: "With God, all things
[ar]e possible"

[Nic]kname: Buckeye State

[Rep]tile: Black Racer Snake
(Coluber constrictor
constrictor)

[Son]g: "Beautiful Ohio" by
[B]allard MacDonald

[Tre]e: Ohio Buckeye
(Aesculus globra)

[Sta]tehood: March 1, 1803;
[17]th state admitted to the
[U]nion

[Pop]ulation: (2000 estimate)
[11],353,140

[Are]a: 44,828 square miles of
[la]nd and water; 34th largest
[sta]te

[High]est Point: Campbell
[Hi]ll; 1550 feet above sea
[le]vel

[Low]est Point: Ohio River;
[43]3 feet above sea level

[Cap]ital: Columbus

[Larg]est City: Columbus

[Maj]or Crops: Soybeans,
[wh]eat, dairy products, corn,
[oa]ts, tomatoes, hogs, cattle,
[po]ultry, eggs, apples, grapes,
[pe]aches, strawberries

[Maj]or Industry:
[Tra]nsportation equipment
[an]d car part production,
[rub]ber production, jet
[en]gines, fabricated metal
[pro]ducts, glass production,
[ma]chinery, food processing,
[ele]ctrical equipment,
[tou]rism

Ohio

Name: Ohio's name comes from a Native American Iroquois word that was used to describe the river that forms most of the state's eastern and entire southern border. Ohio means "good" or "fine river."

Did You Know?

Many inventions don't seem like inventions at all—more like innovations. Take the "pop top" for instance. Ermal Fraze of Kettering, Ohio, invented the pop top for the Schlitz Brewing Company, which changed forever the way drinks were canned and sold.

Seal: The circular state seal displays a scene with a rising sun behind a mountain range. Beneath the mountains is a river with a broad plain and two shocks of wheat in the foreground. The words, *The Great Seal of the State of Ohio,* surround the scene.

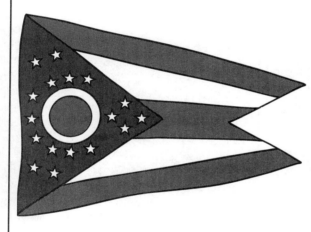

Flag: The state flag has a swallowtail design called a burgee. The blue triangle is symbolic of the hills and valleys of Ohio, the stripes of the roads and waterways. The "O" symbolizes Ohio and the buckeye for which the state received its nickname. The 13 five-point stars clustered around the "O" represent the original states, while the four stars in the peak of the triangle represent the four states that joined the Union after the first 13. Ohio was the 17th.

Johnny Appleseed

John Chapman was born in 1774, in Massachusetts. According to tradition, when he was 18 he persuaded his half brother Nathaniel to go west with him. After a few years of moving around they found a place to call home in Ohio. The land was fertile and farming was good compared to the New England soil they had left behind.

In 1800, John made his way to Licking County, Ohio. At that time, the U.S. Congress was offering land grants to new settlers, 160 to 2240 acres. John decided to plant apple nurseries before the new settlers arrived. For the next half century, John Chapman (Johnny Appleseed) moved ahead of the flood of immigration planting apple trees.

The Way He Lived

If Johnny Appleseed needed to stay for any length of time at one of his nurseries, he would build a hut made of poles with a bark roof. His needs were very simple. He owned only a kettle, a plate and a spoon, and slept on a bed of leaves. He insisted that no man or animal would hurt him as long as he lived by the law of love your neighbor. A wolf he saved from a trap adopted Johnny and followed him wherever he went. Johnny made friends with local Indian tribes and learned to speak their languages. Believing he was touched by the Great Spirit, they allowed him to listen during their council meetings.

Frontiersmen from all over came to meet him and purchase his apple trees. He was an honest businessman and asked fair prices. Sometimes he traded with people who could not afford to pay him— a cast off garment, a pot or pan, or some food was all he took. He even gave some seed-lings away. He appeared to be poor, but he had money hidden under rocks and in holes, which he spent sparingly.

In 1842, more than 40 years after he began his journey, Johnny found his way back to Licking County, Ohio. Living in harmony with nature and man, Johnny's religious views were simple but profound. He gave more than he took and was loved and respected by all. Like a living monument, his apple trees still bear fruit today.

Celebrate Johnny Appleseed's birthday on September 26th or during National Apple Month in October.

Ohio

Notable Natives

Neil Alden Armstrong (1930-), first person to walk on the moon, Wapakoneta

Halle Berry (1966-), Oscar-winning actress, Cleveland

Drew Carey (1958-), comedian, actor, Cleveland

Nancy Cartwright (1959-), voice of Bart Simpson, Kettering

Tracy Chapman (1964-), singer, Cleveland

George Armstrong Custer (1839-1876), general, New Rumley

Charles Dawes (1865-1951) U.S. Vice President, Nobel Prize winner, Marietta

Doris Day (Doris Kappelhoff) (1924-), singer, actress, Cincinnati

Clarence Seward Darrow (1857-1938), lawyer, Kinsman

Phyllis Diller (1917-), comedienne, Lima

Phil Donahue (1935-), television talk show host, Cleveland

Hugh Downs (1921-), television broadcaster, Akron

Thomas Alva Edison (1847-1931), world's most prolific inventor, Milan

Carmen Electra (Tara Patrick) (1973-), actress, model, Cincinnati

Jamie Farr (1934-), actor, Toledo

Clark Gable (1901-1960), actor, Cadiz

James Abram Garfield (1831-1881), 20th President (1881), Orange

Lillian Gish (Lillian de Guiche) (1893-1993), actress, Springfield

John Herschel Glenn (1921-), astronaut, U.S. senator, Cambridge

Ulysses Simpson Grant (1822-1885), 18th President (1869-1877), Point Pleasant

Zane Grey (1875-1939), Western novelist, Zaneville

Arsenio Hall (1955-), television talk show host, Cleveland

Rutherford Birchard Hayes (1822-1893), 19th President (1877-1881), Delaware

Patricia Heaton (1958-), actress, Bay Village

Warren Gamaliel Harding (1865-1923), 29th President (1921-1923), near Corsica

Benjamin Harrison (1833-1901), 23rd President (1889-1893), North Bend

Carol Kane (1952-), comedic actress, Cleveland

Charles F. Kettering (1876-1958), engineer, inventor, Loundonville

Kennesaw Mountain Landis (1866-1944), first commissioner of baseball, Millville

Maya Ying Lin (1959-), architect of the Vietnam Veterans Memorial, Athens

Dean Martin (Dino Paul Crocetti) (1917-1995), actor, singer, Steubenville

Maureen McGovern (1949-), singer, Youngstown

William McKinley (1843-1901), 25th President (1897-1901), Nile

Toni Morrison (1931-), Nobel Prize winning writer, Lorain

Paul Newman (1925-), actor, Cleveland

Jack Nicklaus (1940-), six-time Masters-winning golfer, Columbu

Annie Oakley (Phoebe Anne Oakley Moses) (1860-1926), sharpshoot near Woodland

Sarah Jessica Parker (1965-), actre Nelsonville

Luke Perry (1966-), actor, Fredericktown

Tyrone Power (1913-1958), actor, Cincinnati

Eddie Rickenbacker (1890-1973), Congressional Medal of Honor WWI aviator, Columbus

Boz Scaggs (1944-), singer, Canto

Arthur M. Schlesinger, Jr. (1917-), Pulitzer Prize-winning historian, Columbus

Martin Sheen (1940-), actor, Dayt

William Tecumseh Sherman (1820-1891), Civil War Army general, Lancaster

Steven Spielberg (1946-), Oscar-winning film director, Cincinnat

Gloria Steinem (1934-), feminist, writer, Toledo

William Howard Taft (1857-1930), 27th President (1909-1913), Cincinnati

Tecumseh (1768-1813), Shawnee chief, Old Piqua

James Thurber (1894-1961), short story writer, cartoonist, Colum

Ted Turner (1938-), broadcaster, founder of CNN, Cincinnati

Debra Winger (1955-), actress, Cleveland

Orville Wright (1871-1948), co-inve tor of the airplane, Dayton

Cy Young (Denton True Young) (186 1955), famed baseball pitcher, Gilmore

Apple Dolls

Materials

* 1 Golden Delicious apple
* apple peeler
* plastic knife
* lemon juice
* thick thread and carpet needle
* cotton fabric or pillowcase
* 24" long and 10" long wire
* clay
* fabric
* straw or old cloth

Instructions

1. Peel the apple, leaving only the skin around the stem. (Figure 1)
2. Shape a face in the apple with a knife, cutting indentations for eyes, cheeks and nose. (Figure 2)
3. Dunk the apple in lemon juice to keep it from browning. (Figure 3)
4. String the apple on thread, using the carpet needle to poke the thread through it. Store the apple in a dry, warm place. (Figure 4)
5. If you have several apples drying on a long string, keep them from touching. Drying the apples will take a few weeks depending on room temperature. If the room is moist, drying time will be longer. Keep the apples away from heat as they are drying. (Figure 5)
6. As the apple dries, occasionally pinch it to make a more defined nose, cheek, etc. (Figure 6) (Optional: Dry the apple head in an oven set on low for 24 hours.)
7. Fold the 24" wire. Twist it approximately 6" from the top. (Figure 7)
8. Make arms out of the 10" length of wire. Twist it around the body several times to secure it. (Figure 8)
9. Form simple hands on the wire arms out of clay. (Figure 8)
10. Use fabric or a pillowcase to make clothing as elaborate or simple as you want. (Figure 9) Use the patterns on page 160.
11. Stuff the body with straw or old cloth.

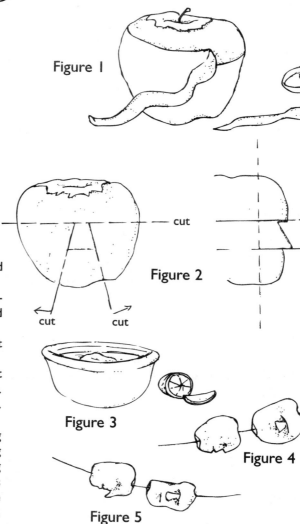

Figure 1

Figure 2

Figure 3

Figure 4

Figure 5

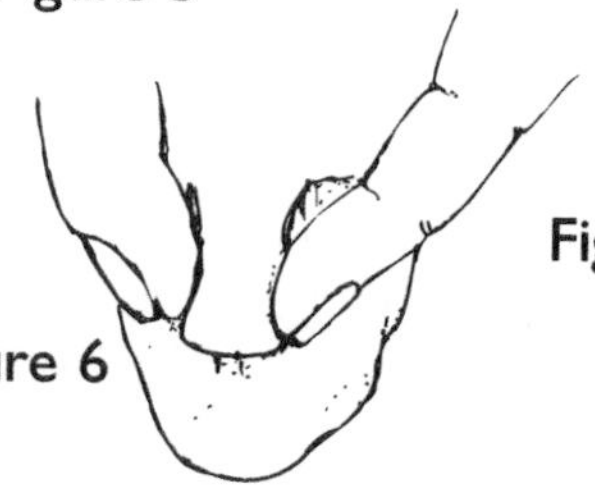

Figure 6

Figure 7

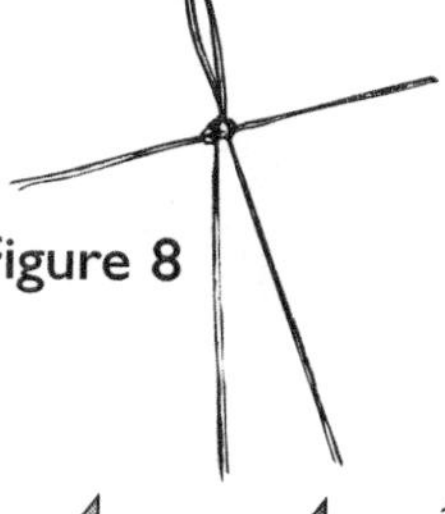

Figure 8

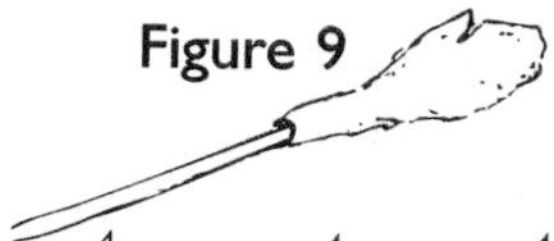

Figure 9

159

Name _____

Apple Doll Clothing

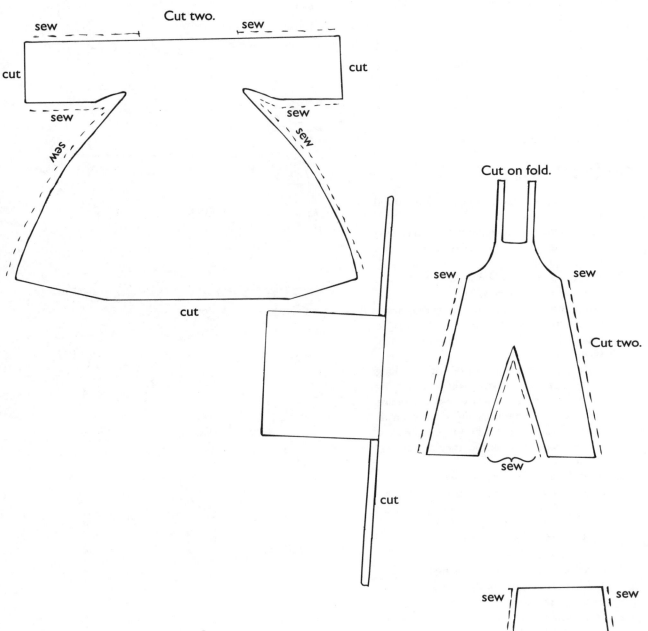

Cut two.
sew   sew
cut   cut
sew
sew   sew
sew
cut

Cut on fold.
sew   sew
Cut two.
sew

cut

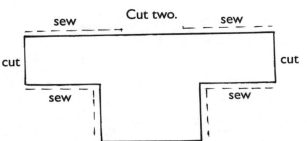

Cut two.
sew   sew
cut   cut
sew   sew

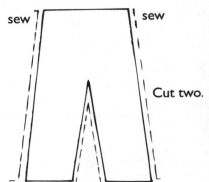

sew   sew
Cut two.

Fun Facts

Amphibian: Bell Frog (Rana catesbeiana)

Animal: American Buffalo or Bison (Bison bison)

Game Animal: White-Tailed Deer (Odocoileus virginianus)

Bird: Scissor-Tailed Flycatcher (Muscivora forficata)

Butterfly: Black Swallowtail (Papilio polyxenes)

Game Bird: Wild Turkey (Meleagris gallopavo)

Fish: White or Sand Bass (Morone chrysops)

Flower: Mistletoe (Phoradendron serotinum)

Fossil: Very Large Predatory Dinosaur (Saurophaganax maximus)

Furbearer: Raccoon (Procyon lotor)

Wildflower: Indian Blanket (Gaillardia pulchella)

Grass: Indiangrass (Sorghastrum nutans)

Insect: Honeybee (Apis mellifera)

Motto: "Labor omnia vincit" (Labor conquers all things)

Nickname: Sooner State

Reptile: Collared Lizard or Mountain Boomer (Crotaphytus collaris)

Rock: Barite Rose

Song: "Oklahoma!" by Oscar Hammerstein II

Tree: Redbud (Cercis canadensis)

Statehood: November 16, 1907; 46th state admitted to the Union

Population: (2000 estimate) 3,450,654

Area: 69,903 square miles of land and water; 20th largest state

Highest Point: Black Mesa; 4,973 feet above sea level

Lowest Point: Little River; 287 feet above sea level

Capital: Oklahoma City

Largest City: Oklahoma City

Major Crops: Cattle, hogs, sorghum, hay, wheat, milk, poultry, cotton, peanuts

Major Industry: Oil refining; natural gas production; transportation equipment; machinery; electrical products; rubber and plastic products; food processing; meat packing; mining—zinc, coal, copper, silver; tourism

Name: *Oklahoma was named by a Native American. The name of the territory was first proposed by Reverend Allen Wright, a Choctaw preacher. He suggested the name* Oklahoma, *a Choctaw word meaning "red man."*

Did You Know?

The world's very first parking meter was installed on an Oklahoma City street on July 16, 1935, much to the displeasure of people driving cars. Carlton Cole Magee invented the parking meter in Oklahoma to cut down on parking congestion. Today, the parking meter is also an important source of revenue for many large cities.

Flag: The flag is colored sky blue and pays homage to many Native American tribes in the United States. In the center of the flag is an Osage warrior battle shield of tan buckskin with small white crosses on it, used by Indians to depict stars. Seven feathers hang from the edge of the shield. Two symbols of peace, an olive branch and a peace pipe or calumet, cross over each other. Under the shield in bold white letters is the word *Oklahoma*.

Seal: The circular seal is dominated by a large five-point star. In the center of the star is a wreath with figures from the seal of the territory of Oklahoma. In each of the five points of the star is a symbol representing a Native American tribe:

* Chickasaw—a warrior holding a bow and shield

* Cherokee—a wreath of oak leaves

* Choctaw—a tomahawk, a bow and three crossed arrows

* Creek—a sheaf of wheat and a plow

* Seminole—a hunter paddling a canoe

The large star is surrounded by 45 small five-point stars, representing the 45 states that made up the Union when Oklahoma became a state.

Trail of Tears

The Trail of Tears is a historically significant event in American history. The term refers to the forced removal of over 90 thousand Native Americans from their homelands to Indian territory now known as Oklahoma. It was the result of the Indian Removal Act of 1830, an attempt to confine the Cheyenne, Cherokee, Choctaw, Chickasaw, Creek, Delaware, Fox, Ottawa, Pawnee, Potawatomi, Sawk, Shawnee and Seminole tribes together in one location. Most of the Native Americans were driven from their homes at gunpoint and forced to walk as many as 2000 miles. Others were corralled into railroad cars with no food or water. The trips were great hardships for all, especially the elderly, weak and sick. Some died from the cold and starvation. By the end of the removal, many Native Americans had died along the way.

The Parflech Bags & Ledger Art

The parflech bag is an article attributed to the various Native American tribes across the plains. Made of buffalo hide, parflech bags carried food, tobacco and other supplies.

Pictographs were Native American art forms now known as ledger art. Initially, pictographs were made on buffalo hide or canvas teepees, shields and clothing. When Native Americans were given pads of ledger paper to draw on, a new medium of expression began. Both ledger art and the original pictographs portray Native American life.

Notable Natives

Carl Bert Albert (1908-2000), U.S. Speaker of the House, McAlester

Chet Baker (1929-1988), jazz trumpet player, Yale

Johnny Bench (1947-), baseball player, Oklahoma City

Garth Brooks (1962-), country singer, Tulsa

Don Cherry (1936-1995), jazz trumpet player, Oklahoma City

Blake Edwards (1922-), film director, Tulsa

Ralph Ellison (1914-1994), writer, Oklahoma City

John Hope Franklin (1915-), historian, Rentiesville

James Garner (1928-), actor, Norman

Vince Gill (1957-), country singer, Norman

Woodrow "Woody" Wilson Guthrie (1912-1967), folksinger, Okemah

Roy Ellsworth Harris (1898-1979), composer, Lincoln County

Paul Harvey (1918-), radio broadcaster, Tulsa

Rosella Hightower (1920-), dancer, choreographer, Ardmore

Anita Hill (1956-), attorney, professor, Morris

Ron Howard (1954-), actor, film director, Duncan

Jeane Kirkpatrick (1926-), diplomat, former ambassador to the U.N., Duncan

Mickey Charles Mantle (1931-1995), baseball player, Spavinaw

Rue McClanahan (1934-) actress, Healdton

Reba McEntire (1955-), country singer, actress, McAlester

Shannon Miller (1977-) Olympic gymnast, Edmond

Bill Moyers (1934-), public television journalist, Hugo

Daniel Patrick Moynihan (1927-2003), U.S. senator, Tulsa

Chuck Norris (1946-), actor, Ryan

Brad Pitt (1963-), actor, Shawnee

Tony Randall (1920-2004) Emmy-winning actor, Tulsa

Oral Roberts (1918-), evangelist, near Ada

Will Rogers (1879-1935) humorist, Oolagah

Dan Rowan (1922-1987) comedian, Beggs

Ted Shackelford (1946- actor, Oklahoma City)

Maria Tallchief (1925-), ballerina, Fairfax

James "Jim" Francis Thorp (1887-1953), Olympic medal-winning athlete, Prague

Alfre Woodard (1953-), actress, Tulsa

Parflech Bag & Ledger Art

Materials for the Parflech Bag

* large brown grocery bag
* water
* scissors
* tempera paints: blue, red, white, green, yellow, black
* ruler
* brushes
* shoelace or leather string
* hole punch
* pencil

Materials for the Ledger Art

* yellow ledger paper pad
* pencil
* colored pencils

Instructions

Making the Parflech Bag

1. Cut a grocery bag down its seam and bottom. Soak it in water, then crumple the bag to squeeze the water out. Lay it on the floor to dry.
2. Fold the bag 2" vertically on both edges. (Figure 1)
3. Fold it into three equal parts horizontally. (Figure 2)
4. Keep the bag folded as you draw the geometric parflech design on it. Use the pattern on page 164. (Figure 3)
5. Reopen the bag and paint it. Let it dry. (Figure 4)
6. Punch a hole in the top flap and insert the leather string. Knot both ends. (Figure 5)
7. Wrap the leather string around the parflech bag. Tie the two ends together to secure them in place. (Figure 6)

Making the Ledger Art

8. Copying ledger art designs on page 165, draw your own Native American stories. (Write a story of life as a warrior or create several narratives on many sheets of ledger paper.) Use your imagination to create other images not shown.
9. Fold the ledger art and place it in the parflech bag.

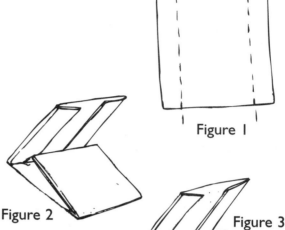

fold

Figure 1

Figure 2

Figure 3

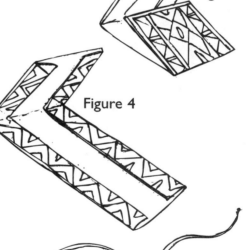

Figure 4

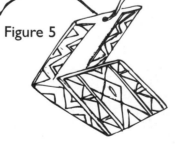

Figure 5

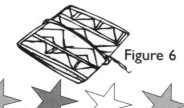

Figure 6

Parflech Design

Ledger Art Designs

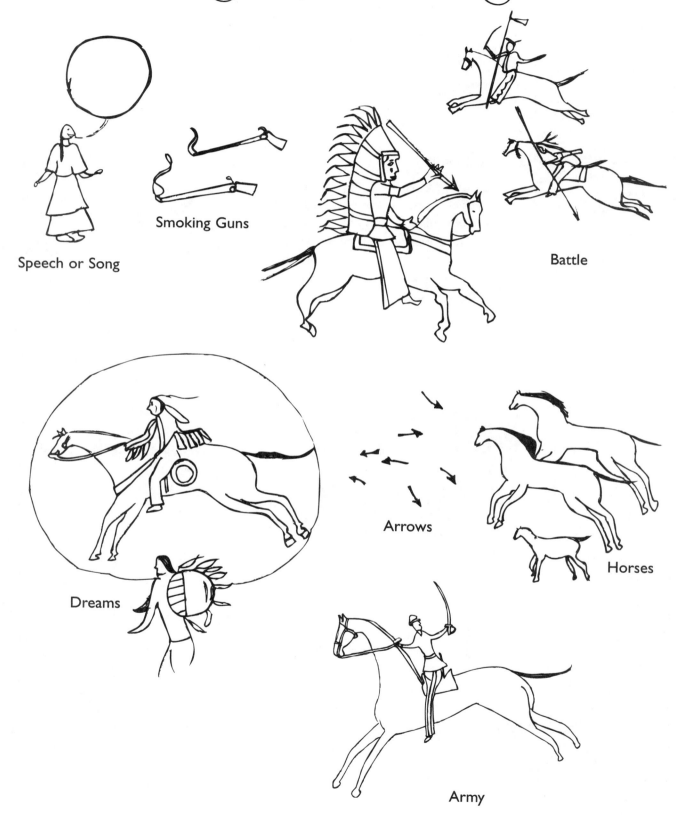

Speech or Song

Smoking Guns

Battle

Dreams

Arrows

Horses

Army

Fun Facts

Animal: American Beaver (Castor canadensis)

Bird: Western Meadowlark (Sturnella neglecta)

Fish: Giant King Salmon also called Chinook Salmon (Oncorhynchus tshawytscha)

Flower: Orange Grape (Mahonia aquifolium, AKA Berberis aquifolium)

Gem: Oregon Sunstone

Insect: Oregon Swallowtail (Papilio oregonius)

Motto: "Alis Volat Propiis" (She Flies with Her Own Wings)

Mushroom: Pacific Golden Chanterelle (Cantharellus formosus)

Nickname: Beaver State

Nut: Hazelnut (Corylus avellana)

Rock: Thunder-Egg (Geode)

Shell: Oregon Hairy Triton (Fusitriton oregonensis)

Song: "Oregon, My Oregon" by J.A. Buchanan

Tree: Douglas Fir (Pseudotsuga menziesii)

Statehood: February 14, 1859; 33rd state admitted to the Union

Population: (2000 estimate) 3,421,399

Area: 98,386 square miles of land and water; 9th largest state

Highest Point: Mount Hood; 11,239 feet above sea level

Lowest Point: Pacific coast; sea level

Capital: Salem

Largest City: Portland

Major Crops: Cattle; salmon fishing; vegetables; fruits—boysenberries, black and red raspberries, prunes; hazelnuts; dairy products; wheat; hops

Major Industry: Lumber and wood products, paper production and manufacturing, tourism, food processing, machinery, scientific instruments

Oregon

Name: *No one is quite sure of the origin of Oregon's name. Some suggest that the word is derived from a French map published in 1715 showing the Wisconsin River as "Quaricon-sint." Others say the first written record of the state name was from Major Robert Rogers in 1765, when proposing a journey. He spelled the name of the area as "Ouragon." It wasn't until 1778, when Captain Jonathan Carver published a book about his travels in North America that the current spelling, Oregon was used.*

Did You Know?

The flag of Oregon is the only one of the 50 state flags that has a different image on each side. One side displays the state seal; the other, has a beaver in the center on the field of navy blue. The beaver is the state animal and gives the state its nickname, the Beaver State.

Flag: On the front of the navy blue flag, is the state seal. Over the seal in gold letters are the words *State of Oregon.* Below the shield in gold letters is the year *1859.* The reverse side of the flag has a beaver in the center of the field of navy blue.

Seal: The circular seal is dominated by a shield surrounded by 33 five-point stars signifying Oregon's entry into the Union as the 33rd state. On the shield is a scene with a departing English war ship and an arriving American merchant ship next to a setting sun on the Pacific Ocean. It represents the declining influence of the British and the rising influence of the Americans. Below that is a wagon pulled by a team of oxen, coming out of an Oregon forest of pine trees. Under the team is a ribbon bearing the words *The Union.* Underneath the ribbon is a plow, a pickaxe and a sheaf of wheat which symbolize agriculture, mining and farming. Above the shield is an American eagle with its wings spread. On the outside of the seal are the words *State of Oregon* and the year Oregon became a state, *1859.*

Oregon Trail

Only the bravest pioneers faced the Oregon Trail in covered wagons. Before the 2000-mile trek began, early immigrants congregated at "jumping off" places such as St. Louis, Omaha and Independence to purchase supplies and hook up with other travelers going to the same locations. They waited for winter ice to thaw and spring grass to grow. Grass had to be high enough so their animals—mules, oxen and horses—could graze along the trail. The new immigrants used basic farm wagons for the trip because they were easier to maneuver even though they were very small, only about 4 feet wide by 10 feet long. A family of four had to carry 1000 pounds of food to sustain them on their long, arduous trek. After a few miles, most realized they had overloaded their wagons, and began throwing unnecessary items out. The Oregon Tail was littered with bags of food, cast iron stoves, furniture and even toys. Young children were lucky to keep their dolls from being discarded along the trail.

Notable Natives

James Beard (1903-1981), food expert, cookbook author, Portland

Bonnie Bird (1914-1995), dancer, teacher, Portland

Raymond Carver (1939-1988), short story writer, poet, Clatskine

Beverly Cleary (Beverly Atlee Bunn) (1916-), children's book writer, McMinnville

Imogen Cunningham (1883-1976), photographer, teacher, Portland

Douglas Englebart (1925-), inventor of the computer "mouse," Portland

Alfred Carlton Gilbert (1884-1961), toy inventor, Salem

Matt Groening (1954-), *The Simpsons'* cartoonist, Portland

Brent Musburger (1939-), sportscaster, Portland

Linus Carl Pauling (1901-1994), Nobel Prize-winning chemist, Portland

Jane Powell (1929-), actress, Portland

Steve Prefontain (1951-1975), track athlete, Coos Bay

Doc Severinsen (1927-), Grammy-winning musician, band leader, Arlington

Sally Struthers (1948-), actress, Portland

Rag Doll

Materials

* 26" square cotton cloth
* quilt batting
* brown, yellow or black yarn
* stick pins
* thread and sewing needle
* fine-point, permanent marker
* 2" x 3" cardboard
* ball-point pen
* knitting needle

Instructions

1. Make two copies of the pattern on page 169. Carefully pin each pattern to a piece of fabric and cut out. (Figure 1)
2. Lay the fabric doll shapes on top of each other and pin them together. Sew them together with a 1/4" seam along the side. Leave a 5" gap open at the hip. (Figure 2)
3. Turn the doll inside out by pulling the cloth through the open area.
4. Slip a piece of cardboard through the gap up to the face. Use a ball-point pen to draw a face, then go over it with a permanent marker. Remove the cardboard from the body. (Figure 3)
5. Stuff the doll with quilt batting. Sew up the gap. (Figure 4)
6. Cut yarn strips 12" long. Take six strands of yarn and fold them in the middle over a knitting needle. Sew them together to make one unit. Continue until all the yarn is sewn into units. (Figure 5)
7. Sew the hair units from the back of the doll's head, moving forward. Continue on all sides of the head to build the hair. (Figure 6)
8. Copy the clothing pattern on page 170.
9. Follow the directions on page 170 to make a skirt for the doll.

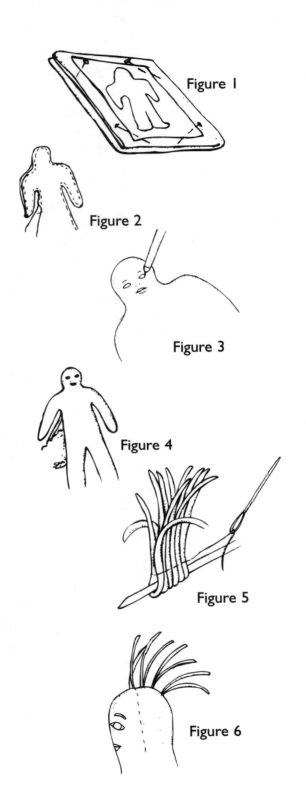

Figure 1

Figure 2

Figure 3

Figure 4

Figure 5

Figure 6

Name _____

Rag Doll Pattern

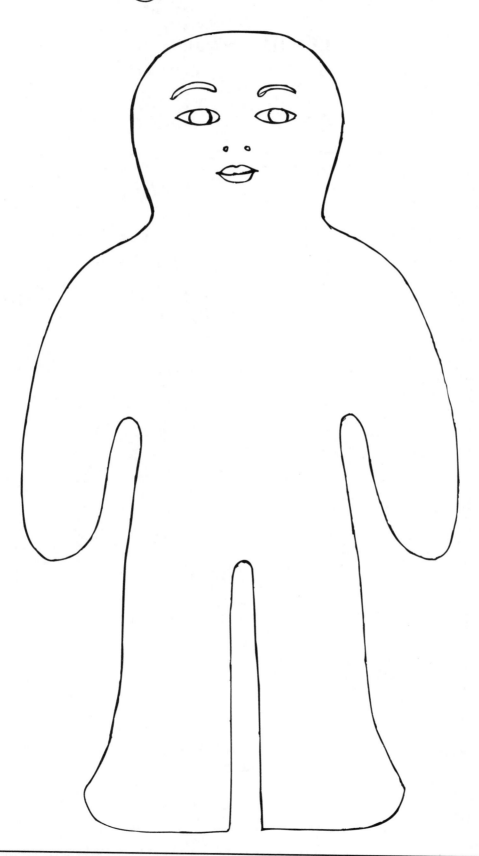

Clothing Pattern

Cut a length of fabric 6½" x 24". Sew 6½" edges together. Baste along top 24" edge with a running stitch. Pull thread to gather fabric around doll's waist. Tie ends of thread together to secure. (Figure 1)

Clothes (Enlarge to fit.)

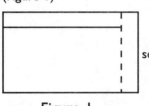

Figure 1

sew

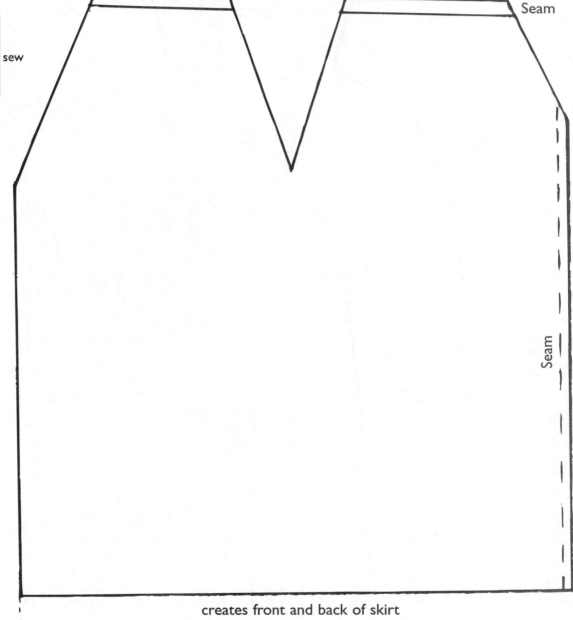

Seam

Seam

creates front and back of skirt

Place on fold

Fun Facts

Pennsylvania

Name: Pennsylvania translates into "Penne's woodland." The land grant was named after Admiral William Penn in 1681. King Charles II of England owed him a large sum of money and awarded the tract of land in America as partial payment of the debt.

Did You Know?

Pennsylvania is called the "Keystone Sate." A keystone is a central piece in an arch that helps lock the other pieces in place. All the other pieces depend on it. No one knows for sure how the state got this name, though it's been called that for more than 200 years. Pennsylvania's vote for independence in the Continental Congress was the deciding or "keystone" vote. Perhaps that is where it got its name. In 1802 the state was referred to as " . . . the keystone of the federal union" at a republican presidential victory rally for Thomas Jefferson. Whatever the origin of the nickname, Pennsylvania has earned it over the years.

Flag: The flag's field is national blue, the same blue used on the United States flag. On the flag is the state coat of arms. On either side are horses above a ribbon bearing the state motto, "Virtue, Liberty, and Independence."

Seal: The circular seal of the state contains a shield in the center. The shield is divided into thirds. At the top is a sailing ship, at the middle a plow and at the bottom three sheaves of wheat. On the left is a stalk of Indian corn and on the right is an olive branch. Above the shield is an American eagle. Encircling all of this are the words *Seal of the State of Pennsylvania.*

Barn Designs

The Dutch settled in southern, central and southwestern Pennsylvania in the 17th and 18th centuries. They were deeply religious people who incorporated their beliefs and symbols into their folk art. Many of their distinctive designs were placed on their magnificent red barns. Some barns were huge—90 feet long and three stories high! Included in the designs were unique geometric shapes that were good luck symbols. The tradesman who painted them was called a "hexenmeister."

Today, these symbols are signs of the Pennsylvania Dutch heritage. They remain a breathtaking aspect of a distinct culture.

Notable Natives

Louisa May Alcott (1832-1888), writer, Germantown

Frankie Avalon (1939-), singer, actor, Philadelphia

Kevin Bacon (1958-), actor, Philadelphia

John Barrymore (1882-1942), actor, Philadelphia

Stephen Vincent Benet (1898-1943), poet, Pulitzer Prize-winning writer, Bethlehem

Daniel Boone (1735-1820), frontiersman, Reading

Peter Boyle (1933-), actor, Philadelphia

James Buchanan (1791-1868), 15th President (1857-1861), near Mercersburg

Alexander Calder (1898-1976), mobile sculptor, Lawnton

Rachel Carson (1907-1964), science writer, Springdale

Mary Cassatt (1844-1926), Impressionist painter, Allegheny

Bill Cosby (1937-), comedian, Emmy-winning actor, North Philadelphia

Kim Delaney (1961-), actress, Philadelphia

Jimmy Dorsey (1904-1957), band leader, Shenandoah

Tommy Dorsey (1905-1956), band leader, Mahoney Plane

Fabian (1943-), singer, Philadelphia

Lola Falana (1943-), singer, dancer, Philadelphia

W.C. Fields (William Claude Dukenfield) (1879-1946), comedic actor, Philadelphia

Robert Fulton (1765-1815), engineer, inventor, Lancaster County

Richard Gere (1949-), actor, Philadelphia

Martha Graham (1894-1991), choreographer of modern dance, Pittsburgh

Jeff Goldblum (1952-), actor, Pittsburgh

Sherman Helmsley (1938-), actor, Philadelphia

Lee Iacocca (1924-), auto executive, Allentown

Reggie Jackson (1946-), baseball player, Wyncote

Joan Jett (1960-), singer, Philadelphia

Shirley Jones (1934-), actress, Smithto

Michael Keaton (1951-), actor, Pittsburgh

Gene Kelly (1912-1996), dancer, actor, Pittsburgh

Jack Klugman (1922-), actor, Philadelphia

Patti LaBelle (1944-), singer, Philadelphia

George C. Marshall (1880-1959), statesman, Nobel Prize winner, Uniontov

George McClellan (1826-1885), Civil W general, Philadelphia

Margaret Mead (1901-1978), anthropologist, Philadelphia

Abraham F. Murray (1939-), actor, Pittsburgh

Arnold Palmer (1929-), four-time Masters-winning golfer, Youngstown

Robert E. Peary (1856-1920), explorer Cresson Springs

Man Ray (Emanuel Rabinovitch) (1890-1976), photographer, Philadelphia

Betsy Ross (1752-1836), flagmaker, seamstress, Philadelphia

James Stewart (1908-1997), Oscar-winning actor, Indiana

Teller (1948-), magician, Philadelphia

John Updike (1932-), Pulitzer Prize-winning writer, Shillington

Bobby Vinton (1935-), singer, Canonsburg

Honus Wagner (1874-1955), baseball player, Carnegie

Andy Warhol (1928-1987), pop artist, Pittsburgh

Andrew Wyeth (1917-), painter, Chad Ford

17th Century Barn Hot Plate

Caution! These painted tiles are not to be used with heat or as hot plates unless you use with ceramic paint. Always follow manufacturer's instructions. Use only as directed.

Figure 1

Materials

* 1 red or white ceramic tile (from hardware store)
* tracing paper
* masking tape
* paint: water-based ceramic paints, if available. These can be baked in the oven to "fix" paint. Always read manufacturer's instructions. (Optional paint: White enamel. It cannot be used in an oven or near heat as a hot plate. Instead, use it for decorative purposes only. Use white paint on red tile, red paint on white tile.)
* thin paintbrushes
* soft-leaded pencil
* scissors
* ball-point pen
* turpentine or paint thinner

Optional:
* Epoxy glue and picture hanger (if using as a wall display)

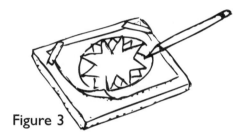

Figure 2

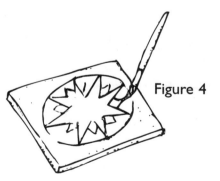

Figure 3

Instructions

1. Copy a Pennsylvania Dutch farm design from page 174 onto tracing paper. Enlarge or reduce as desired.
2. Make sure the tile is clean and dry before you begin. Cut out a design and color the back of it with a soft pencil. (Figure 1)
3. Center the design on the tile and tape it down. (Figure 2)
4. Press hard on the pen as you trace the design to make an impression on the tile. (Figure 3)
5. Go over the lines you drew with paint. Thin out the paint as necessary. Allow it to dry. (Figure 4)
6. If you are using the tile as a decorative wall piece, flip it over. Mix epoxy glue. Place a sawtooth hanger 1/2" from the top middle. Glue each edge and let it dry. (Figure 5)

Figure 4

Figure 5

Pennsylvania Dutch Farm Designs

(Enlarge pattern to fit tile.)

Fun Facts

Bird: Rhode Island Red
(Gallus gallus)

Fish: Rockfish or Striped Bass
(Morone saxatilis)

Flower: Common Meadow
Violet (Viola sororia)

Fruit: Rhode Island Greening
Apple (Malus domestica)

Mineral: Bowenite

Motto: "Hope"

Nicknames: Ocean State,
Little Rhody

Rock: Cumberlandite

Shell: Quahog
(Mercenaria mercenaria)

Song: "Rhode Island's It for
Me" by Charlie Hall

Tree: Red Maple
(Acer rubrum)

Statehood: May 29, 1790;
13th state admitted to the
Union

Population: (2000 estimate)
1,048,319

Area: 1545 square miles;
the smallest state

Highest Point: Jerimoth Hill;
812 feet above sea level

Lowest Point: Atlantic coast

Capital: Providence

Largest City: Providence

Major Crops: Fishing,
seafood, vegetables, grapes,
dairy products, nursery
stock, eggs

Major Industry: Fashion
jewelry, machinery, plastic
manufacturing, shipbuilding,
boat building, tourism

Rhode Island

Name: *The origin of Rhode Island's name is uncertain. Some speculate that the name honors the Greek island of Rhodes. Others believe that the Dutch explorer Adriaen Block named the area "Roode Eylandt" because of the red clay found in the soil.*

Did You Know?

For over 100 years, children have delighted in riding carousels, merry-go-rounds that often have ornately carved animals. One of the oldest carousels still in operation is the Flying Horse Carousel at Watch Hill in Westerly, Rhode Island. One of the unique characteristics about this carousel, other than its age, is that it is a "flying" carousel. The horses are not attached to poles on which they go up and down, but suspended from the top of the carousel. When the carousel turns, the horses "fly" over the ground like swings. The carousel has 66 individually hand-carved figures, most of them horses.

Seal: The circular seal has an anchor in the center, with a ribbon above it with the state's motto, "Hope." Encircling it are the words *Seal of the Great State of Rhode Island and Providence Plantations* and the date *1636.*

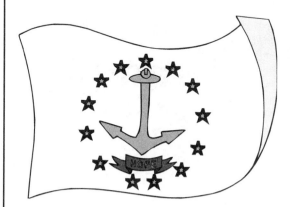

Flag: The flag is white. In the center is a gold ship's anchor, surrounded by a circle of 13 gold five-point stars. Directly under the anchor on a blue ribbon is the state's motto, "Hope."

Precious Quahog Shells

Rhode Island is right in the middle of "quahog" shell country. These shells are so highly regarded and such an important part of Rhode Island history, they have been designated as the official state shell. The Native Americans treasured the quahog for its meat and its shell. They shaped the shells into beads used for necklaces and other adornments as well as a form of money known as "wampum." Wampum belts were symbols of authority and power in the Iroquois Federation. The purple colored quahog shell was considered more valuable than the white shell.

The word *quahog* comes from the indigenous Native Americans of Rhode Island, the Narragansetts. They, however, called the shell, poquauhock. Even today, quahogs are a popular food. They grow quickly when they are young and their age is determined by the number of rings on the shells. It is estimated that a 4" quahog is about 40 years old.

Quahogs are found all along the Atlantic Coast, from Canada down to Texas. However, the purple northern quahog, lives only between New Jersey and Maine. Quahogs bury themselves in sand and mud and feed on plankton from the ocean.

Notable Natives

Nelson Wilmarth Aldrich (1841-1915), politician, Foster

Harry Anderson (1952-), magician, actor, Newport

William Ellery Channing (1780-1842), clergyman, essayist, Newport

George M. Cohan (1878-1942), songwriter, Providence

George William Curtis (1824-1892), journalist, Providence

Nelson Eddy (1901-1967), singer, actor, Providence

William Ellery (1727-1820), signer of the Declaration of Independence, Newport

Robert Gray (1755-1806), explorer, Tiverton

Raymond M. Hood (1881-1934), architect, Pawtucket

Van Johnson (1916-), actor, Newport

H.P. Lovecraft (1890-1937), science fiction writer, Providence

Matthew C. Perry (1794-1858), naval officer, Newport

Oliver Hazard Perry (1785-1819), naval officer, South Kingstown

Gilbert Stuart (1755-1828), portrait painter, North Kingstown

Meredith Viera (1953-), actress, television talk show host, Providence

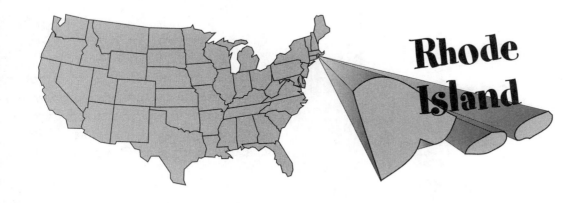

Rhode Island

Quahog Shell Jewelry

Materials

* 2 sheets of white paper
* 1 piece of purple paper
* wood nails or knitting needles
* scissors
* petroleum jelly
* glue stick or a small amount of prepared wallpaper paste
* clear varnish or clear nail polish
* string
* 2 feet elastic thread cut in two pieces

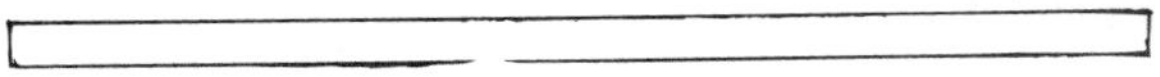

Figure 1

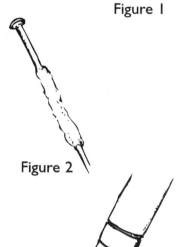

Figure 2

Figure 3

Instructions for Making the Beads

1. Cut white and purple paper into thin strips 1/4" x 6". (Figure 1)
2. Cover a nail or knitting needle with a thick coat of petroleum jelly. (Figure 2)
3. Coat one side of a paper strip with glue. (Figure 3)
4. Roll the strip of paper onto the nail. Secure the end with glue. Remove the paper bead from the nail and set it aside to dry. (Figure 4)
5. Repeat this process for each bead you make. The purple paper represents the purple quahog and is therefore more valuable. Use it sparingly for this reason. (Figure 5)
6. When the beads have dried, slip them back onto the nail covered with petroleum jelly. Varnish all sides of the beads, then set them aside to dry. (Figure 6)
7. String the beads on elastic and tie the ends together with a knot for a necklace. (Figure 7)

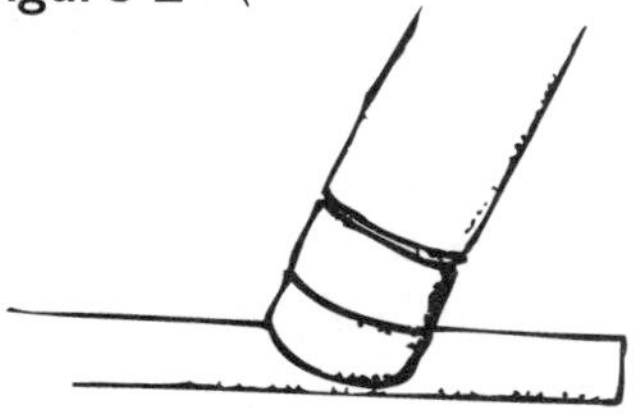

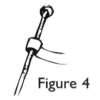

Figure 4

Figure 5

Figure 6

Figure 7

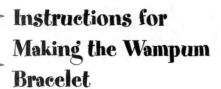

Instructions for Making the Wampum Bracelet

8. Follow the necklace directions (1-7) to make the bracelet, but use the large bead design on the right to make 12 or more wampum beads.
9. Thread the large beads, arranging them side by side. Slip the elastic over one bead and through to the second bead as shown. Follow the flow through all the beads until you reach the end. Secure it with a knot. (Figure 8)
10. Slip another piece of elastic through the opposite side of the beads. (Figure 9)
11. When you join two beads together with the second elastic, gently pull the threads to make it more secure. (Figure 10)
12. Knot the ends when you're done weaving the threads through the beads.

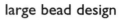

large bead design

(Start rolling this bead at the large end and work toward the small.)

Figure 8

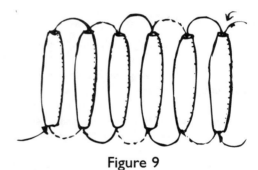

Figure 9

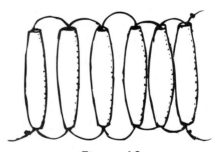

Figure 10

Quahog Shell Beads

standard shape

oval shape

bracelet

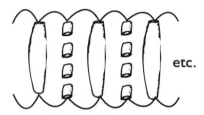

etc.

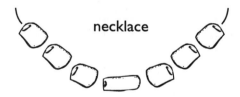

necklace

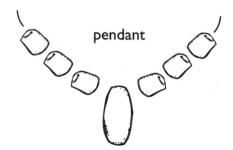

pendant

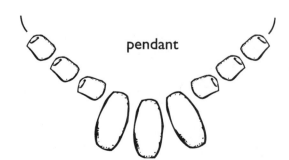

pendant

Fun Facts

Amphibian: Spotted Salamander (Ambystoma maculatum)

Animal: White-Tailed Deer (Odocoileus virginianus)

Bird: Great Carolina Wren (Thyothorus ludovicianus)

Butterfly: Eastern Tiger Swallowtail (Pterourus glaucus)

Dog: Boykin Spaniel (Canis familiaris)

Game Bird: Wild Turkey (Meleagris gallopavo)

Fish: Rockfish or Striped Bass (Morone saxatilis)

Flower: Yellow Jessamine (Gelsemium sempervirens)

Fruit: Peach (Prunus persica)

Gem: Amethyst

Grass: Indiangrass (Sorghastrum nutans)

Insect: Carolina Mantis (Stagmomantis carolina)

Mottoes: "Animis Opibusque Parati" (Ready in soul and resource); "Dum Spiro Spero" (While I breathe, I hope)

Nickname: Palmetto State

Reptile: Loggerhead Sea Turtle (Caretta caretta)

Shell: Lettered Olive (Oliva sayana)

Songs: "Carolina" by Henri Timrod; "South Carolina on My Mind" by Hank Martin and Buzz Arledge

Spider: Carolina Wolf Spider (Hogna carolinensis)

Stone: Blue Granite

Tree: Cabbage Palmetto (Sabal palmetto)

Statehood: May 23, 1788; 8th state admitted to the Union

Population: (2000 estimate) 4,012,012

Area: 32,007 square miles of land and water; 40th largest state

Highest Point: Sassafras Mountain; 3560 feet above sea level

Lowest Point: Atlantic coast; sea level

Capital: Columbia

Largest City: Columbia

Major Crops: Tobacco, peaches, commercial tea, broilers, cattle, calves, turkeys, dairy products, watermelons, peanuts, soybeans, hogs

Major Industry: Textile goods, steel products, chemical products, apparel, wood pulp, paper products, machinery, tourism

South Carolina

Name: South Carolina is named after an English monarch. King Charles I of England gave a large tract of land to Sir Robert Heath in 1619. The land was to be called the province of Carolana. *Carolana* is the Latin word for "Charles." In 1710, King Charles II of England granted land rights to others and divided Carolina into North and South.

Did You Know?

South Carolina is one of the top three peach producers in the United States. It has the perfect climate—hot, humid and subtropical—for growing the South American fruit. Spaniards first brought peaches to North America. Now California, South Carolina and Georgia are the top peach-producing states in the Union. South Carolina alone grows over 100 million pounds of peaches each year!

to the center of the flag after the heroic defense by Moultrie of the palmetto-log fort on Sullivan's Island against the attack by the British fleet on June 28, 1776.

Flag: The state flag has its history in the Revolutionary War. The Revolutionary Council of Safety asked Colonel William Moultrie to design a flag for use by the South Carolina troops. He chose a dark blue field to match the color of the soldiers' uniforms. In the upper left-hand corner of the flag is a silver crescent moon, the same image on the front of the soldiers' caps. A palmetto tree was added

Seal: The circular state seal has two ovals of equal size. The oval on the left contains a palmetto tree; the one on the right shows a woman. In the ovals are the words *South Carolina* and the state's two mottoes: "Dum Spiro Spero" and "Animis Opibusque Parati."

Mini Winnowing Basket

Down in South Carolina's "Low Country" live the Gulla. Some believe that the term *Gulla* is a term used by slave traders for the African nation of Angola. The Gulla are a combination of many African groups who were accosted by slave traders and shipped to the first colonies from the 17th to 19th centuries. They became slaves and were critical to the economy and survival of the south. They survived unspeakable hardships, but the Gulla might be considered luckier than most slaves. They worked in South Carolina's isolated coast and islands harvesting rice. The isolation of the islands and the scope and size of the rice plantations allowed the Gulla to gain a level of independence most slaves did not have.

Their working structures were unique. They worked in what is called a "task system" which gave them more autonomy, responsibility (and, eventually, independence) in their jobs and lives than most slaves had.

One of the cultural traditions of the Gulla is a beautifully woven basket made of sweet grass, bulrush and pine needles from the marshy swamplands of South Carolina. Gulla baskets were a necessity for storing grain and cotton and were used as fish containers. The art and craft of making Gulla baskets, particularly the winnowing baskets for rice, was passed down from father to son.

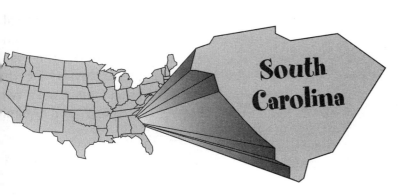

South Carolina

Notable Natives

Washington Allston (1779-1843), poet, painter, Waccamaw

James Mark Baldwin (1861-1934), psychologist, editor, Columbia

Bernard Baruch (1870-1965), statesman, financier, Camden

Mary McLeod Bethune (1875-1955), educator, Mayesville

James Brown (1933-), soul singer, Barnwell

John C. Calhoun (1782-1850), U. S. senator, Vice President, politician, Calhoun Mills

Andy Dick (1965-), comedic actor, Charleston

Joe Frazier (1944-), world heavyweight champion boxer, Beaufort

Robert F. Furchgott (1916-), Nobel Prize-winning physiologist, Charleston

James Gadsen (1788-1858), soldier, statesman, Charlestwon

Althea Gibson (1927-), tennis player, Silver

Dizzy Gillespie (1917-1993), jazz trumpeter, Cheraw

Joseph Leonard Goldstein (1940-), Nobel Prize-winning molecular geneticist, Sumter

Angelina Emily Grimke (1805-1879), abolitionist, women's rights advocate, Charleston

Sarah Moore Grimke (1792-1873), abolitionist, women's rights advocate, Charleston

Robert Young Hayne (1791-1839), politician, Pon Pon Plantation, St. Paul's Parrish, Colleton District

Lauren Hutton (1943-), super model, actress, Charleston

Andrew Jackson (1767-1845), 7th President (1829-1837), in the Waxhaw District

Jesse Louis Jackson (1941-), civil rights leader, Greenville

Jasper Johns (1930-), sculptor, painter, Allendale

Eartha Kitt (1927-), singer, North

Francis "Swamp Fox" Marion (c.1732-1795), Revolutionary War general, Winyah

Andie McDowell (1958-) actress, Gaffney

Mary-Louise Parker (1964-), actress, Fort Jackson

John Rutledge (1739-1800), statesman, U.S. Supreme Court Justice, Charleston

William Westmoreland (1914-), soldier, Army chief of staff, Spartanburg

Vanna White (1957-), game show co-host, television personality, North Myrtle Beach

Winnowing Baskets

Materials

* 1-2 bunches of raffia (per basket) or a skein of yarn
* thread and carpet needle or glue

Instructions

1. Lay out raffia or yarn—enough to form a bundle $1/4$"-$1/2$" in diameter—about 36" in length. (If the raffia strands are not long enough, overlap strands to desired length. (Figure 1)
2. Tie strands at about 3"-intervals. (Figure 2)
3. Hook one end over about 1" and tie together. (Figure 3)
4. Build basket as you would a clay coil pot, tying or glueing each row as you go. (Figure 4)
5. When you have finished coiling the basket, tie the ends and glue in place.

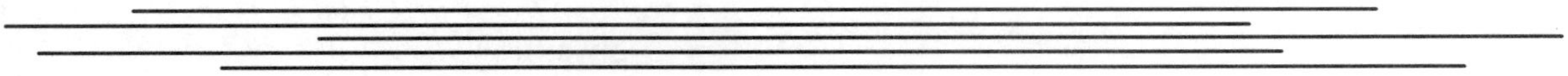

Figure 1

Figure 2

Figure 3

Figure 4

Gulla Winnowing Design

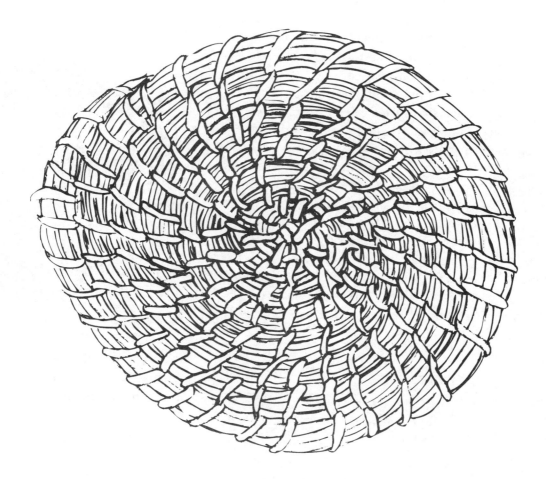

Fun Facts

Animal: Coyote
(Canis latrans)

Bird: Chinese Ring-Necked
Pheasant (Phasianus
culchicus)

Fish: Walleye
(Stizostedion vitreum)

Flower: Pasque Flower
(Pulsatilla hirsutissima)

Fossil: Triceratops
(Triceratops horridus)

Gem: Fairburn Agate

Grass: Western Wheat Grass
(Agropyron smithii)

Insect: Honeybee
(Apis mellifera)

Mineral: Rose Quartz

Motto: "Under God the
People Rule"

Nicknames: Mount
Rushmore State,
Coyote State

Slogan: "Great Faces, Great
Places"

Song: "Hail, South Dakota" by
Deecort Hammitt

Tree: Black Hills Spruce
(Picea glauca densata)

Statehood: November 2,
1889; 40th state admitted to
the Union

Population: (2000 estimate)
754,844

Area: 77,121 square miles of
land and water; 17th largest
state

Highest Point: Harney Peak;
7242 feet above sea level

Lowest Point: Big Stone
Lake; 962 feet above sea
level

Capital: Pierre

Largest City: Sioux Falls

Major Crops: Cattle, hogs,
flaxseed, sunflower seed,
wheat, rye, hay, soybeans,
milk, corn

Major Industry: Lumber and
wood products, durable
goods manufacturing,
tourism

South Dakota

Name: South Dakota takes its name from a Native American word. Dakota is a Sioux word which means "ally" or "friend." South comes from the fact that of the two states named Dakota, South Dakota is farthest south.

Did You Know?

Artist Gutzon Borglum's granite sculpture of the four presidential faces—George Washington, Thomas Jefferson, Abraham Lincoln and Theodore Roosevelt—on Mount Rushmore is one of the most famous monuments in America. Each face is over six stories tall with each presidential nose about 20 feet long! A grown man can stand inside the eyes of the sculpture. The massive granite mountain statue took 14 years to blast and carve. But would it have been so famous and beloved if the original idea for the mountain carving had been completed? The original idea for the carving was to memorialize Civil War General George Armstrong Custer, western hero Buffalo Bill Cody and explorers Meriwether Lewis and William Clark!

Flag: The state seal, surrounded by a golden sun, is set in the middle of a sky-blue field. Around the sun in a circle are the words *South Dakota the Mount Rushmore State.*

Seal: The circular seal depicts the state's commerce and resources. A bucolic scene of South Dakota land is cut in half by a winding river and a smokestack and steamship, both with smoke billowing toward the sky. In the foreground is a farmer with horses plowing a field. Over the scene is a ribbon with the state's motto, "Under God the People Rule." Encircling the scene, are the words *Great State of South Dakota Seal* and the date *1889.*

184

Mount Rushmore & Crazy Horse

The massive granite walls of the Black Hills of South Dakota have inspired artisans to create two gigantic and historic memorials. The first, on Mount Rushmore, is known as the Shrine of Democracy. It shows the faces of George Washington, Thomas Jefferson, Theodore Roosevelt and Abraham Lincoln. The head of each President stands 60 feet high. These Presidents were chosen by sculptor, Gutzon Borglum, because of their importance in American history.

The four Presidents represent the birth, growth, preservation and development of our nation and its dedication to democracy and individual freedom.

Gutzon Borglum was a respected artist, one of America's most prolific sculptors.

He studied under the famous sculptor, Rodin, in Paris. In September 1924, Borglum proposed that he carve a work historically relevant and representative of what this country stands for. Borglum's challenge was to create a work of art with images equal to the monumental landscape of the Black Hills.

Also South Dakota's Black Hills is a privately funded public artwork known as the Crazy Horse memorial. After seeing Mount Rushmore, Lakota Chief Henry Standing Bear wanted people to recognize Native American heroes as well. Famed sculptor, Korczak Ziolkowski, began the arduous task of blasting and chipping away rock in 1949 to create his masterpiece of Crazy Horse. The Crazy Horse memorial is more than a sculpture, it shows the spirit of the man and his people. Crazy Horse proudly sits astride his war pony pointing out towards the land they once roamed.

Notable Natives

Gene Myron Amdahl (1922-), computer scientist, businessman, Flandreau

Sparky Anderson (1934-), baseball manager, Bridgewater

Tom Brokaw (1940-), television anchorman, Webster

Thomas Daschle (1947-), U.S. senator, Aberdeen

Ella Deloria (1889-1971), novelist, White Swan

Crazy Horse (Sioux name—Ta-Sunko-Witko) (c.1849-1877), Oglala chief, Dakota Territory

Hubert Humphrey (1911-1978), U.S. senator, Vice President, presidential candidate, Wallace

Cheryl Ladd (1951-), actress, Huron

George McGovern (1922-), U.S. senator, Democratic presidential candidate, Avon

Russell Means (1939-), Native American rights activist, Pine Ridge Indian Reservation

Sitting Bull (Sioux name—Tatanka Iyotake) (c.1834-1890), Sioux chief, near Grand River

Mamie Van Doren (1931-), actress, Rowena

Mount Rushmore & Crazy Horse

Materials

* plastic wrap
* carving tools
* wooden board or flat surface
* 5 pounds self-hardening clay (gray)
* clear varnish
* permanent felt-tip black marker
* tape
* water
* paper towels

Figure 1

Instructions

1. Enlarge and copy the Mount Rushmore and/or Crazy Horse designs on page 187.
2. Tape a sheet of plastic wrap over the design and tape it down. Trace the design on the plastic with a black marker. (Figure 1)
3. Soften the clay into a slab larger than the design you plan. Daub it with water to keep it moist.
4. Lay the plastic sheet with the design on top of the clay slab. Trace over it with a carving tool incising, or making an impression, in the clay. (Figure 2)
5. Pull off the plastic and refine all impressions.
6. Slightly lift the design and poke a hole in the back for a hanger. (Figure 3)
7. Varnish when the clay is completely dry.

Figure 2

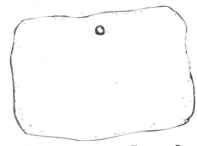

Figure 3

Mount Rushmore & Crazy Horse Designs

Cut out on the dotted lines.
Press down where black lines and dark shadowed areas are shown.

Cut

Cut

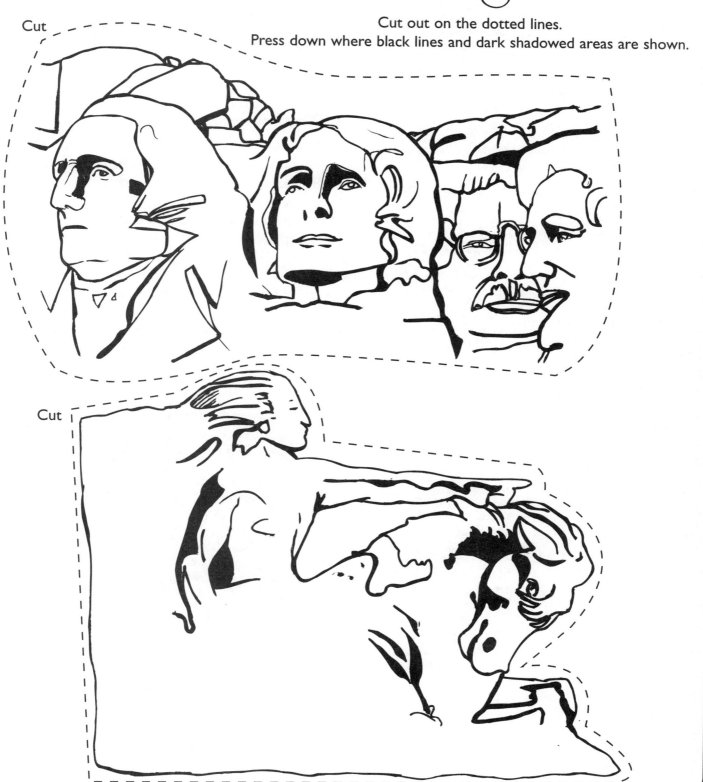

Fun Facts

Amphibian: Cave Salamander (Gyrinophilus palleucus)

Animal: Raccoon (Procyon lotor)

Bird: Mockingbird (Mimus polyglottos)

Game Bird: Bobwhite Quail (Colinus virginianus)

Butterfly: Zebra Swallowtail (Eurytides marcellus)

Fish: Channel Catfish (Ictalurus punctatus)

Game Fish: Largemouth or Black Bass (Micropterus salmoides)

Flower: Iris (Iridaceae)

Wildflower: Passion Flower (Passiflora incarnate)

Gem: Tennessee River Pearls

Insects: Ladybug (Coccinella novemnotata), Firefly (Poturis pennsylvanica De Geer)

Agriculture Insect: Honeybee (Apis mellifera)

Motto: "Agriculture and Commerce"

Nickname: Volunteer State

Reptile: Eastern Box Turtle (Terrapene carolina)

Rock: Limestone

Songs: "The Tennessee Waltz" by Redd Stewart

"Tennessee, My Homeland" by Nell Grayson Taylor

"Tennessee" by Vivian Rorie

"When It's Iris Time in Tennessee" by Willa Waid Newman

"My Tennessee" by Frances Hannah Tranum

"Rocky Top" by Boudleaux and Felice Bryant

Tree: Tulip Tree or Tulip Poplar (Liriodendron tulipifera)

Statehood: June 1, 1796; 16th state admitted to the Union

Population: 5,689,283

Area: 42,146 square miles of land and water; 36th largest state

Highest Point: Clingmans Dome; 6643 feet above sea level

Lowest Point: Mississippi River; 182 feet above sea level

Capital: Nashville

Largest City: Memphis

Major Crops: Soybeans, greenhouse products, cotton, tobacco, dairy products, cattle, hogs

Major Industry: Chemicals, textiles and apparel production, lumber, transportation equipment, leather goods, rubber, plastics, marble quarrying, zinc mining

Tennessee

Name: _Tanasi_ or _Tennessee_ was a Native American Cherokee word for some villages along what is now known as the Tennessee River.

Did You Know?

The Cherokee Nation in Tennessee never had a written language until a man named Sequoyah developed one. His father was half Cherokee and his mother was a full blood. His English name was George Guess. He broke the language down into 85 symbols that were easy to learn. But instead of being applauded for his work, Sequoyah was charged with witchcraft! When he was able to prove that the symbols he wrote down represented talking, his accusers dropped their charges and began learning the symbols themselves. In 1824 the Cherokees awarded him a silver medal for his contribution to the tribe. Sequoyah singlehandedly brought literacy to his people.

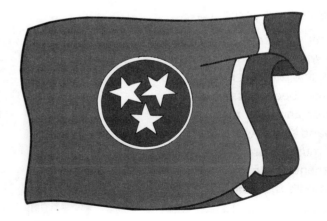

Flag: In the center of a field of red is a blue circle with three five-point stars, representing the three landforms in Tennessee—mountains, highlands and lowlands. These are held together by a small white unbroken circle. A narrow strip of white and a larger strip of blue edges the flag.

The image of the seal may not be reproduced without express permission from the State of Tennessee. This product is not sanctioned or authorized by the State of Tennessee.

Seal: The circular seal is a visual representation of the state motto, "Agriculture and Commerce." In the top half of the circle, are the Roman numerals, XVI, which symbolize Tennessee as the 16th state to enter the Union. Below that is a plow, a sheaf of wheat and a cotton stalk, sitting on the word *agriculture*, all symbolizing the importance of agriculture on the state's future and past. In the bottom half of the circle is a riverboat, floating over the word *commerce* showing the importance of the river as a place of commerce and transportation. The words *The Great Seal of the State of Tennessee* and the date *1796* encircle the seal.

Rural Americana Music

Rural music from Tennessee reflects the sound of our country's south with timeless melodies of days gone by. The music of dulcimers and zithers, now played at state fairs and around campfires, has been passed down from father to son, mother to daughter and into history. Familiar tunes are: "I Was Born Ten Thousand Years Ago," "Kum Ba Ya" and "On Top of Old Smokey." Rural music from Tennessee is often played with homemade instruments such as spoons or bones. By making the simple instruments that follow, you can begin your own Tennessee band.

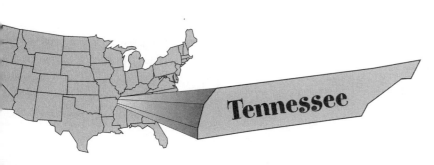

Tennessee

Notable Natives

James Agee (1909-1955), poet, Pulitzer Prize-winning novelist, Knoxville

Gregg Alman (1951-), singer, Nashville

Eddy Arnold (1918-), singer, Henderson

Chet Atkins (Charles Burton) (1924-2001), guitarist, Lutrell

Howard Henry Baker, Jr. (1925-), politician, statesman, Huntsville

Edward Emerson Barnard (1857-1923), astronomer, Nashville

Kathy Bates (1948-), actress, Memphis

Julian Bond (1940-), politician, civil rights leader, Nashville

Hattie Caraway (1878-1950), first elected woman senator, Bakerville

Dixie Carter (1939-), actress, McLemoresville

Rita Coolidge (1945-), singer, Nashville

Davy Crockett (1786-1836), frontiersman, Greeneville

Shannon Doherty (1971-), actress, Memphis

David Farragut (1801-1870), first American vice admiral, Knoxville

Lester Flatt (1914-1979), bluegrass guitarist, Overton County

Tennessee Ernie Ford (1919-1991), singer, Bristol

Morgan Freeman (1937-), actor, Memphis

Aretha Franklin (1942-), singer, Memphis

George Hamilton (1939-), actor, Memphis

Isaac Hayes (1942-), composer, Covington

Benjamin Hooks (1925-), civil rights leader, Memphis

Cordell Hull (1871-1955), Nobel Peace Prize-winning statesman, Overton

Samuel L. Jackson (1948-), actor, Chattanooga

Mary Noailles Murfree (pen name Charles Egbert Craddock) (1850-1922), writer, Murfreesboro

Dolly Parton (1946-), singer, actress, Sevierville

Minnie Pearl (Sarah Ophelia Cannon) (1912-1996), country singer, Centerville

Wilma Rudolph (1940-1994), Olympic gold-medal runner St. Bethlehem

Sequoyah (c.1770-1843), Cherokee scholar, Tennessee

Cybil Shepard (1950-), actress, Memphis

Dinah Shore (1917-1994), actress, singer, Winchester

Tina Turner (Annie Mae Bullock) (1939-), singer, Brownsville

Alvin York (1887-1964), World War I hero, Fentress County

Shoe Box Harp

Materials

* shoe box
* plywood (to fit snugly on the walls of the shoe box)
* X-acto™ knife
* 6 rubber bands of varying widths (large enough and strong enough to fit the shoe box lengthwise)
* wooden stick or matchstick

Instructions

1. Glue the plywood inside the box to make it sturdy. (Figure 1)
2. Cut notches equal in distance and length to each other in the top ends of the box. (Figure 2)
3. Stretch six rubber bands across and under the box, resting in the notches.
4. Experiment with rubber bands of different lengths and widths for a variety of tones. (Figure 3)
5. Pick the strings with your fingers or a small stick to create musical sounds.

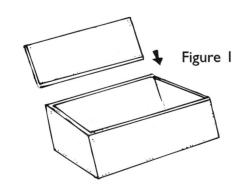

Figure 1

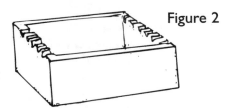

Figure 2

Figure 3

Bone Rattle

Materials

* 5-8 small dried round bones (preferably pork loin or lamb chops) boiled, dried and cleaned
* 2 feet of bendable wire (or coat hanger)
* wire cutters or pliers
* electrical tape

Instructions

1. Bend the wire into a 4" to 5" circle. (Figure 4)
2. Slip the round bones onto the wire. (Figure 5)
3. To make a handle, twist the remaining wire from both sides of the circle. (Figure 6)
4. Wrap tape around the handle several times to cover the wire and make it easy to handle. (Figure 7)
5. Shake the bone rattle with musical accompaniment.

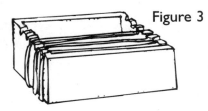

Figure 4

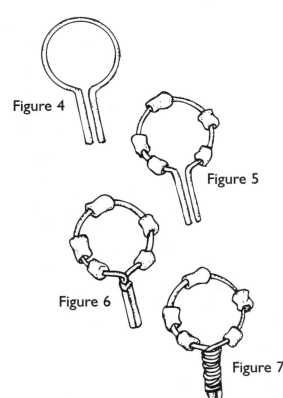

Figure 5

Figure 6

Figure 7

Triangle

Materials

* 20" long aluminum tubing
* 12" x 1/2" steel rod
* cotton cord
* pliers
* metal file

Instructions

1. Make points on both ends of the tubing by filing them down. (Figure 1)
2. Use pliers to bend the tubing at 7". Create two additional triangle sides by bending them to approximately 8" on either side. (Figure 2)
3. Tie cotton cord to the two longest sides and hold the triangle in the air. (Figure 3)
4. Strike the triangle with the steel rod. Practice various sounds. You may find you need to alter the points by filing them down further. Also try different sounds by striking it in different ways. (Figure 4)

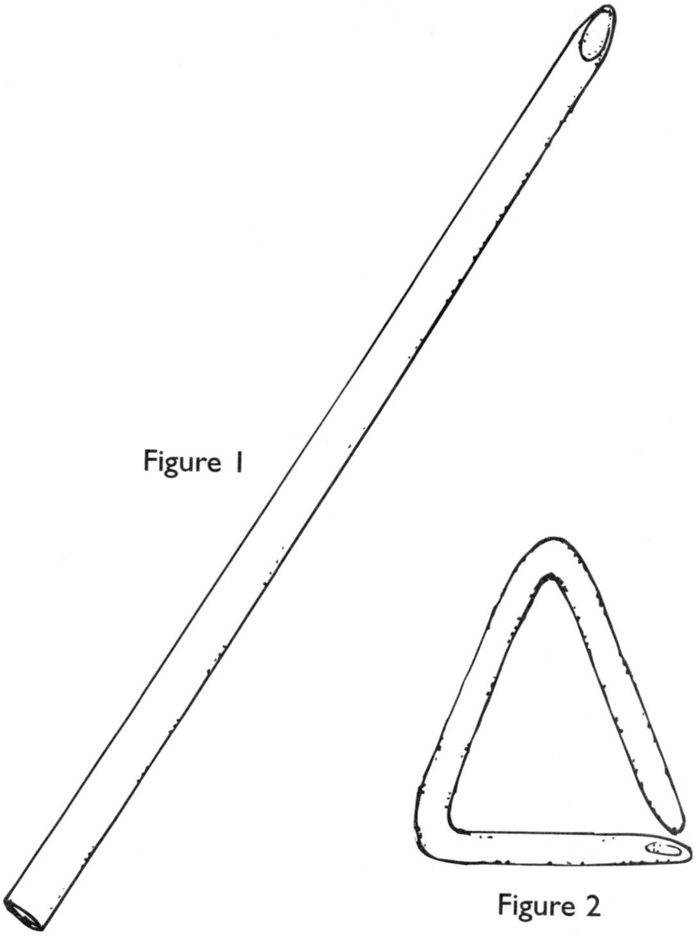

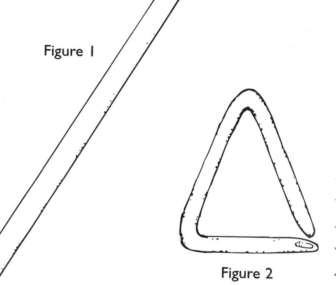

Figure 1

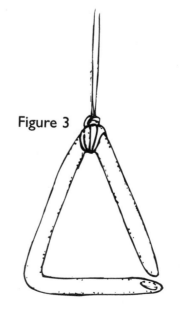

Figure 2

Figure 4

Figure 3

Mouth Bow

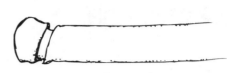

Figure 1

Materials

* pliable cherry, white birch or maple 3" branch. (Some experts believe that the type of wood used in a mouth bow is important. These are the recommended types.)
* X-acto™ knife
* steel guitar string
* guitar pick

Note: One side of the branch should be 1/2" wide, the other 3/4" to 1" wide. The branch should be cut and stripped.

Figure 2a

Figure 2b

Instructions

1. Cut a slight groove in the branch about 1" in on either side and no more than 1/4" deep. (Figure 1)
2. The guitar string should have a metal loop attached to it. Pull the string through it and attach it to the branch at the groove. (Figures 2a and 2b)
3. Press the branch down lightly and slowly to make a "c" shaped bow. (Figure 3)
4. Tie the other end of the guitar string around the opposite groove. Keep it taut while wrapping the string several times around the groove. (Figures 4a and 4b)

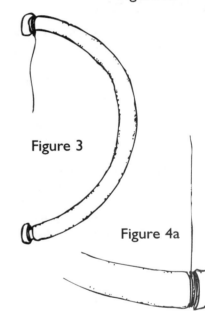

Figure 3

Figure 4a

How to Play

Hold the mouth bow in one hand. Press the small end to your cheek near your mouth. Your mouth acts as an echo chamber, so keep it open. Keep the bow close to your mouth but not touching it. Open your mouth to change the tones of the notes as you strum with your opposite hand. Make different notes by slightly bending the bow.

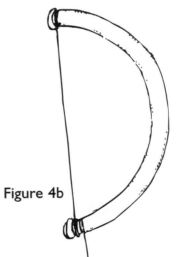

Figure 4b

Rural Musical Instruments

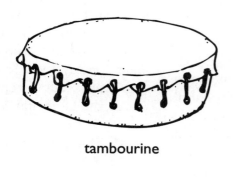

tambourine

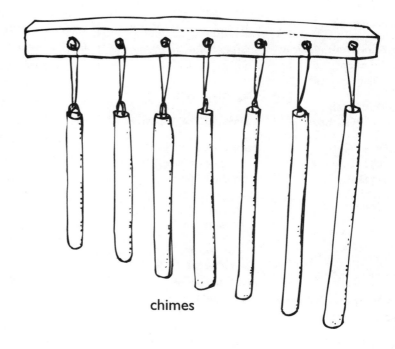

chimes

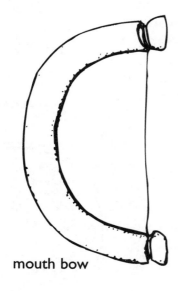

mouth bow

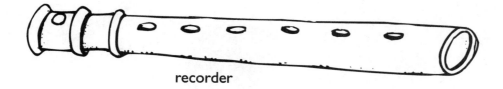

recorder

Fun Facts

Bird: Mockingbird
(Mimus polyglottos)

Dinosaurs: Brachiosaur
Sauropod, Pleurocoelus

Fish: Guadalupe Bass
(Micropterus treculi)

Flower: Bluebonnet
(Lupinus subcarnosus or
Lupinus texensis)

Fruit: Texas Red Grapefruit
(Citrus paradisi)

Gem: Texas Blue Topaz

Grass: Sideoats Grama
(Bouteloua curtipendula)

Insect: Monarch Butterfly
(Danaus plexippus)

Flying Mammal: Mexican
Free-Tailed Bat
(Tadarida brasilensis)

Large Mammal:
Longhorn (Bos bos)

Small Mammal:
Armadillo (Dasypus
novemcinctus)

Motto: "Friendship"

Nickname: Lone Star
State

Health Nut: Pecan

Native Pepper: Chiltepin
(Capsicum var. aviclualre)

Pepper: Jalapeno
(Capsicum annum)

Plant: Prickly Pear Cactus
(Opuntia)

Reptile: Horned Lizard
(Phrynosoma cornutum)

Shell: Lightning Whelk
(Busycon perversum
pulleyi)

Shrub: Crape Myrtle
(Lagerstroemia indica)

Song: "Texas, Our Texas"
by Gladys Y. Wright and
William J. Marsh

Stone: Petrified Palmwood
(Palmoxylon)

Tree: Pecan
(Carya illinioensis)

Vegetable: Sweet Onion
(Allium)

Statehood: December 29,
1845; 28th state admitted
to the Union

Population: (2000
estimate) 20,851,820

Area: 268,601 square miles
of land and water;
2nd largest state

Highest Point: Guadalupe
Peak; 8749 feet above sea
level

Lowest Point: Gulf of
Mexico; sea level

Capital: Austin

Largest City: Houston

Major Crops: Cattle,
sheep, cotton, dairy
products, poultry, eggs,
sorghum, corn, sugarcane,
rice, wheat, peanuts,
fruits, vegetables

Major Industry: Chemical
manufacturing, oil and
natural gas, food
processing, meat packing,
electrical equipment,
machinery, mining,
tourism

Name: Texas' state name comes from the Native American Caddo word, techas meaning "friends" or "allies." The Caddo were native to the areas now known as Arkansas, East Texas and Louisiana.

Did You Know?

Pharmacist, Charles Alderton, in Waco, Texas, invented Dr. Pepper™. In 1850, Alderton was working in Morrison's Old Corner Drug Store stirring up various recipes of soft drinks and letting customers try them. The recipe eventually known as Dr. Pepper™ became a quick favorite. At first, it was called "Waco," but eventually the soda pop was named after a doctor friend of Morrison, owner of the drug store.

Flag: The flag is made up of three colors—red for bravery, white for strength and blue for loyalty. The single five-point star represents Texas, the Lone Star State.

Seal: The circular state seal of Texas has a large five-point star at the center, surrounded by garlands of leaves. On the outer ring of the seal are the words *The State of Texas.*

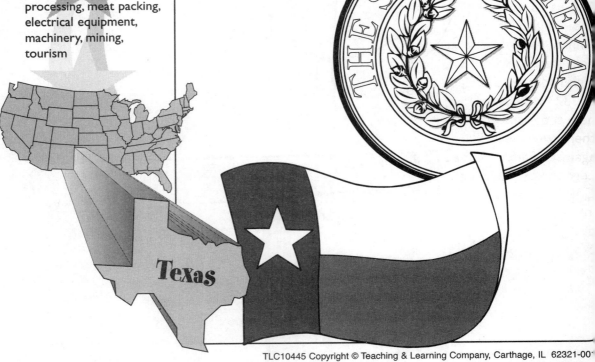

The Alamo

In the early 1800s, the Spanish military stationed a cavalry unit at the mission, San Antonio de Valero, also known as the "Alamo." This mission, turned army barracks and fortress, became a home for Revolutionaries, Royalists and soldiers during Mexico's decade-long struggle for independence from Spain. By December 1835, Texans wanted to annex their territory from Mexico and have their own independent state. They began a revolution against Mexican troops stationed at the Alamo and the surrounding town of San Antonio. After five grueling days of house-to-house battles, the Mexican soldiers were forced to surrender. The Texans and local Tejanos quickly occupied the fortified Alamo.

By February 1836, the Mexican army's general, Antonio López de Santa Anna, reached San Antonio with 5000 troops. His goal was to reclaim the lost territory, including the Alamo. For 13 days the Tejanos and Texans fought valiantly against the mighty force of Santa Anna's army. Early pleas for help were sent out and on the eighth day of the siege a band of 32 volunteers arrived to help the Alamo defenders. Still, there were less than 200 men against Santa Anna's 4000. Legend says that the Alamo's Col. Travis, seeing their impending doom, drew a line in the dirt and asked any man who chose to stay and fight to step over the line. All but one man chose to stay.

Two who remained were already famous—Jim Bowie was a gunfighter and Davy Crockett was a frontiersman and congressman from Tennessee.

The final attack on the besieged garrison came just before daybreak on March 6, 1836. Mexican soldiers moved through the darkness toward the Alamo as cannons blasted. At first, the Alamo defenders thwarted the assaults, but Mexican troops regrouped, scaled the walls and rushed inside. The fight became desperate and the defenders were overwhelmed. By sunrise when the battle ended, Santa Anna had reclaimed the Alamo.

A symbol of fighting against tyranny and oppression, and courage in the face of death, the Alamo remains Texas' most hallowed ground.

Fireback

Firebacks, made as early as the 1600s, were decorated pieces of flat iron were placed inside hearths. The iron firebacks captured the heat of a fire and radiated the warmth long after the fire burned out. Firebacks were usually decorated with historical symbols and patriotic images. The Alamo would have been a perfect icon for a fireback.

Notable Natives

Debbie Allen (1950-), actress, dancer, Houston

Lance Armstrong (1971-), Tour de France-winning cyclist, Plano

Gene Autry (1907-1998), singer, Tioga

Carol Burnett (1933-), comedienne, San Antonio

Kate Capshaw (1953-), actress, Fort Worth

Cyd Charisse (Tula Ellice Finklea) (1921-), actress and dancer, Amarillo

Dabney Coleman 1932-), actor, Austin

Joan Crawford (Lucille le Sueur) (1904-1977), actress, San Antonio

Mildred Ella Didrickson (Babe) Zaharias (1914-1956), athlete, Port Arthur

Hilary Duff (1987-), actress, Houston

Dwight David Eisenhower (1890-1969), 34th President (1953-1961), Denison

Morgan Fairchild (1950-), actress, Dallas

Farrah Fawcett (1947-), actress, Corpus Christi

A.J. Foyt (1935-), four-time Indy 500 winner, Houston

Jennifer Garner (1972-), actress, Houston

Larry Hagman (1931-), actor, Fort Worth

Woody Harrelson (1961-), actor, Midland

Ethan Hawke (1970-), actor, Austin

Ben Hogan (1912-1997), four-time U.S. Open winning golfer, Dublin

Buddy Holly (Charles Hardin) (1936-1959), musician, Lubbock

Howard Hughes (1905-1976), aviator, industrialist, film producer, Houston

Lyndon Baines Johnson (1908-1973), 36th President (1963-1969), Stonewall

George Jones (1931-), singer, Saratoga

Tommy Lee Jones (1946-), actor, San Saba

Janis Joplin (1943-1970), singer, Port Arthur

Barbara Jordan (1936-1996), public official, Houston

Beyonce Knowles (1981-), singer, Houston

Lyle Lovett (1957-), singer, Klein

Mary Martin (1913-1990), singer, actress, Weatherford

Steve Martin (1945-), actor, Waco

Larry McMurtry (1936-), novelist, Wichita Falls

Meat Loaf (1951-), singer, Dallas

Roger Miller (1936-1992), singer, Fort Worth

Audie Murphy (1924-1971) war hero, Kingston

Willie Nelson (1933-), singer, Abbot

Sandra Day O'Connor (1930-), first woman U.S. Supreme Court Justice, El Paso

Roy Orbison (1936-1988), singer, Vernon

Buck Owens (1929-), country singer, Sherman

Fess Parker (1925-), actor, hotel developer, Fort Worth

Dennis Quaid (1954-), actor, Houston

Randy Quaid (1950-), actor, Houston

Dan Rather (1931-), TV anchorman, Wharton

Sissy Spacek (1949-), actress, Quitman

Aaron Spelling (1928-), TV producer, Dallas

Patrick Swayze (1952-), dancer, actor, Houston

Rip Torn (Elmore Rual Tom, Jr.) (1931-), actor, Temple

Tommy Tune (1939-), dancer, Wichita Falls

Framed Mini Alamo Fireback

This project should not be used with fire or flame.

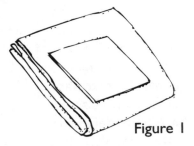

Figure 1

Figure 2

Materials

* tracing paper
* 8" x 10" wooden frame
* 3 mm ¹/₈" tin sheet (8" x 10")
* 8" x 10" heavy card stock
* glue
* scissors
* hammer
* steel awl or nail
* newspapers

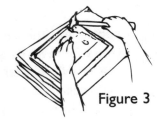

Figure 3

Instructions

1. Copy the Alamo template on page 197. Enlarge, if necessary, to fit the tin sheet.
2. Lay the tin sheet on several layers of newspaper. (Figure 1)
3. Tape the template on the tin sheet. (Figure 2)
4. Starting at the middle of the template, lightly hammer the awl or nail to make small dents to texture the tin. Do not punch through the tin. (Figure 3)
5. When you have outlined the Alamo template with punched lines, remove it and continue making texture marks on the tin. Fill in areas that need additional texture. (Figure 4)
6. Spread glue over the back of the tin and on the frame's cardboard backing. Glue the tin design in position. Let it dry, then attach the frame. (Figure 5)

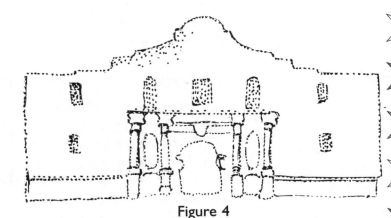

Figure 4

Figure 5

Name _____

Alamo Template

Fun Facts

Animal: Rocky Mountain Elk (Cervus canadensis)

Bird: Common American Gull (Larus californious)

Emblem: Beehive

Fish: Bonneville Cutthroat Trout (Salmo clarki)

Flower: Sego Lily (Calochortus nuttallii)

Fossil: Allosaurus (Allosaurus fragilis)

Fruit: Cherry

Gem: Topaz

Grass: Indian Rice Grass (Oryzopsis hymenoides)

Insect: Honeybee (Apis mellifera)

Mineral: Copper

Motto: "Industry"

Nickname: Beehive State

Rock: Coal

Song: "Utah . . . This Is the Place" by Sam Francis and Gary Francis

Tree: Blue Spruce (Picea pungens)

Vegetable: Spanish Sweet Onion

Historic Vegetable: Sugar Beet

Statehood: January 4, 1896; 45th state admitted to the Union

Population: (2000 estimate) 2,233,169

Area: 84,904 square miles of land and water; 13th largest state

Highest Point: Kings Peak; 13,528 feet above sea level

Lowest Point: Beaverdam Creek; 2000 feet above sea level

Capital: Salt Lake City

Largest City: Salt Lake City

Major Crops: Cattle, calves, hogs, dairy products, hay, turkeys

Major Industry: Machinery; mining—coal, copper, silver, lead, gold, zinc; aerospace; food processing; electrical equipment; tourism

198

Utah

Name: Utah got its name from a Native American word, <u>yuttahih</u>, meaning "one that is higher up."

Did You Know?

Nestled in the middle of everyone's body is the navel. A small Utah town of a little more than 400 residents, in the middle of the state, in the Juab Valley is like a navel on the body. You can't name a town after the navel just because it is in the center of the state can you? Some people believe the name, Le Van, was chosen by Mormon leader, Brigham Young, and had no relation to the town's location. But others believe the town was named for its location in the middle of the state of Utah. Residents didn't think they should name their town Belly Button or Navel, so, they named it Levan, *navel* spelled backwards!

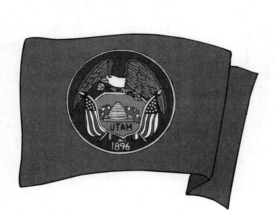

Flag: The state flag has the state seal in the middle of a field of dark blue.

Seal: The circular seal has the state emblem, a beehive, at its center in a shield. Above it is the state motto, *industry*. Below the beehive is the date, *1847*, the year the Mormons entered what is now the state of Utah. On either side of the shield is an American flag. Above it is an American eagle. In the outer ring of the seal are the words *The Great Seal of the State of Utah* and the year in Utah became a state, *1896*.

The First Transcontinental Railroad

On May 10, 1869, one of the most dramatic and important events in American history was the completion of the first Transcontinental Railroad at Promontory, Utah. Before that time, no railroad connected the eastern side of the continent to the west. This monumental industrial feat could be compared to the 20th century first moon landing in its historical, scientific and popular significance. Continental travel had generally taken six months or longer, but the Transcontinental Railroad reduced travel time to six days. Even the cost savings was considerable. Cross-country travel had cost around $1000, but the railroad reduced travel expenses to an average of $70.

During the final days leading up to the railroad's connection, rival workers from the Union Pacific and the Central Pacific pushed to outdo one another. While Union Pacific workers boasted that they could lay six miles of track a day, Central Pacific workers claimed to lay down 10 miles in a day. Bets were made, and the race was on. Newspapers around the country gave daily reports about each team's progress. On April 28, 1869, Central Pacific workers laid down an unheard of 10 miles of track in 12 hours. (This feat was accomplished without the aid of modern equipment.) As the gap narrowed between the two railroads, it became apparent that they would meet at Promontory Point, Utah.

A little after 11:00 on the morning of May 10, 1869, Governor Leland Stanford of California arrived at Promontory in a Central Pacific train. At the same time, the Union Pacific rolled in with its officer, Thomas C. Durant. By noon, the trains faced each other and the last tie was laid down. It was made of California laurel and had a silver plate in the middle with the date and names of the railroad officers of the two railroads engraved on it.

As the final four spikes (two silver and two gold) were about to be driven into the ties, telegraph offices wired newspapers around the country of the historic event. Governor Stanford stood on the north side of the track and Durant on the south. Both were ready to hammer the final two golden spikes with specially made silver hammers. Governor Stanford missed on his first try, but, the telegraphs wired . . . "Done!" and history was made.

Utah

Railroad Spikes

Materials

* 4 toilet paper tubes
* silver spray paint
* gold spray paint
* clay carving tools
* packaging tape
* 4 cups plaster of Paris
* 4 cups vermiculite, (organic potting material found in gardening centers)
* 4 cups water
* stir stick
* medium-sized plastic bowl

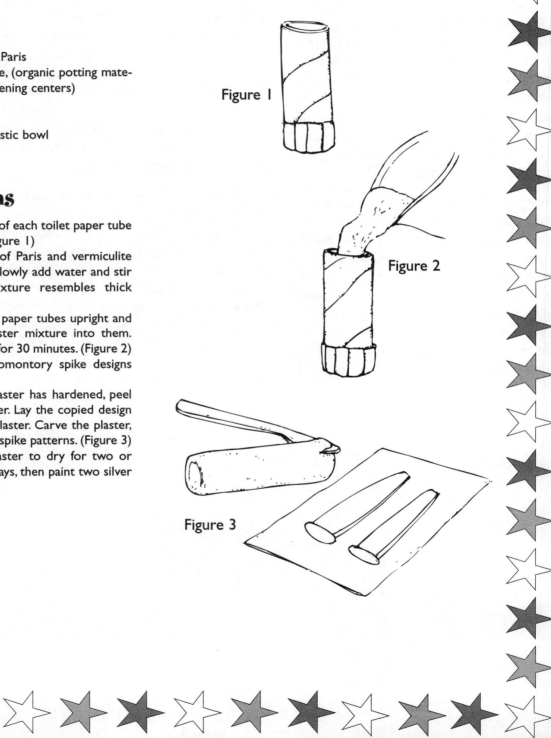

Figure 1

Figure 2

Figure 3

Instructions

1. Seal one end of each toilet paper tube with tape. (Figure 1)
2. Pour plaster of Paris and vermiculite into a bowl. Slowly add water and stir until the mixture resembles thick gravy.
3. Set the toilet paper tubes upright and pour the plaster mixture into them. Let them set for 30 minutes. (Figure 2)
4. Copy the promontory spike designs on page 201.
5. When the plaster has hardened, peel away the paper. Lay the copied design next to the plaster. Carve the plaster, following the spike patterns. (Figure 3)
6. Allow the plaster to dry for two or three more days, then paint two silver and two gold.

Promontory Spike Designs

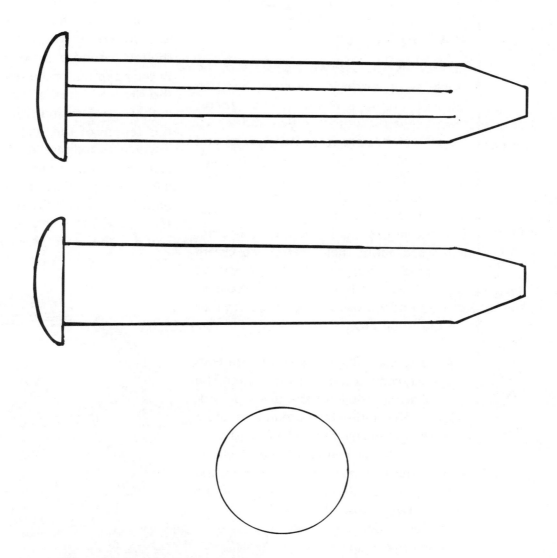

Fun Facts

Amphibian: Northern Leopard Frog (Rana pipiens)

Animal: Morgan Horse (Equus caballus)

Bird: Hermit Thrush (Catharus guttatus)

Butterfly: Monarch Butterfly (Danaus plexippus)

Fish: Brook Trout (Salvelinus fontinalis), Walleye Pike (Stizosedion vitreum)

Flower: Red Clover (Trifolium pratense)

Fossil: White Whale (Delphinapterus leucas)

Fruit: Apple (Malus pumila)

Gem: Talc

Insect: Honeybee (Apis mellifera)

Motto: "Freedom and Unity"

Nickname: Green Mountain State

Rocks: Granite, Marble and Slate

Song: "These Green Mountains" by Diane Martin

Tree: Sugar Maple (Acer saccharum)

Statehood: March 4, 1791; 14th state admitted to the Union

Population: (2000 estimate) 608,827

Area: 9615 square miles of land and water; 45th largest state

Highest Point: Mt. Mansfield; 4393 feet above sea level

Lowest Point: Lake Champlain; 95 feet above sea level

Capital: Montpelier

Largest City: Burlington

Major Crops: Dairy products, cattle, hay, apples, maple syrup, maple products

Major Industry: Electronic equipment, fabricated metal products, printing and publishing, paper products, tourism

Vermont

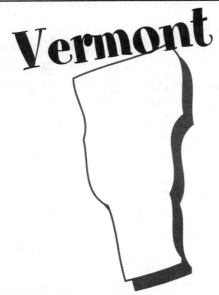

Name: Vermont's name has its origins in two French words. When the state was being formed in 1777, Dr. Thomas Young suggested naming the state Vermont, combining two French words—verd meaning "green" and mont meaning "mountain."

Did You Know?

Vermont is not just sweet because of the maple syrup made in the state, but also because of the ice cream made there! Vermont is the home of Ben and Jerry's Ice Cream™, started by Ben Cohen and Jerry Greenfield, friends since junior high school gym class. In 1963, they opened an ice cream store in a converted gas station, selling one scoop of ice cream at a time. Ben and Jerry's™ became a local favorite and word about their creamy ice cream was spread. People from all over wanted some. Ben and Jerry's™ is now sold all throughout the world, one of the premier ice cream brands.

Flag: The state flag is a field of blue with the state coat of arms in the center. The coat of arms contains a shield with a landscape of Vermont—high mountains and a blue sky extending into yellow. There is a pine tree in the center of the shield as well as three sheaves of yellow grain, and a red cow standing to the right of the tree. Two crossed pine branches under the shield extend halfway up the sides. Beneath is a ribbon with the state's name, *Vermont,* and the motto, "Freedom and Unity." Above the shield is the crest, a profile of a deer head with antlers.

Seal: The circular design of the seal has several key elements. It contains four sheaves of grain and a cow, probably representing agriculture in the state. (The four sheaves of grain may also represent the four counties in existence at the time of the adoption of the seal.) At the top of the circle are several wavy lines, probably indicating water and sky. The pine tree in the center of the seal has 14 branches, possibly to indicate Vermont as the 14th state to join the Union. An arrow on the left may mean that part of the state was unsafe at the time the seal was adopted in the late 1700s. Near the bottom of the seal are the word *Vermont* and the state motto, "*Freedom & Unity.*"

Maple Fudge Bars

Known for its breathtaking scenery and colorful seasons, Vermont may also be the nation's sweetest state. It is the chief supplier of maple sugar and syrup. Native Americans of the region were the first to tap the sugar maple trees. When early colonists settled the area, they soon added the tasty sweetener to their diet.

The process of harvesting maple sap has remained relatively unchanged for 300 years. The harvesting season usually begins in mid-January to mid-April, depending on the weather since cold nights and warm days encourage the sap to flow. Most professional "tappers" search for mature trees more than 10" in diameter. They drill a harvest hole into the trunk of the maple tree about four feet from the base. Pails hanging from nails above the sap hole capture the oozing liquid. One tree might have four pails attached to it. After the sap is gathered, it is immediately boiled down to concentrate the sugar through evaporation. Great care is taken not to overheat or burn the sap or sugar. The syrup is then filtered and poured into stylized jars. Harvesting sap is a time-consuming process. It takes approximately 40 gallons of sap to make one gallon of syrup.

Notable Natives

Chester Alan Arthur (1830-1886), 21st President (1881-1885), Fairfield

Orson Bean (1928-), actor, comedian, Burlington

Myra R. Bradwell (1831-1894), lawyer, women's rights advocate, Manchester

Orestes Augustus Brownson (1803-1876), clergyman, writer, Stockbridge

Calvin Coolidge (1872-1933), 30th President (1923-1929), Plymouth

Donald James Cram (1919-2001), Nobel Prize-winning chemist, Chester

John Deere (1804-1886), inventor of the steel plow, Rutland

George Dewey (1837-1917), admiral, Montpelier

John Dewey (1859-1952), philosopher, educator, Burlington

Stephen A. Douglas (1813-1861), U.S. senator, presidential candidate, Brandon

Andrew Ellicott Douglass (1867-1962), astronomer, Windsor

George Franklin Edmunds (1828-1919), U.S. senator, politician, Richmond

James Fisk (1834-1872), financial speculator, Bennington

Richard Morris Hunt (1827-1895), architect, Brattleboro

Elisha Graves Otis (1811-1861), inventor, Halifax

Rudy Vallee (1901-1986), singer, Island Pond

Brigham Young (1801-1877), Mormon Church leader, Whittingham

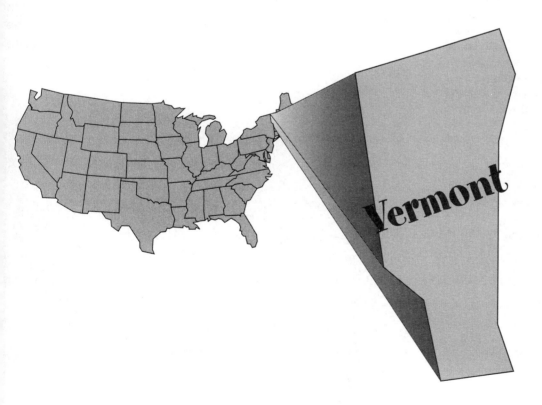

Tapping Maple Trees the Old-Fashioned Way

This project requires heat.

Instructions

Here's how to make homemade maple syrup:

1. Drill a small hole about 3" into a mature sugar maple tree. (Get permission from the owner!)
2. Push a metal or plastic spout into the sap hole. (Figure 1)
3. Hang a collection pail or bucket on a nail under the spout and allow the sap to drip. (Figure 2) Be sure to cover the bucket to keep out rain, leaves and insects.
4. After you've gathered the sap (You will need about 10 gallons to make one quart of syrup.), you will need to boil out the water. Pour some of the sap into a large pan and bring to a boil (do not let the sap burn, it will affect the taste). Add more sap as the water evaporates. The syrup should reach 219°F on a candy thermometer.
5. Pour the cooled syrup though a filter into sterilized containers. (Figure 4) Store in a cool place, or freeze.
6. Before using, reheat syrup to 180°F.

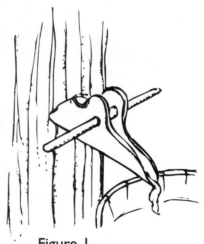

Figure 1

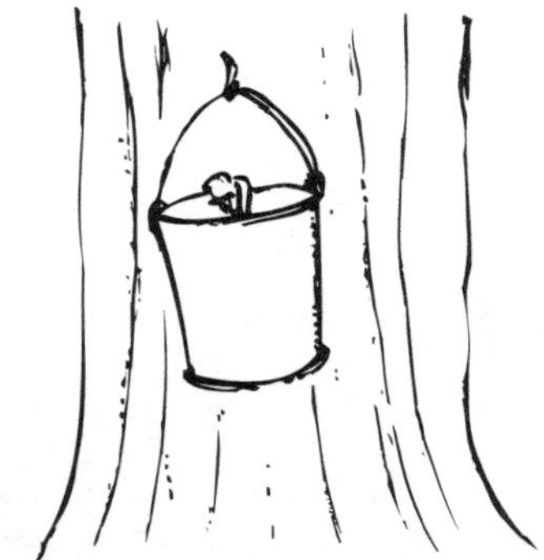

Figure 2

Figure 3

Maple Candy

This project requires heat.

Colonial children poured their maple syrup onto bowls of snow for dessert. Native Americans used maple syrup for many things, including as a seasoning or glaze for moose meat. What do you use maple syrup for?

Follow the recipe for easy-to-make maple candy.

Materials

* 4 cups maple syrup
* 1 cup cream
* 1/4 cup butter
* 1 cup chopped walnuts (optional)
* 1 teaspoon lemon juice
* butter
* 9" baking dish
* saucepan
* hot pads or mitt

Figure 1

Figure 2

Instructions

1. Bring the maple syrup, cream and butter to a boil. Turn the heat down and simmer an additional 10 minutes. (Figure 1)
2. Using hot pads or a mitt, remove the pan from the heat and stir in walnuts and lemon juice. (Figure 2)
3. Butter a baking dish and pour the mixture into it. Allow it to cool, then cut into small squares. (Figure 3)

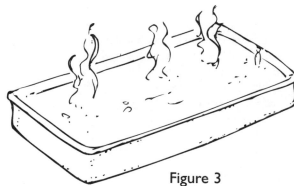

Figure 3

Snowflake Jar

Materials for One Jar

* 12" squares of thin paper
* jam jar
* 12" ribbon
* scissors
* nail
* hammer
* rubber band (optional)

Instructions

Study the snowflake designs on page 207. Create your own snowflake with these basic steps:

1. Cut out a paper circle two times larger than the jar lid. (Figure 1)
2. Fold the circle in half. (Figure 2)
3. Fold it three more times. (Figure 3)
4. Draw half a heart 1/4" from the bottom edge of the paper. Cut out the shape. (Figure 4)
5. Repeat the process on the other side of the folded paper. (Figure 5)
6. Place the folded paper on a hard surface and use a hammer and nail to create a series of dots in it. (Figure 6)
7. Trim the bottom with two equally spaced triangles. (Figure 7)
8. Unfold and flatten the paper snowflake and place it over a jar filled with the maple candy you made (page 205). Secure it with a ribbon tied into a bow. If necessary, use a rubber band to secure the cover before adding the ribbon. (Figure 8)

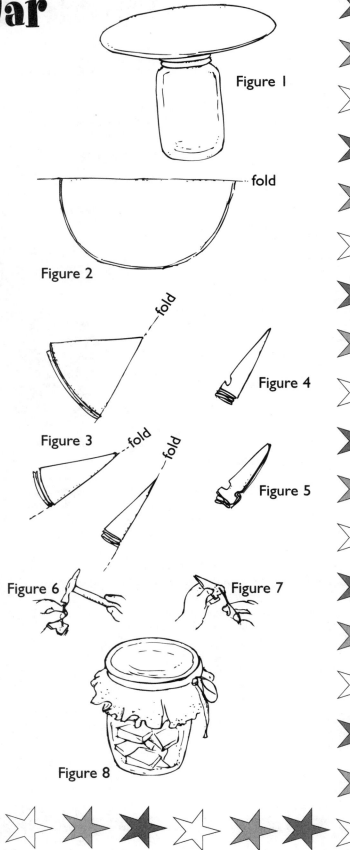

Figure 1

fold

Figure 2

fold

Figure 4

Figure 3

fold

fold

Figure 5

Figure 6

Figure 7

Figure 8

Snowflake Designs

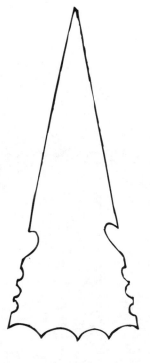

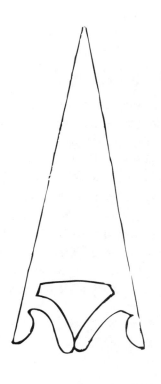

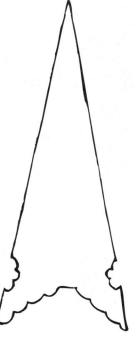

Fun Facts

Bird: Cardinal (Cardinalis cardinalis)

Dog: American Fox Hound (Canis familiaris)

Fish: Brook Trout (Salvelinus fontinalis)

Flower: Flowering Dogwood (Cornus florida)

Insect: Tiger Swallowtail (Papilio glaucus Linne)

Motto: "Sic Semper Tyrannis" (Thus Always to Tyrants)

Nicknames: Old Dominion, Mother of Presidents

Shell: Oyster (Crassostraea virginica)

Song: "Carry Me Back to Old Virginia" by James A. Bland

Tree: Flowering Dogwood (Cornus florida)

Statehood: June 25, 1788; 10th state admitted to the Union

Population: (2000 estimate) 7,078,515

Area: 42,769 square miles of land and water; 35th largest state

Highest Point: Mt. Rogers; 5729 feet above sea level

Lowest Point: Atlantic coast; sea level

Capital: Richmond

Largest City: Virginia Beach

Major Crops: Cattle, broilers, turkeys, hogs, dairy products, tomatoes, tobacco, potatoes, soybeans, peanuts, apples, beans

Major Industry: Lumber, furniture, transportation equipment, textiles and apparel, food processing, printing, electric equipment, data and computer processing, chemical production

Name: Like some other U.S. states, Virginia was named after an English monarch. Sir Walter Raleigh named the area, Virginia in honor of Elizabeth I, the virgin Queen, who ruled England from 1558 until her death in 1603.

Did You Know?

Most people think the largest office building in the world would be in a city like New York, Chicago or London. But it isn't. The largest office building in the world is not a commercial building, but the Pentagon located in Arlington, Virginia. It was designed by architect George Bergstrom in the 1940s to house the Department of Defense. The five-sided Pentagon is the workplace for nearly 23,000 employees each day!

Seal: The circular seal depicts the Roman goddess Virtus, representing the spirit of the Commonwealth, dressed as an Amazon with a sheathed sword in one hand, a spear in the other and one foot on the form of Tyranny. He lies with a broken chain in his left hand, a scourge in his right and his fallen crown nearby, implying struggle that has ended in complete victory. Virginia's motto, "Sic Semper Tyrannis" appears at the bottom of the seal with the state name at the top.

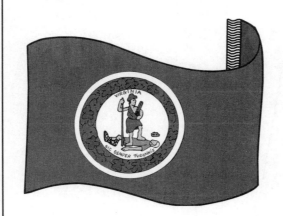

Flag: The light blue flag has a white circle in the center with the state seal in it. The right edge of the flag has a white silk fringe.

Virginia's Botanist President

Virginia was a farming state in America's early history. Its beauty inspired many, particularly President Thomas Jefferson. He was a curious botanist, known for his personal notebooks on plants he found in his own fields and backyard. However, Jefferson's most significant collections were the newly found plants and animals of North America gathered by Lewis and Clark and the Corps of Discovery.

In tribute to the famous Virginia farmer, President and botanist, create a notebook of plants found in your own backyard.

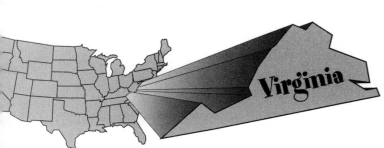

Notable Natives

Arthur Ashe (1943-1993), tennis player, Richmond

Stephen Fuller Austin (1793-1836), colonizer, "Father of Texas," Austinville

Pearl Bailey (1918-1990), actress, singer, Newport News

Warren Beatty (1937-), actor, Richmond

Francis Preston Blair (1791-1876), editor, politician, Abingdon

James "Jim" Bridger (1804-1881), trapper, storyteller, Richmond

Sandra Bullock (1964-), actress, Arlington

Richard Byrd (1888-1957), polar explorer, Winchester

Willa Cather (1873-1947), Pulitzer Prize-winning writer, Winchester

Roy Clark (1933-), country musician, Meaherrin

William Clark (1770-1838), explorer, Caroline County

Henry Clay (1777-1852), U.S. senator, Hanover County

Patsy Cline (Virginia Petterson Hensley) (1932-1963), country singer, Winchester

Jerry Falwell (1933-), television evangelist, Lynchburg

Ella Fitzgerald (1917-1996), singer, Newport News

William Henry Harrison (1733-1841), 9th President (1841), Berkeley

Patrick Henry (1736-1799), Revolutionary War hero, Hanover County

Sam Houston (1793-1863), soldier, political leader, statesman, near Lexington

Thomas Jefferson (1743-1826), 3rd President (1801-1809), Shadwell

Robert E. Lee (1807-1870), Confederate Civil War general, Westmoreland County

Meriwether Lewis (1774-1809), explorer, Albemarle County

Shirley McLaine (1934-), actress, Richmond

Rob Lowe (1964-), actor, Charlottesville

James Madison (1751-1836), 4th President (1809-1817), Port Conway

John Marshall (1755-1835), U.S. Supreme Court Chief Justice, near Germantown

James Monroe (1758-1831), 5th President (1817-1825), Westmoreland County

Mackenzie Phillips (1959-), actress, Alexandria

Walter Reed (1851-1902), Army surgeon, Belroi

Tim Reid (1944-), actor, Norfolk

Bill Bojangles Robinson (1878-1949), dancer, Richmond

George C. Scott (1927-1999), actor, Wise

Sam Snead (1912-2002), three-time PGA and Masters-winning golfer, Hot Springs

Zachary Taylor (1784-1850), 12th President (1849-1850), near Barboursville

John Tyler (1790-1862), 10th President (1841-1845), Greenway

Booker T. Washington (1856-1915), educator, Franklin County

George Washington (1732-1799), 1st President (1789-1797), Westmoreland County

Woodrow Wilson (1856-1924), 28th President (1913-1921), Staunton

Tom Wolfe (1931-), journalist, critic, novelist, Richmond

Backyard Botany Journal

Materials

* 8 sheets watercolor paper (8½" x 11")
* hole punch
* few long strands of raffia
* various tubes of watercolor paints
* watercolor palette or ice cube tray
* brushes
* liquid soap (mild)
* spray bottle
* paper towels
* journal cover (white butcher paper, newsprint—not newspaper)
* various garden leaves and flowers from your yard

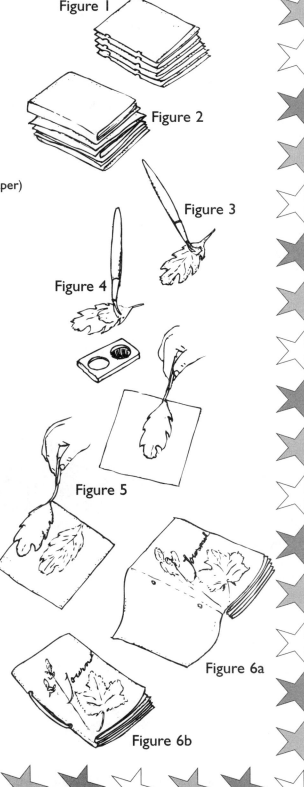

Figure 1

Figure 2

Figure 3

Figure 4

Figure 5

Figure 6a

Figure 6b

Instructions

1. Fold the watercolor papers in half. Lay them in a stack and snip two half circle punches on the folded edges. (Figure 1)
2. Prepare paper by spritzing it with water, then putting it in a plastic bag between paper towels. Stack a heavy book or block on top for weight. Allow the paper to absorb the water, but not buckle. The paper should be slightly damp when you begin your prints. (Figure 2)
3. Squeeze a pea-shaped blob of watercolor onto the palette. Add the same amount of water to it and stir until it is the consistency of pudding or thick cream. Mix ¾ teaspoon of liquid soap with the paint and water and stir.
4. Paint a fine coat of soap on a leaf or flower. (Figure 3)
5. With the same brush, coat the soaped area carefully with paint. Spray with water to keep the paint and soap moist through this process. (Figure 4)
6. Work quickly lifting the stem of the flower or leaf and placing the inked side down onto the damp paper. (Figure 5)
7. Cover with a paper towel and press firmly with the heel of your palm, trying not to move the plant.
8. Slowly remove the paper towel off the leaf. Lift the leaf off the paper by grabbing the stem and tipping it up. (Figure 5)
9. Continue making impressions of leaves and flowers, using this process.
10. Copy the cover design on page 211. Punch two holes in the cover to match the other pages. When the pages have dried, gather them together, thread raffia through the holes and tie it. (Figures 6a and 6b)

Name _____

Cover Design

fold here

My Journal

Date

Fun Facts

Bird: American Goldfinch or Wild Canary (Carduelis tristis)

Fish: Spearhead Trout (Salmo gairdnerii)

Flower: Coast Rhododendron (Rhododendron macrophyllum)

Fossil: Columbian Mammoth (Mammuthus columbi)

Fruit: Apple (Malus pumila)

Gem: Petrified Wood

Grass: Bluebunch Wheatgrass (Agropyron spicatum-pursh)

Insect: Green Darner Dragonfly (Anax junius Drury)

Motto: "Alki" (Bye and Bye)

Nickname: Evergreen State

Song: "Washington, My Home" by Helen Davis

Folk Song: "Roll on, Columbia, Roll On" by Woodie Guthrie

Tree: Western Hemlock (Tsuga heterophylla)

Statehood: November 11, 1889; 42nd state admitted to the Union

Population: (2000 estimate) 5,894,121

Area: 71,303 square miles of land and water; 18th largest state

Highest Point: Mt. Rainier; 14,410 feet above sea level

Lowest Point: Pacific coast; sea level

Capital: Olympia

Largest City: Seattle

Major Crops: Seafood, lentils, peas, dairy products, apples, pears, apricots, cherries, grapes, cattle, hops, wheat, potatoes, spearmint oil, asparagus

Major Industry: Aerospace, shipbuilding, software development, refined aluminum, food processing, paper products, lumber and wood products, chemical products, tourism

Washington

Name: Washington is the only state in the Union named after a President, George Washington, the first President of the United States, called "The Father of Our Country."

Did You Know?

One of the biggest days for the greeting card business is Father's Day, but it wasn't always a holiday. Sonora Smart Dodd of Spokane, Washington, first proposed the idea in 1909. She wanted to honor her own father, who had raised all six of his children by himself after their mother had died giving birth to the sixth child. The first Father's Day was observed on June 19, 1910, in Spokane. In 1966, President Lyndon Baines Johnson proclaimed it a national holiday.

Flag: The state flag has the state seal in the center of a field of green.

Seal: The state seal displays a portrait of George Washington in the center of a circle with the words *The Seal of the State of Washington* and the year *1889*.

Volcanic Cascade Mountain Range

The Cascade Mountain Range divides the state of Washington to the east and west. This rich and beautiful mountain range is the home of five snow-capped volcanoes: Mt. Adams, Mt. Baker, Glacier Peak, Mt. St. Helens and Mt. Rainier.

Volcanoes are created over the span of millions of years, each with characteristics all its own. Mt. Adams straddles the crest of the Cascades. It is considered to be a quiet volcano, but scientists have discovered sulfur deposits on its summit which reveal that it still has life burning within it. Unique to Mt. Adams are several bubble caves formed by pockets of air that puffed up from molten lava. Mt. Baker is located in the northern part of the Cascades. It is the youngest of all five volcanoes and shows signs of life, emiting steam plumes at its glaciers. Glacier Peak sits west of the Cascade crest and is the most remote of all Washington's volcanoes. It shows very little life, but scientists continue to monitor its rumblings.

Mt. Rainier, the largest volcanoe in the Cascade Range, last erupted 2200 years ago. Some of the trees on this mountain are between 500 and 1000 years old. The most famous of all these volcanoes is Mt. St. Helens, which erupted on May 18, 1980. Its northern face slid off and its powerful blast was heard as far as Vancouver, British Columbia. Mt. St. Helens continues to show signs that it is gearing up for another eruption.

The Science Behind Volcanoes

A volcano is a vent in the Earth's surface. Through it blows molten rock, ash and solid rock. How the volcano erupts depends upon the shape of the vent hole. When the vents are unclogged, the eruptions seem to be quiet and the lava flow is slow and runny. If the vent is plugged or clogged, the internal pressure builds up so much energy, it explodes with a violent eruption up to 20 miles high. Learn the basic science behind volcanoes by making your own with simple materials.

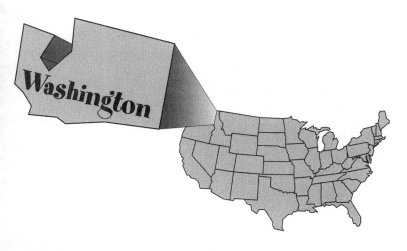

Notable Natives

Philip Abelson (1913-), physical chemist, Tacoma

Bob Barker (1923-), television game show host, Darrington

Max Brand (Frederick Schiller Faust) (1892-1944), journalist, short story writer, Seattle

Trisha Brown (1936-), choreographer, Aberdeen

Dyan Cannon (1937-), actress, Tacoma

Chester Floyd Carlson (1906-1968), inventor of photocopy technology, Seattle

Carol Channing (1921-), actress, Seattle

Judy Collins (1933-), singer, Seattle

Bing Crosby (Harry Lillis) (1903-1977), singer, actor, Tacoma

Merce Cunningham (1919-), choreographer, dance teacher, Centralia

Frederick Russell Eggan (1906-1991), cultural anthropologist, Seattle

John Albert Elway (1960-), football player, Port Angeles

Frances Farmer (1914-1970), actress, Seattle

Kenny G. (1956-), musician, Seattle

Bill Gates (1955-), computer scientist, software giant, Seattle

Jimi Hendrix (1942-1970), guitarist, Seattle

George Herbert Hitchings (1905-1998), Nobel Prize-winning physiologist, Hoquiam

Robert Joffrey (Abdullah Jaffa Anver Bey Kahn) (1930-1988), choreographer, Seattle

Kenny Loggins (1948-), singer, Everett

Hank Ketcham (1920-2001), cartoonist known for Dennis the Menace, Seattle

Craig T. Nelson (1946-), actor, Spokane

Seattle Dwamish (1786-1866), Suquamish chief

Hilary Swank (1974-), actress, Bellingham

Blair Underwood (1964-), actor, Tacoma

Adam West (1928-), television actor, star of Batman, Walla Walla

Volcano Science

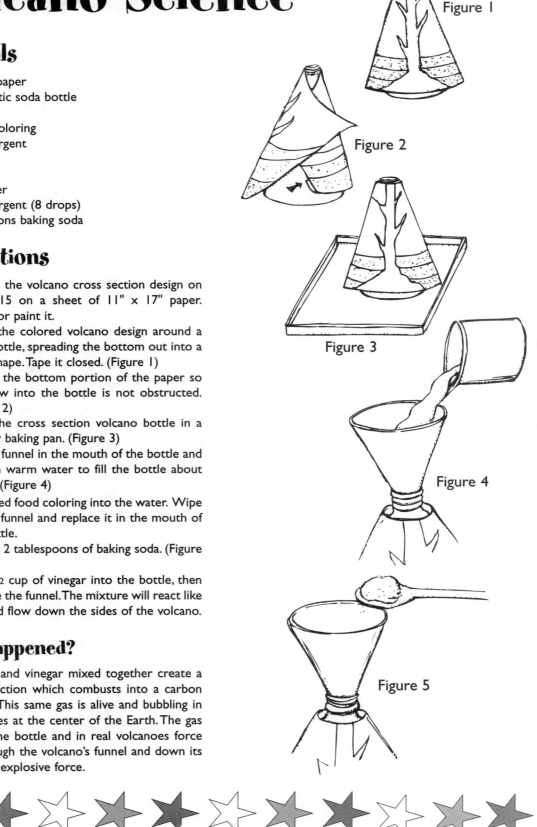

Figure 1

Figure 2

Figure 3

Figure 4

Figure 5

Materials

* 11" x 17" paper
* 1 liter plastic soda bottle
* baking pan
* red food coloring
* liquid detergent
* vinegar
* funnel
* warm water
* liquid detergent (8 drops)
* 2 tablespoons baking soda

Instructions

1. Enlarge the volcano cross section design on page 215 on a sheet of 11" x 17" paper. Color or paint it.
2. Wrap the colored volcano design around a soda bottle, spreading the bottom out into a cone shape. Tape it closed. (Figure 1)
3. Fold in the bottom portion of the paper so the view into the bottle is not obstructed. (Figure 2)
4. Place the cross section volcano bottle in a shallow baking pan. (Figure 3)
5. Place a funnel in the mouth of the bottle and pour in warm water to fill the bottle about $^3/_4$ full. (Figure 4)
6. Drop red food coloring into the water. Wipe off the funnel and replace it in the mouth of the bottle.
7. Pour in 2 tablespoons of baking soda. (Figure 5)
8. Pour $^1/_2$ cup of vinegar into the bottle, then remove the funnel. The mixture will react like lava and flow down the sides of the volcano.

What Happened?

Baking soda and vinegar mixed together create a chemical reaction which combusts into a carbon dioxide gas. This same gas is alive and bubbling in real volcanoes at the center of the Earth. The gas bubbles in the bottle and in real volcanoes force lava up through the volcano's funnel and down its side with an explosive force.

Volcano Cross Section Design

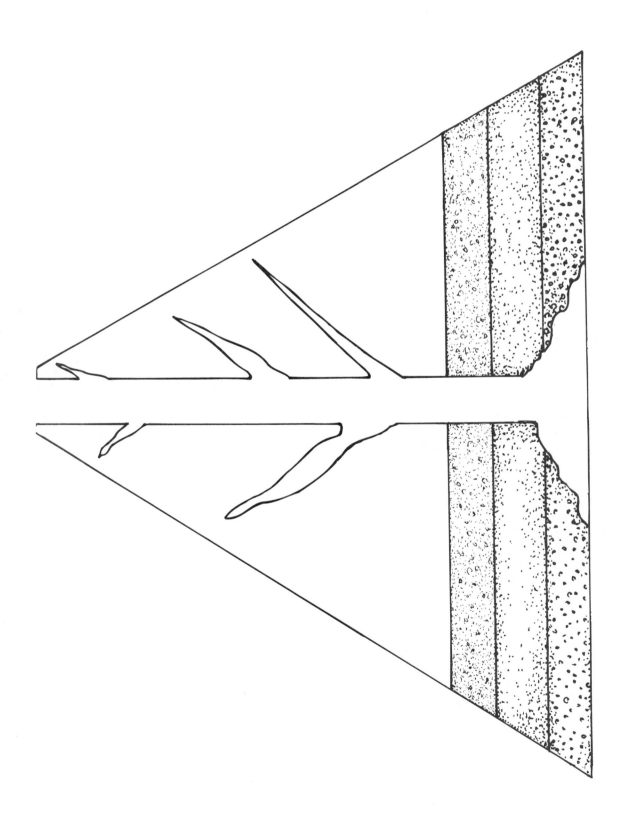

Fun Facts

Animal: Black Bear (Ursus americanus)

Bird: Cardinal (Cardinalis cardinalis)

Butterfly: Monarch (Danaus plexippus)

Fish: Brook Trout (Salvelinus fontinalis)

Flower: Big Laurel (Rhododendron maximum)

Fruit: Golden Delicious Apple (Malus pumila)

Gem: Mississippian Fossil Coral (Lithostrotionella)

Insect: Honeybee (Apis mellifera)

Motto: "Montani semper liberi" (Mountaineers are always free)

Nickname: Mountain State

Songs: "The West Virginia Hills" by Ellen King

"This Is My West Virginia" by Iris Bell

"West Virginia, My Home Sweet Home" by Julian G. Hearne Jr.

Tree: Sugar Maple (Acer saccharum)

Statehood: June 20, 1863; 35th state admitted to the Union

Population: (2000 estimate) 1,808,344

Area: 24,231 square miles of land and water; 41st largest state

Highest Point: Spruce Knob; 4863 feet above sea level

Lowest Point: Potomac River; 240 feet above sea level

Capital: Charleston

Largest City: Charleston

Major Crops: Cattle, dairy products, poultry, eggs, apples

Major Industry: Coal mining; steel production; chemical products; primary metals, stone, clay, and glass products; tourism and recreation

216

West Virginia

Did You Know?

Stone marbles were used in Ancient Egypt as long ago as 4000 B.C.! Glass marbles became popular in the United States in the 1880s. Children as well as adults enjoy playing with marbles, often joining in the many marble tournaments held throughout the United States. The leading producer of marbles in the United States is the Vitro Agate Company which operates a factory in Williamstown, West Virginia.

Flag: The white flag has a border of dark blue. In the center of the flag is the state coat of arms, showing a scene of two men, a rock and a motto encircled by a wreath of rhododendron, with the name of the state above it on a red ribbon.

Name: Sir Walter Raleigh named the area of Virginia in honor of Queen Elizabeth I of England, the virgin Queen, who ruled from 1558 until her death in 1603. In 1863, the western counties refused to secede from the Union during the Civil War and became a separate state.

Seal: The seal is a circle that contains the words *State of West Virginia* and the state motto, "Montani Semper Liberi." On the inside circle are a farmer with an ax, representing farming, and a miner holding a pick, representing industry. Between them is a large rock, symbolizing strength, with the date, *June 20, 1863*, on it. In front of the rock are two crisscrossed rifles. Where the two rifles meet is a liberty cap or Phrygian cap, symbolizing that hard-fought freedom was won and will be maintained by force if necessary.

Differences

Prior to the Civil War, the Appalachian mountains divided the state of Virginia in half. The state also differed in customs, cultures and even religions. The eastern part of the state had smooth rolling hills with good farmland, and the citizens were wealthy land owners. The western side of the state was drastically different. The land was rugged and mountainous, and the citizens' small farms barely squeezed out enough food to feed their families. Eastern Virginians were accused of exploiting their western neighbors and cheating them out of land and money. Western Virginians resented the easterners and wanted to separate into their own state and have more governmental control. However, the only way the boundaries of a state can be changed is through approval, and eastern Virginians refused.

In 1861, the Civil War began and southern states began seceding from the Union to join the Confederate States of America. Since this secession was illegal in the eyes of the federal government, it gave an opportunity to western Virginians to slip away from the control of eastern Virginians. The westerners formed a new, separate government which they called the Restored Government of Virginia and committed themselves to join the Union. The federal government approved the new government and the new boundaries. On June 20, 1863, the state of West Virginia became official.

A thaumatrope is a toy played with in colonial times. When it's held steady, both sides are different. When it's spun, it exemplifies the split and similarities between the two Virginias for when the ropes are twisted the images of the thaumatrope merge.

Notable Natives

John Peale Bishop (1892-1944), poet, writer, Charleston

George Brett (1953-), baseball player, Glendale

Pearl Buck (1892-1973), Nobel Prize-winning writer, Hillsboro

Harry Flood Byrd (1887-1966), politician, Martinsburg

Joyce DeWitt (1941-), actress, Wheeling

Henry Louis Gates Jr. (1950-), historian, Keyser

George Howard Herbig (1920-), astronomer, Wheeling

Thomas "Stonewall" Jackson (1824-1863), Confederate Civil War general, Clarksburg

Don Knotts (1924-), actor, Morgantown

Peter Marshall (1927-), actor, Huntington

Mary Lou Retton (1973-), gymnast, Fairmont

Cyrus Vance (1917-2002), diplomat, politician, Clarksburg

Chuck Yeager (1923-), test pilot, Myra

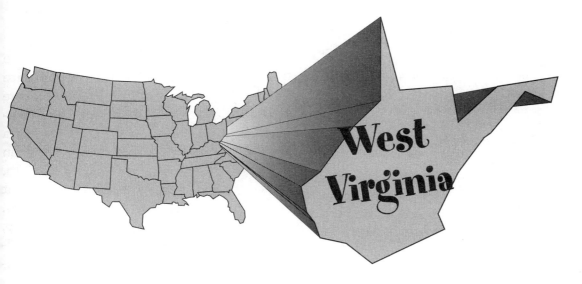

West Virginia

Thaumatrope
(Wonder-Turner)

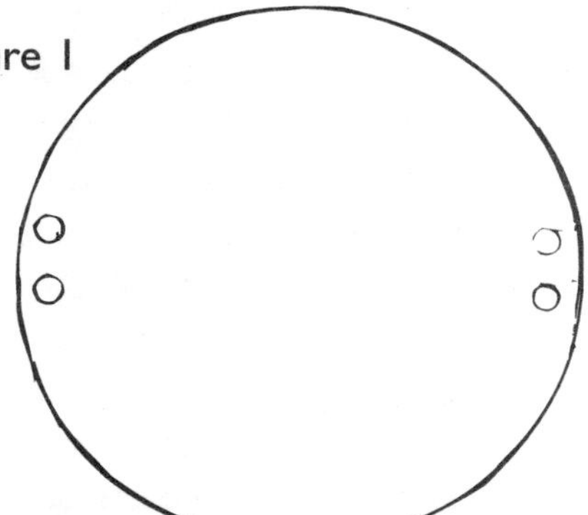

Figure 1

Materials

* drawing compass
* 4¹/₂" piece of plywood (or 4" plastic lid with edge trimmed away)
* awl
* 2—2¹/₂" x ¹/₄" dowels
* 2¹/₂' of strong string or mason's line (2)
* sandpaper
* saw or utility knife or scissors
* acrylic paints: white or pink, red, brown, yellow, green
* fine- and medium-bristle paintbrushes

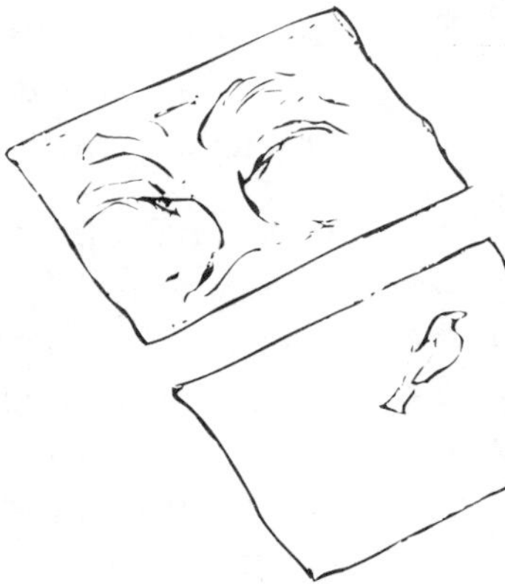

Figure 2

Instructions

1. Draw a 4" circle with a compass on plywood. Cut it out with a saw or utility knife and sand the rough edges.

2. Punch or drill two small holes into the right edge of the disk at the middle. Allow a ¹/₂" between the marks. Repeat on the left side of the disk in exactly the same positions. Make the holes large enough for the string to go through. (Figure 1)

3. Copy the cardinal and dogwood tree designs on page 220. Reduce or enlarge them to fit on the disk, one on each side. (Figure 2) Paint the cardinal red and the tree pink or white and let them dry. (Figure 3)

4. Glue the designs to the disk, one right side up, the other upside down.

5. Thread a string through one hole of the disk to the hole ¹/₂" away and back out. Repeat on the opposite side. (Figure 4)

6. Pull the strings on both sides taut and tie to a dowel on each side. (Figure 5)

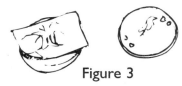

Figure 3

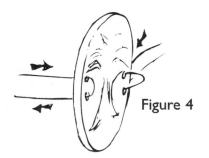

Figure 4

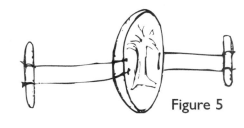

Figure 5

How to Work
the Thaumatrope

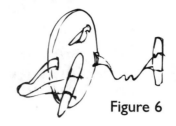

Figure 6

7. Wind up the disc by holding your hands the full length of the two strings. Keep the strings fairly loose in the beginning. (Figure 6)

8. Move the strings in a circular motion, twisting them. (Figure 7)

9. Continue until you have 20 or so strong twists on each side of the thaumatrope. (Figure 8)

10. Move your hands as if playing an accordion and allow the strings of the thaumatrope to unwind flipping the disk rapidly to see the cardinal in the dogwood tree. (Figure 9)

Figure 7

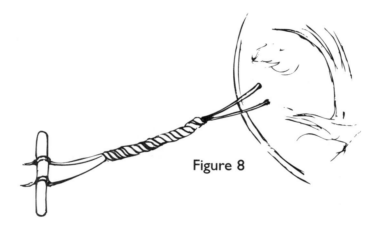

Figure 8

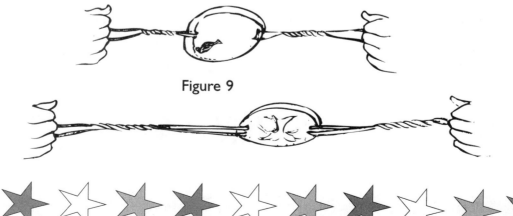

Figure 9

Cardinal &
Dogwood Designs

Color Key

a. yellow
b. red
c. white or pink
d. brown

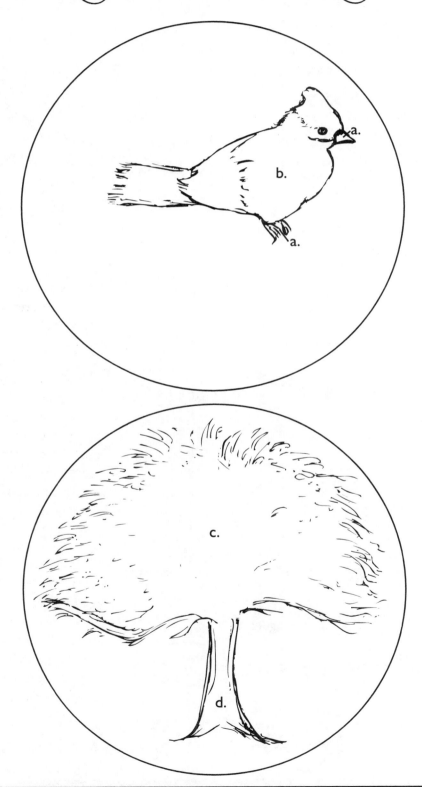

Fun Facts

Animal: Badger (Taxidea taxus)

Domestic Animal: Dairy Cow (Bos taurus)

Wild Animal: White-Tailed Deer (Odocoileus virginianus)

Bird: American Robin (Turdus migratorius)

Dog: American Water Spaniel (Canis familiaris)

Fish: Muskellunge (Esox masquinongy masquinongy)

Flower: Wood Violet (Viola papilionacea)

Fossil: Trilobite

Grain: Corn (Zea mays)

Insect: Honeybee (Apis mellifera)

Mineral: Galena

Motto: "Forward"

Nickname: Badger State

Rock: Red Granite

Song: "On, Wisconsin" by J.S. Hubbard and Charles D. Rosa

Tree: Sugar Maple (Acer saccharum)

Statehood: May 29, 1848; 30th state admitted to the Union

Population: (2000 estimate) 5,363,675

Area: 65,503 square miles of land and water; 23rd largest state

Highest Point: Timms Hill; 1951 feet above sea level

Lowest Point: Lake Michigan Shore; 581 feet above sea level

Capital: Madison

Largest City: Milwaukee

Major Crops: Cheese, milk, cattle, hogs, sugar beets, potatoes, vegetables, oats, hay, corn, cranberries

Major Industry: Mining—copper, iron ore, zinc, lead; automobile manufacturing; food processing; paper products; electrical equipment; fabricated metal products; tourism

Wisconsin

Did You Know?

By now kindergarten classrooms are commonplace in America. But in 1856, when Margarethe Meyer Schurz, a recent German immigrant, began teaching the young children of Watertown, Wisconsin, it was a brand-new concept, the first kindergarten in the United States. Margarethe taught her daughter, Agathe, and other neighbor children music, arts and crafts. Her system was adopted all across America.

Coat of Arms: The coat of arms shows a shield divided into quarters. In the top left quarter is a plow, representing farming. In the top right is a pick and ax crossed, representing mining. In the lower left is an arm and hammer to represent manufacturing. The bottom right quarter shows an anchor to represent navigation. In the center of the shield in a circle is the United States coat of arms and motto, "E Pluribus Unum" which means, "one out of many." Above the shield is a badger, and above that is a ribbon bearing the state's motto, "Forward." Below the shield is a cornucopia, symbolizing plenty, and a pyramid of 13 lead ingots, representing the mineral wealth of Wisconsin and the 13 original states. On the left side of the shield is a seaman and on the right a laborer holding a pick. These two men represent labor on water and land. Thirteen stars are under this entire scene to represent the original colonies.

Flag: The flag is dark blue with the state coat of arms in the center. Above the coat of arms is the state name and below it, 1848, the year Wisconsin became a state.

Dairy Land & Milk-Based Soaps

In 1845, a group of 190 Swiss immigrants left their homeland for better economic opportunities in America. They traveled 49 days across the Atlantic, were ferried in canal boats over rivers and rattled in rail cars across the land. Their final trek was a 60-mile march to 1200 acres of land in Wisconsin. The Swiss called the land, New Glarus, a tribute to the homeland they had left behind. They brought with them their culture, language, religion and unique dairy farming skills. As a result of the Swiss influence, Wisconsin's dairy industry is the most productive in the world, able to supply our entire nation with milk and its by-products.

Notable Natives

Roy Chapman Andrews (1884-1960), paleontologist, author, Beloit

Karole Armitage (1954-), dancer, choreographer, Madison

Harold Delos Babcock (1882-1968), physicist, astronomer, Edgerton

John Bardeen (1908-1991), two-time Nobel Prize-winning scientist, Madison

Walter Bradford Cannon (1871-1945), physiologist, Prairie du Chien

Carrie Chapman Catt (1859-1947), suffragette, Ripon

Seymour Cray (1925-1996), computer designer, Chippewa Falls

Edward Sheriff Curtis (1868-1952), photographer of Native Americans, Madison

Tyne Daly (1946-), actress, Madison

Willem Defoe (1955-), actor, Appleton

Conrad Arnold Elvehjem (1901-1962), biochemist, academic, McFarland

Zona Gale (1874-1938), novelist, dramatist, Portage

Hamlin Garland (1860-1940), Pulitzer Prize-winning novelist, West Salem

Herbert Spencer Gasser (1888-1963), Nobel Prize-winning physiologist, Plattville

Arnold Lucius Gesell (1880-1961), psychologist, author, Alma

King Camp Gillette (1855-1932), safety razor inventor, Fond du Lac

Deidre Hall (1947-), actress, Milwaukee

Marcus Lee Hansen (1892-1938), historian, Neenah

Eric Arthur Heiden (1958-), Olympic gold-medal speed skater, Madison

Woody Herman (1913-1987), big band leader, Milwaukee

Lewis Wickes Hine (1874-1940), photographer, Oshkosh

Al Jarreau (1940-), musician, singer, Milwaukee

George F. Kennan (1904-2005), diplomat, Milwaukee

Liberace (1919-1987), pianist, Primrose

Georgia O'Keeffe (1887-1986), painter, Sun Prairie

William Rehnquist (1924-), U.S. Supreme Court Chief Justice, Milwaukee

Gena Rowlands (1936-), actress, Cambria

Tom Snyder (1936-), television talk show host, Milwaukee

Spencer Tracy (1900-1967), actor, Milwaukee

Frederick Jackson Turner (1861-1932), Pulitzer Prize-winning historian, Portage

Orson Welles (1915-1985), actor, Kenosha

Laura Ingalls Wilder (1867-1957), children's book writer, Pepin

Thornton Wilder (1897-1975), Pulitzer Prize-winning playwright, Madison

Frank Lloyd Wright (1867-1959), architect, Richland Center

Bob Uecker (1935-), baseball player, Milwaukee

Hand-Milled Soap

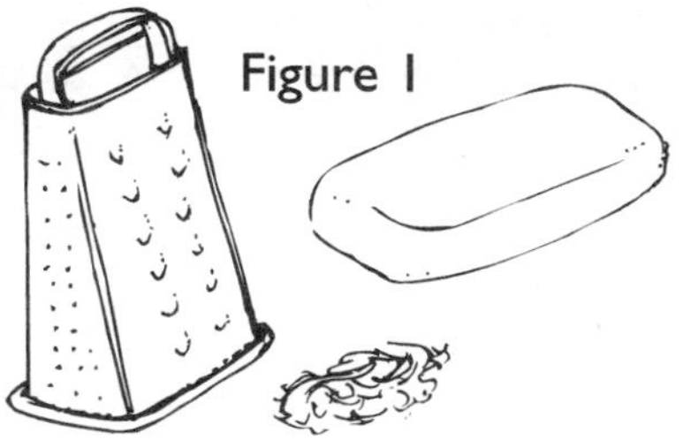

This project requires heat.
This is an easy, less traditional way of making milk soap without the dangers of lye.

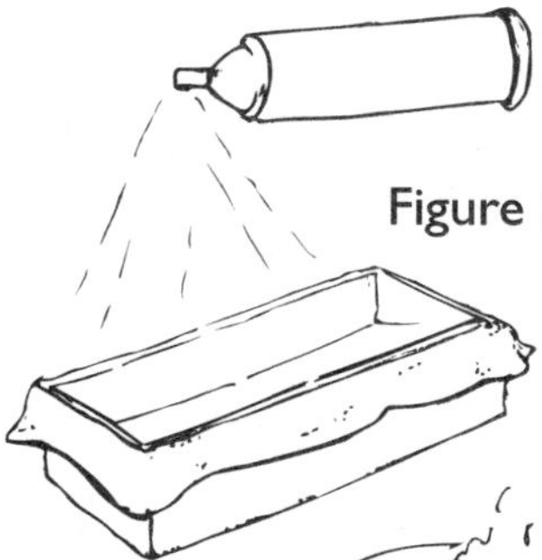

Figure 1

Figure 2

Materials

* safety goggles
* gloves
* paper face mask
* 8-quart pot
* stove
* heavy mixing spoon
* 2 stainless steel pots
* putty knife
* blender
* cooking thermometer
* plastic drying racks
* 5 unscented, hypoallergenic soap bars (Do not use glycerin soap or soaps that have no alcohol!)
* 1/2 cup dry milk

* 20 drops peppermint or other essential fragrance oil
* cheese grater
* shoe box covered in plastic
* cooking spray
* double boiler or microwave
* water (1 cup for every two dry cups of soap)
* mixing spoon
* food processor
* knife (for cutting)
* plastic knife (for carving)
* refrigerator (optional)
* rubber bands

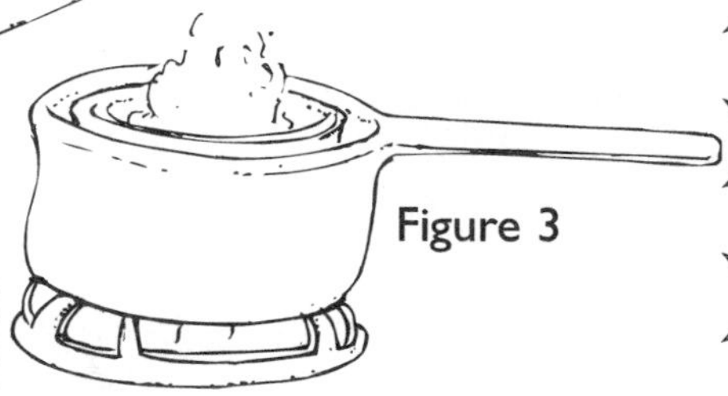

Figure 3

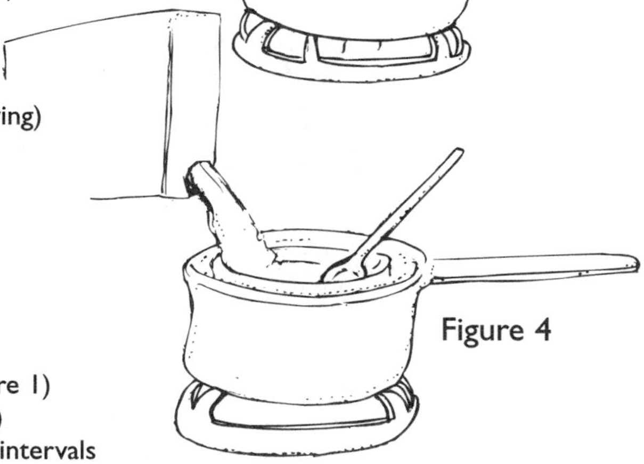

Figure 4

Instructions

1. Grate the soap bars for your soap base. (Figure 1)
2. Spray the molds with cooking spray. (Figure 2)
3. Melt the soap base in the microwave in short intervals or use a double boiler, gently stirring the soap base until melted. (Figure 3)
4. Add dry milk and your choice of fragrance to the melted soap base while stirring. (Figure 4)
5. Pour the soap into a plastic covered shoe box and allow to cure at least two hours. When firm, remove the soap from its mold and cut into squares similar in size to the soap designs on page 224.
6. Copy the soap designs on page 224. Cut out the designs and lay them on top of the cured soap. Slip a rubber band around the soap and design. (Figure 5)
7. Carve the soap, following around the design. (Figure 6)
8. Place the soap on plastic drying racks to cure for several days.

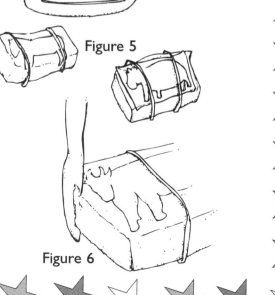

Figure 5

Figure 6

Name _____

Hand-Milled Soap Designs

Wyoming

Name: Wyoming comes from a Native American Algonquin word meaning "large prairie place" or "on the great plain." Algonquin was a family of spoken languages by nearly 20 different Native American peoples.

Did You Know?

Coal was formed from the remains of plants—ferns, trees and other plants that lived at the time of the dinosaurs. Over millions of years, heat, pressure and geologic processes compressed the bits of plant life together into coal. We use coal to make electricity in power plants all across the country. In fact, coal is one of the main sources of electricity in the United States. Much of it comes from Wyoming, the third largest producer of coal in the country!

Flag: The flag is a blue rectangle with a red border and a white line separating the two. A large white silhouette of a bison with the state seal on it dominates the flag.

Seal: Three figures are on the state seal: A woman standing on a pedestal, symbolizing the exalted position women hold in Wyoming, is holding a staff with the words *equal rights* written on the banner, a reminder that Wyoming was the first state to grant women the right to vote. She stands between two columns with scrolls twisting around them. On them are the words *livestock, mines, grains* and *oil* to represent Wyoming's wealth. The male figures on either side of the woman represent the mining and livestock industries so important to the state. An eagle and a five-point star bearing the number 44 on a shield represent Wyoming's entry into the Union as the 44th state.

Women of Wyoming

Wyoming opened its doors to new opportunities for women as early as 1869 when it became the first state to give women the right to vote. It would take the federal government 61 more years to give women across the nation the same privileges. True to Wyoming's sense of justice and constitutional freedoms, in 1870, Esther Hobart Morris became the nation's first female judge. By 1920, the federal government passed the 19th Amendment to the Constitution which gave women the right to vote. Five years later, Nellie Taloe Ross was elected the first female governor of Wyoming.

The nature of this project requires you to find three women you respect or who have changed your life. They may be family members, friends or acquaintances. You may also investigate three historical women who impacted women's rights or civil rights in general. The women you chose should be extraordinary in your opinion. Incorporate their images into a favorite Victorian pasttime, the silhouette, with a triptych frame.

Notable Natives

Lynne Cheney (1941-), political commentator, Casper

Jackson Pollock (1912-1956), painter, Cody

Triptych

Figure 1

Materials

* 3 sheets of black card stock or black construction paper
* 3—8¹/₂" x11" sheets of paper
* pencil
* scissors
* white glue
* spotlight or flashlight
* utility knife
* 3—4¹/₂" x 6¹/₂" pieces of cardboard
* 1" white paper tape
* clear, self-adhesive paper
* paint (any color) and paintbrush

Optional:
* instant camera and film to shoot profiles; or profiles of famous women cut from magazines

Figure 2

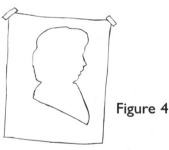

Figure 3

Instructions

1. Set a chair close to a white wall and invite your first special woman sit in profile. (Figure 1)
2. Place the flashlight on the table a few feet away from your subject. Turn off all other lights in the room and focus the flashlight on your subject. Adjust its position to give a clear, crisp profile shadow against the wall. (Figure 2)
3. Tape a piece of white paper to the wall where the profile is visible. (Figure 3)
4. Trace the subject's profile carefully. (Figure 4)
5. Turn on the light. Reduce the drawing on a copier to approximately 4".
6. Tape it to a sheet of black paper or card stock. (Figure 5)
7. Cut out. (Figure 6)
8. Repeat for additional profile portraits.

Figure 4

Figure 5

Figure 6

Optional Profiles

Choose three of the silhouettes on page 229 and copy them. Copy, then tape to black paper. Cut out.

Figure 7

Instructions for the Frame

8. To make a triptych, paint three pieces of cardboard then tape them together, side by side. Run the tape along the front and back of each. (Figure 7)
9. Cover the front and back of the triptych with clear, self-adhesive paper. (Figure 8)
10. Cut out the portraits and glue them to the inside of the triptych. Stand it up as a frame. (Figure 9)

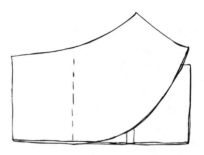

Figure 8

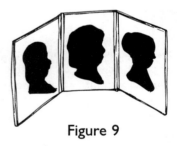

Figure 9

Profiles of Some Women Who Changed the Course of American History

Elizabeth Cady Stanton

Susan B. Anthony

Nellie Taloe Ross

Ester Morris

Soda "Pop" Quiz

How well do you know where different kinds of drinks were first invented?
Match the letter of the state to the correct drink.

_____	1. Dr. Pepper™	A. California
_____	2. Pepsi-Cola™	B. Georgia
_____	3. Coca-Cola™	C. Florida
_____	4. 7-Up®	D. Michigan
_____	5. Kool-Aid™	E. Missouri
_____	6. A & W Root Beer™	F. Nebraska
_____	7. Gatorade™	G. North Carolina
_____	8. Ginger ale	H. Texas

Bonus: Which two drinks listed in the quiz are NOT soda pops?

_____   _____

TLC10445 Copyright © Teaching & Learning Company, Carthage, IL 62321-0010

State Bird Matching

Some birds are very popular and have been chosen as the state bird by many states.
See if you can match the birds to the states that have chosen them.

_____ 1. Western Meadowlark

_____ 2. Cardinal

_____ 3. Mockingbird

_____ 4. American Robin

_____ 5. Eastern Goldfinch

_____ 6. Bluebird

_____ 7. Chickadee

_____ 8. Mountain Bluebird

A. Missouri, New York

B. Illinois, Indiana, Kentucky, North Carolina, Ohio
   Virginia, West Virginia

C. Iowa, New Jersey

D. Connecticut, Michigan, Wisconsin

E. Maine, Massachusetts

F. Kansas, Montana, Nebraska, North Dakota,
   Oregon, Wyoming

G. Arkansas, Florida, Mississippi, Tennessee, Texas

H. Idaho, Nevada

Bonus: Which bird has been chosen the most times as an official state bird?

_____

Name _____

State Mottoes Quiz 1

Many state mottoes are written in Latin, an ancient language.
Read the state mottoes below and translate them in your own words.

1. Alabama's motto—"Audemas jura nostra defendere"

   _____

2. Arizona's motto—"Ditat Deus"

   _____

3. Arkansas' motto—"Regnat Populus"

   _____

4. Colorado's motto—"Nil Sine Numine"

   _____

5. Connecticut's motto—"Qui Transtulit Sustinet"

   _____

6. Idaho's motto—"Esto Perpetua"

   _____

7. Kansas' motto—"Ad Astra Per Aspera"

   _____

8. Maine's motto—"Dirigo"

   _____

9. Maryland's motto—"Fatti Maschii Parole Femine"

   _____

10. Massachusetts' motto—"Ense Petit Placidam Sub Libertate Quietem"

    _____

11. Michigan's motto—"Si Quaeris Peninsulam Amoenam, Circumspice"

    _____

12. Mississippi's motto—"Virtute et Armis"

    _____

State Mottoes Quiz 2

Many of the state mottoes are written in Latin, an ancient language.
Read the state mottoes below and translate them into your own words.

1. Missouri's motto—"Salus Populi Suprema Lex Esto"

   _____

2. Montana's motto—"Oro y Plata"

   _____

3. New Mexico's motto—"Crescit Eundo"

   _____

4. New York's motto—"Excelsior"

   _____

5. North Carolina's motto—"Esse Quam Videri"

   _____

6. Oklahoma's motto—"Labor Omnia Vincit"

   _____

7. Oregon's motto—"Alis Volat Propiis"

   _____

8. South Carolina's mottoes—"Animas Opibusque Parati" and "Dum Spiro Spero"

   _____

9. Virginia's motto—"Sic Semper Tyrannis"

   _____

10. Washington's motto—"Alki"

    _____

11. West Virginia's motto—"Montani Simper Liberi"

    _____

Name _____

Presidential Match

Match the letter of the President with the state in which he was born.

_____ 1. George Washington   A. Arkansas

_____ 2. John Adams   B. California

_____ 3. Martin Van Buren   C. Connecticut

_____ 4. Abraham Lincoln   D. Georgia

_____ 5. Ulysses S. Grant   E. Illinois

_____ 6. Grover Cleveland   F. Ohio

_____ 7. Benjamin Harrison   G. Kentucky

_____ 8. Calvin Coolidge   H. Massachusetts

_____ 9. Harry Truman   I. Missouri

_____ 10. Dwight Eisenhower   J. New Jersey

_____ 11. Richard Nixon   K. New York

_____ 12. Jimmy Carter   L. Ohio

_____ 13. Ronald Reagan   M. Texas

_____ 14. George W. Bush   N. Vermont

_____ 15. Bill Clinton   O. Virginia

Bonus: Which state has had more of its native citizens become President than any other?

_____

Star Match

Many movie stars and musicians changed their names before they became famous.
Look at the list of names at the right and write the "star" name next to the name they were born with.

_____ 1. Frances Gumm

_____ 2. Nicolas Coppola

_____ 3. Marion Michael Morrison

_____ 4. Donnabelle Mullenger

_____ 5. Charles Carter

_____ 6. Robert Allen Zimmerman

_____ 7. Frederick Austerlitz

_____ 8. John Francis Bongiovi, Jr.

_____ 9. Bernard Schwartz

_____ 10. Tara Patrick

Carmen Electra

John Wayne

Charlton Heston

Bob Dylan

Fred Astaire

Tony Curtis

Nicolas Cage

Judy Garland

Donna Reed

Jon Bon Jovi

Did You Know?

Next to the sentence, write the name of the state from which the invention or innovation came.

_____ 1. The lollipop machine was invented in this state.

_____ 2. The famous and delicious Milky Way™ candy bar was invented in this state.

_____ 3. The very first Pizza Hut™ opened in this state.

_____ 4. Nylon was invented in this state.

_____ 5. Yummy chocolate chip cookies were first baked here.

_____ 6. Jell-O™ was invented in this state.

_____ 7. Much to the disappointment of car owners everywhere, the parking meter was invented and first appeared in this state.

_____ 8. Ben and Jerry's Ice Cream™ was first made and sold in this state.

_____ 9. The Cracker Jack™ confection was first made and sold in this state.

_____ 10. This was the place where the "pop top" was invented.

State Names 1

State names originated from many sources. Some were named for English monarchs. One was named after a wealthy land owner. Match the name of each person to the state that was named in his honor. This could be tricky because you'll use two names twice and you won't use two names at all!

_____ 1. Georgia	A. Admiral William Penn
_____ 2. Louisana	B. Queen Elizabeth I
_____ 3. Maryland	C. King George II
_____ 4. New York	D. King George III
_____ 5. North Carolina	E. Duke of York
_____ 6. South Carolina	F. King Charles I
_____ 7. Pennsylvania	G. King Louis XIV
_____ 8. Virginia	H. Mary Queen of Scots
_____ 9. West Virginia	I. Queen Henrietta Maria

Bonus: Which monarch listed above was French?

_____

State Names 2

Most state names are derived from Native American words.
Match the state name to its Native American meaning.

_____ 1. Chippewa word meaning "grassy place"

_____ 2. Dakota word meaning "cloudy" or "sky-tinted water"

_____ 3. Oto word meaning "broad water" or "flat river"

_____ 4. Creek word meaning "tribal town"

_____ 5. Algonquin word meaning "large prairie place"

_____ 6. Iroquois word meaning "meadowland"

_____ 7. Algonquin word meaning "river of the big canoes"

_____ 8. Sioux word meaning "downstream place"

_____ 9. Chippewa word meaning "great water"

_____ 10. Sioux word meaning "south wind people"

A. Alabama

B. Arkansas

C. Kansas

D. Kentucky

E. Michigan

F. Minnesota

G. Missouri

H. Nebraska

I. Wisconsin

J. Wyoming

State Flag Match

Under each flag, write the name of the state it belongs to.

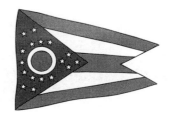

1. _____

2. _____

3. _____

4. _____

5. _____

6. _____

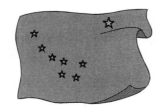

7. _____

8. _____

9. _____

10. _____

Answer Key

Soda "Pop" Quiz, page 230

Bonus: Gatorade™ and Kool-Aid™

1. H		5. F	
2. G		6. A	
3. B		7. C	
4. E		8. D	

State Bird Matching, page 231

1. F		5. C	
2 B		6. A	
3. G		7. E	
4. D		8. H	

Bonus: Cardinal

State Mottoes Quiz 1, page 232

Alabama: "We dare defend our rights"
Arizona: "God enriches"
Arkansas: "The People Rule"
Colorado: "Nothing Without Providence"
Connecticut: "He who transplants sustains"
Idaho: "Let it be perpetual"
Kansas: "To the stars through difficulty"
Maine: "I lead"
Maryland: "Strong deeds, gentle words"
Massachusetts: "By the sword we seek peace, but peace only under liberty"
Michigan: "If you seek a pleasant peninsula, look about you"
Mississippi: "By valor and arms"

State Mottoes Quiz 2, page 233

Missouri: "Let the welfare of the people be the supreme law"
Montana: "Gold and Silver"
New Mexico: "It grows as it goes"
New York: "Ever upward"
North Carolina: "To be, rather than to seem"
Oklahoma: "Labor conquers all things"
Oregon: "She flies with her own wings"
South Carolina: "Ready in soul and resource" and "While I breathe, I hope"
Virginia: "Thus always to tyrants"
Washington: "Bye and bye"
West Virginia: "Mountaineers are always free"

Presidential Match, page 234

Bonus: Virginia with 8 Presidents, Ohio with 7 is the runner-up.

1. O		6. J		11. B	
2 H		7. F		12. D	
3. K		8. N		13. E	
4. G		9. I		14. C	
5. L		10. M		15. A	

Star Match, page 235

1. Judy Garland		6. Bob Dylan	
2 Nicolas Cage		7. Fred Astaire	
3. John Wayne		8. Jon Bon Jovi	
4. Donna Reed		9. Tony Curtis	
5. Charlton Heston		10. Carmen Electra	

Did You Know? page 236

1. Connecticut		6. New York	
2 Minnesota		7. Oklahoma	
3. Kansas		8. Vermont	
4. Delaware		9. Illinois	
5. Massachusetts		10. Ohio	

State Names 1, page 237

1. C		4. E		7. A	
2 G		5. F		8. B	
3. I		6. F		9. B	

Bonus: King Louis XIV

State Names 2, page 238

1. I		6. D	
2 F		7. G	
3. H		8. B	
4. A		9. E	
5. J		10. C	

State Flag Match, page 239

1. New Mexico		6. Tennessee	
2 Ohio		7. Alaska	
3. Arizona		8. Rhode Island	
4. South Carolina		9. Maryland	
5. Hawaii		10. Texas	